# A HANDBOOK OF POLL SURVEYS IN MEDIA
# AN INDIAN PERSPECTIVE

A Handbook of

# Poll Surveys in Media

## An Indian Perspective

Dr N. BHASKARA RAO

GYAN

A Handbook of Poll Surveys in Media : An Indian Perspective



ISBN: 978-81-212-1042-3



Published in 2010 in India by
Gyan Publishing House
5, Ansari Road, Darya Ganj
New Delhi-110002
Phones :011-47034999, 9811692060

E-mail: books@gyanbooks.com
Website: www.gyanbooks.com

*Lasser Type Setting by*: Rudra Computer Graphics, Delhi
*Printed at* : Young Art Press, Delhi-92

# Dedication

*Dedicated to those who practised that polls and politics are not all about winning but making a difference in the lives of people and their thinking. Three such leaders who are no more but their legacy is and with whom I had association in that pursuit.*

*Rajesh Pilot truly signalled transition of the country to newer heights and showed how to think national with concern for grassroots. Kakani Venkatratnam and Kalapala Surya Prakash Rao two grassroots leaders of Andhra Pradesh who showed me (1952- 65) what is proactive and propeople is all about.*

# Contents

**Dr. S. Y. QURAISHI**
Election Commissioner of India

भारत निर्वाचन आयोग
*Election Commission of India*

# Foreword

A book on Poll Surveys could not have been more timely. Elections 2009 are just over but the debate whether Opinion and Exit Polls should have been allowed to be published during the days of polling has not fully subsided. Perhaps it is not likely to be. Some of my best friends in the Media have chided me that a wonderfully conducted election was deprived of its due glamour by not allowing the public catering of poll surveys. I am happy that Dr. N. Bhaskara Rao has come out with a well researched and meticulously crafted perspective on a subject that not only holds interest for media and the people but also for politicians and election managers alike.

Public opinion polls, as Nick Moon in his book "Opinion Polls: History, Theory and Practice" says, are 'for good or ill, inextricably wedded to the democratic process.' Needless to stress that opinion poll cannot be a random heap of anecdotal information and must follow a methodical and scientific approach. When, the opinion polls failed to predict the outcome of 1992 British elections, the critics went on to state that 'opinion polls were a pernicious parasite' and that 'they could corrupt democracy itself by reducing an elections to the level of a horse race.'

India is no stranger to poll surveys. With the expansion of reach of the media both electronic and print, such surveys have become a regular feature on the eve of every election during the last two decades. There is apparently no uniform yardstick followed for the surveys. It has been observed that in a multi-phased election, dissemination of results of the poll surveys, tends to influence the electors in the remaining phases. The Election Commission consulted political parties on the issue of poll survey in 1997 and again in 2004. They have come out unanimously against publishing results of any survey between the date of election notification and the completion of poll in all phases.

The Commission prescribed certain guidelines for publishing results of opinion and exit polls during the Lok Sabha elections in 1998 and these were repeated in 1999. The period of restriction was from two days before the poll in the first phase and till the completion of poll in the last phase. Both the print and electronic media followed these guidelines in 1998 general elections. In 1999, however, when the issue again went to the Supreme Court, the Commission opted to withdraw the guidelines based on lacuna that it did not have the punitive powers to enforce the guidelines. Surveys were conducted and results published in all subsequent elections.

Following a second round of consultation with the political parties before the 2004 general elections, the Commission suggested to the Government for appropriate legislation to prohibit survey results from the notification date till the conclusion of poll in all phases. In early 2009, a Bill was introduced in Parliament seeking such prohibition. Immediately prior to the general elections to the 15th Lok Sabha, the Election Commission, backed by Supreme Court directions in a PIL, prohibited publishing of results of opinion and exit polls during the period starting from the time the campaigning ends i.e. 48 hours before the close of poll for the first phase of election and till the completion of poll in all phases. To their credit, media abided by these directions, some of them grudgingly though.

The general complaint cutting across all political parties and formations is that poll surveys and their results are often doctored to suit the interests of those commissioning or financing the survey. Considering the range of ingenuous methods attempted to manipulate the electors, it is difficult to find fault with such a complaint. In the recent elections, we have seen widely varying poll predictions by different agencies and the yawning gap between the projections and the actual results.

While Dr Bhaskara Rao's book promises to the reader the internal dynamics of poll survey and its external processes and consequences, I have three points to make. Coincidentally, none of these is in favour of the surveys during polling days. First, if the intention or even the unintended fallout of the survey is about 'influence', then it is the Election Commission's abundant duty to prevent it. This has to be the case till a way is found to ensure that reporting surveys does not mean campaigning or persuasion of voters. It is relevant to take note of the side effects that could be caused by what Dr Rao conceptualizes as "pre emptive journalism" where surveys tend to draw sweeping conclusions even when the actual voting is yet to take place. The hallucinating impact of such 'make-believe' survey reports could at time be so strong that one of the losing candidates went to the court and argued his case that the poll results were not as per the opinion surveys hence should be quashed!

If the objective of the poll survey is to bring to the audience the drama and excitement of political choice, and also to bolster the TRPs of 'entertainment' channels this can surely wait for a few days in the interest of achieving free and fair polls. As a reader or viewer, I too have an appetite for the results of the poll surveys, though several of them are becoming increasingly less serious and less clean, but I would rather let my senses wait for the counting day than dilute the delivery of a fool-proof democratic election. Free and Fair polls are of supreme and sacred consideration for the Election Commission of India and for its sake, the Commission would like to brook no barriers.

Finally, I would find it difficult to link the issue in any manner with press freedom. The Commission respects the role of the media in Indian democracy and more so in the specific context of conducting elections. It has consciously opted to build in transparency and media scrutiny at every level of the electoral exercise. The Press in return has reposed full trust in the Commission and functioned as its eyes and ears in enforcing fair elections. There is no reason why the restriction on opinion and exit polls should become a thorn in this formidable alliance.

The wisdom of the Indian voters in the exercise their franchise, has seen many a reputation of psephologists and media pundits fall by the way side time and again. The voters have silenced the doomsayers who predict instability and chaos. They are the ones who have proved that the democratic foundations of this great nation are strong, deeply rooted and unshakable. While I expect Dr Bhaskara Rao's book to open for the readers new windows of understanding to poll surveys, I would like the cause of the Indian voter and the cause of Indian democracy to form the twin underpinnings of this understanding.

**July 15, 2009** **S.Y. Quraishi**

# List of Tables

# List of Graphs

# Preface

Gallop polls are known globally. George Gallop, who founded Gallop Polls more than five decades ago in USA, is viewed as father of public opinion surveys world over, including in the context of the Presidential polls of that country. Since then such specialist agencies which conduct poll eve surveys have proliferated, particularly in countries such as India where an electoral democracy is well established, markets are dominant in the economy and news media have a unique stature. George Gallop and I have one thing in common both of us did our Ph.D from the School of Communication, University of Iowa, USA. Of course, I did several years later (1968 – 70). The reason I refer to this is that a senior researcher and editor with Gallop Polls for years, David Moore, in his books "The Opinion Makers (2008)" and "The Super Pollsters (1995)" describe how poll surveys vitiate poll atmosphere and scuttle the same democratic processes for which in fact they came into being. He gives "devastating insider account of their several limitations and misapplications". The revelations in this book have several insights for India. I have been talking and writing about some of these aspects for some years. More recently, on November 1, 2008, I referred to critical ones at the Lok Sabha Speaker's Second Roundtable of eminent people in the Parliament House Annexe. The response I received, made me think of this publication on poll surveys. Unlike in the

USA, the way poll surveys have proliferated, the way they are being covered by the news media and used by political parties/leaders is what I thought should be viewed critically. So that positive potential of surveys is derived in the interest of free and fair polls in India.

The first comment of the editor of the publishing house after going through the manuscript was that I was too involved; Yes, of course, I was. First, as a student activist starting with 1955 landmark Assembly poll in Andhra Pradesh, then as a political scientist and then as a communication researcher engaged in public opinion research and as an analyst of social change. With these concerns overlapping, I have continued my interest in research methods and utilisation of field research. First, I was a participant and witness to intense involvement at grass roots in the electoral process every time there was an election for village panchayats, zilla parishad, Assembly or Parliament. My house was the nodal point in the village for preparation of voters list, enrollment of voters and distribution of voter slips. My father's handwriting was sought after (no type writer, no Xerox) for all such work, election after election. I was a frequent helper in distributing those slips.

My personal encounter with the electoral politics was to do with the Centre (1975 – 77) and the State of Andhra Pradesh (1986 – 91). I have seen how those in the power, concerned with elections, go about influencing the news media and use official information apparatus of the Government in the interests of the party. My experience at the Centre was with tracking public standing of the Government keeping in view the electoral opportunities and challenges. Based on a series of field surveys (1976-77), I indicated that Indira Gandhi government had lost ten percent of votes and the poll outcome was a foregone conclusion. But on seeing my survey report the Minister (V.C. Shukla) debunked it as a "statistical scrap". I was not sure that he ever brought the report to the notice of the Prime Minister. But I came to know from the acknowledgment note sent to me by R K Dhawan later that she did see it and even after that she decided to go to the polls that was when I was asked for a note on poll strategy

(1977) which I did (not meant for media use). It was this paper which later became an issue for the Shah Commission taking more than a couple of days of proceedings. The contentious point relevant today more than before is whether or how far an incumbent "misuses" his position for possible poll advantage.

Six or seven pollsters in the market today (out of about 15) in New Delhi had their origins with me at the ORG or in the CMS or the MDRA. Some of these, though commercially successful got into the surveys reluctantly. I keep hearing about (what I consider) "ugly side" of conducting poll surveys for news media and their use by political parties. Obviously, I am concerned. I also regret for being indirectly responsible for some such examples. But then I am being told that what other pollsters/ psephologists are doing is to be lamented far more!. That is when I realised the criticality of professional training and decided that as an "applied social scientist" I rather devote more time on educational endeavours. I expect this book to serve that purpose. Commercial lure or glare of news media or pampering of politicians in power alone should not be the reason for young researchers getting attracted to psephology. Sample surveys have a lot more potential to contribute for the prosperity and sustaining parliamentary democracy of the country. Also, I expect this book to offer the kind of motivation that my 1995 experimental publication "Perspectives into Mass Media 2020" did. Most of those who purchased that publication (at Rs. 5000) were the ones who have gone beyond their expansion plans in media in the country in the last 15 years. This book I expect would help citizens respond to surveys more responsibly; news media cover surveys not as an end in themselves and survey agencies operate and report more transparently.

I have witnessed early in my long research career what is sponsor bias or source bias and interview bias and even more blatant bias at the analysis stage in interpretation and presentation of findings of field surveys. This is what made me a votary of "independent research". But how could people be aware of any such bias when they see or read about a survey in the news media?. Sensitivity of public to any such bias is the best bet in a "checks and balance" based democracy. That is what I expect this book to serve.

In a nutshell, all that I have tried to say in this book is that the scope and structure of surveys need to be understood better than we seem today, particularly about their potential to effect free and fair conduct of elections. In this process, the news media should be sensitive to the function of surveys of all types. Potential of poll surveys could be unleashed only when there is transparency in conducting and covering them by the news media. There is need for more professional polling agencies to operate with concern about credibility of everyone rather than taking an isolated and primarily commercial view. Today there is need for both news media and agencies to make special efforts to indicate that their surveys are neither manufactured nor manipulated. But the onus is more with the news media, individually and together. This is a reference book for those in the news media covering electoral politics and for political leaders and aspiring candidates. This is also about everything that a voter, candidate and leader should know so that they could benefit from poll surveys. This book reminds researchers and survey agencies challenges of upholding significance of surveys of all kinds in the larger context and long range perspective which they should not lose sight of.

The first chapter gives an overview for the origin of poll survey in India and the concerns and motivation for their proliferation over the years. The second chapter describes how news media had initially taken to field survey as a way for objective reporting and credible coverage of poll campaigns but what goes in reality in that process tends to be detrimental to that very objective. The third chapter on anatomy of surveys deals with their reliability and accuracy aspects, how one should look at surveys for fundamentals. As poll surveys have come to stay as a part of electoral democracy, sensitivity about methodology as to how estimates are made is critical. The fourth chapter indicates the kind of role poll surveys play, what difference they could make and why they are being viewed differently considering their potential to influence the poll process and even the outcome. The fifth chapter deals with unique character of exit polls and peculiarities of their role and the compulsions in restraining them between poll phases. The sixth chapter, gives the elusive nature of public opinion in its very basic character as the reason for illusionary character of poll surveys and various aspects of methodology, in capturing such an elusive phenomenon. The Seventh chapter describes the function of analysts, pollesters and psephologists and even profiles some of them as it is pertinent the know about their credentials as a part of transparency in poll surveys.

The eighth chapter describes persuasive ways of parties to stay ahead in polls and poll surveys and how surveys have become the means for candidate selection. The ninth chapter identifies certain rethink in the media about the very relevance of poll surveys and the compulsions for such a rethink among political .parties and polling agencies about their methods. The tenth chapter outlines the way forward to surveys as potential tool for sustaining and deepening democratic traditions in the country.

**July 15, 2009** **Dr N. Bhaskara Rao, Ph.D**

# Acknowledgements

The provocation for this book is most of poll surveys covered in the media in the recent years. P N Vasanti's column (2008 – 2009) in the *Mint* and elsewhere and the kind of fresh perspective she had offered on media, some of them referred to in this book, deserve to be acknowledged. I acknowledge all out assistance of Regi V John of CMS Academy, I could not have completed this book without his help. I also acknowledge assistance of Raj Kumar of the CMS in constantly coming up with updates. I profusely thank Dr. Shanti Swarup for giving a shape to this book and its title.

I wish to thank **CMS Academy of Communication and Convergence Studies** for facilitating me to write this book, stipulating a deadline of three months.

# 1

# Poll Surveys: The Indian Scene

## Public Opinion and Surveys

In this author's book, "Politics of Leadership in an Indian State" (1967), a chapter was devoted to discuss how media (mostly newspapers) create, mobilize and polarize political opinions as well as political alliances at micro and macro levels within a State (Andhra Pradesh). In the initial years of 1960s it was primarily the opinion of political leaders which mattered. The combined reach of all newspapers, radio and cinema at that time was much lower than 10 percent of adult population. With decentralization and democratization of local-self government in full swing since the 1980s, "public opinion" has become as important for the news media as for the policy makers. In fact, in the 1990s public opinion has become a criterion as to the direction of public policies and political strategies. With persuasive strategies becoming the main stay of political parties to come to power, interest in public opinion surveys has become a yardstick in the 1990s not only in the context of elections to State Assemblies and the Lok Sabha but also otherwise.

Public opinion has never become so relevant and important factor for public policies and political scene as today. It will be even more so in the coming years. Attitudes and images are the outcome of individual perceptions which, when expressed, become public opinions. Perceptions are influenced by exposure to communication channels and experiences of past and present. Public opinions are not permanent, rather they are always in the process of change. It is a very nebulous concept and depends on the prevailing power structure, diffusion process and channels of information.

Since public opinion is not a simple aggregate of the opinions of the numbers of a people at any given time point, one need to understand the character, magnitude of divisions and disparities in the society and between people on various socio-economic and demographic indicators. As public opinion is the "breath of life in the politics of democracy", Government's very validity rests on such opinions.

Public Opinion Surveys help make better decisions and arrive at informed judgments. The policy outcome however should not be *determined* by such polls. Polls obviously bring out what is *popular* but that need not always be what is *right* — even assuming that opinion methodologies are unbiased and have used neutral measuring instruments. U.K's Labour Party leader Roy Hatterslay had said in 1996 that public opinion surveys are "a major disincentive to ideological politics….as they make politicians believe that they can choose between *principle* and *popularity*"… He was of course not referring to Indian political scene. However, this observation aptly describes the trap some of our political parties allow themselves into, as we see these days. In fact Professor Robert Worcester of UK's leading public opinion agency *Mori* went to the extent of observing that when public opinion surveys get into hands of politicians and spin-doctors, as they tend to more often these days, they "become a threat to democratic culture".

To the extent respondents to a public opinion survey are articulate, informed and uninhibited, to that extent opinion polls become reflective and reliable. But that is never the case on ground in a country like India. We need to do something new to equip our future citizens with the ability to discriminate, claim and enjoy the rights of informed, responsible and active citizen. Our schools as well as mass media have a role in this regard by sensitizing children on the importance of expressing opinions in so many different ways.

Public opinion surveys are used by news media all over the world to gauge the needs, moods, aspirations, perceptions and priorities of people – not only to facilitate marketing of products but also in the context of public policies and electoral politics. Indian news media have not lagged behind although the primary concern has been with poll prospects and outcome.

Indian public affairs are no longer centralized. They are state and region specific. Even more so since devolution of power and politics to Panchayats and Nagar Palikas. Coalition Governments and the uncertainties therein, have further added to the significance of public opinion. Not just in the context of elections, but also on policy initiatives of Governments at the Centre and in the States, public opinion has become a very important factor. With more and more communication channels available to a larger public across the country in the coming decades, the role of public opinion would be even more direct.

In this context it would be relevant to recall what GVG Krishnamurthy said as Chief Election Commissioner of India a couple of years ago. After seeing a series of poll surveys in the media on the eve of 1998 Lok Sabha Poll, he observed that many poll surveys were not representative, hence he wondered why the Election Commission should not prevent what he called "manipulative opinion polls" and their "media plant". Subsequent polls in India proved him right. That is how even the Press Council of India tried to, although unsuccessfully, to bring in the much needed transparency in public opinion surveys.

Growth and proliferation of poll surveys recently in India could be attributed to several factors. These include: growth of mass media particularly television, and news channels and the competitive compulsions under which they operate, spread of market research services, growing body of social sciences particularly application of statistical methods, availability of desegregated data on past voting, availability of investigators for countrywide field surveys, and increased uncertainties in party politics nationally and regionally and rise of State parties and emergence of coalition politics that are constantly changing poll configurations. And then of course there is the State-of-art computerization in the country and the availability of sophisticated software packages. A change in a generation at the helm in political parties and also in the media has also facilitated this change in the context of poll studies and surveys by way of their outlook towards survey research methodologies and analytical tools and experimentation in that process. This author could take the credit for market research agencies, like ORG and later MDRA, venturing into business of conducting Pre-poll surveys at national level in early 1970s. CSDS's pioneering contribution since 1990s has given poll survey research a new thrust and standing.

### Concerns in Early Surveys

As long as there was certainty in the polity and no vacuum in leadership, the country did not feel the need for a systematic opinion survey trying to predict a poll outcome in terms of seats and as a part of media coverage of elections. That is how the first such pre-poll field survey at national level could be traced to the beginning of a turmoil in the Congress Party with a split of the party in 1967 when Mrs. Indira Gandhi emerged as a national leader in her own right. The first three general elections (1951, 1957, 1962) were not preceded by any national pre-poll surveys, in sharp contrast to proliferation of such national sample surveys since the 10th election to the Lok Sabha of 1991 and their spread to State Assemblies. Pre-poll surveys received a boost with the rise of regional parties in the States and then with setting in of the coalition era at the Centre since 1996 and even in many States. However, earlier in 1957, the coming to power of Communist Party of India in Kerala, first time ever in a Western type of democracy as an outcome of the Assembly election, had attracted formal research on "voting trends" and "political behaviour" (not on "voting intentions"). But that enquiry was mostly academic. Gravitational pull of Communism was the concern of political scientists like Rajini Kothari, Bashiruddin Ahmed and their colleague in 1965. The main attention during this period was more on "unique" constituencies or "classic contests" rather than at a state or the national level. The concern was not with projecting the outcome of a poll, but on India's transition into an electoral democratic setup. Hence, the representative character of sample of voters was not a concern. It was more a case study approach based on discussions with political activists and media reports. Eric P.W. da'Costa, perhaps, could be credited for undertaking the initial sample surveys in India on elections. His concern to start with however, was more to do with public opinion and not so much with political processes or voting trends.

Most of the surveys were initially concerned primarily with preference of voters around parties. They were more academic. These studies looked into issues concerning public opinion. Newspapers published findings of such studies only as an exception, perhaps because by the time the findings were available, they would have lost their immediate relevance for newspaper readers. Most of the studies remained at best micro in their scope though in a couple of cases they dealt with the national or the state level issues. Such surveys on politics and public policies were mostly by Da'Costa until the 1970s.

In 1967 this author wrote in *Politics of Leadership in an Indian State,* about how public opinion sets the base for leadership and moulds the process journalists cover politics as 'experts'. His concern then was as a sociologist with *perceptions* and *group dynamics.* It was a couple of years later that he turned to *survey research methodology* to enlarge the scope of such inquiries into *preferences* and *practices-as* a political analyst. Until late 1960s, the concern of such surveys in the national context was limited mostly to four metropolitan cities by the doyen of public opinion surveys in India, Eric da'Costa. It was on the return of this author from the United States in 1970 with a

Ph.D. in communication research that national level public opinion surveys were undertaken using country-wide field infrastructure developed by premier market research agency, ORG. Soon thereafter, opinion surveys on public affairs became a focus of market research firms as it helps them to get into news media and their commercially oriented concerns. It was a few years later that poll surveys found sponsors with big news media partners.

Pre-poll surveys became a serious activity once newspapers started taking them as news stories and then started sponsoring them. It was The Hindustan Times which prominently published Eric Da'Costa's poll surveys limited to Delhi first and later to the four metros. The credit for elevating the status of pre-poll surveys belong to the late Girilal Jain of *Times of India*, Arun Purie of *India Today*, and Ramoji Rao of *Eenadu*. This author had the privilege of discussing surveys and sampling and their representative character with each of these eminent editors of India three decades ago and of convincing them of the relevance and objectivity of pre-poll surveys. These publications have sustained public opinion surveys in India over the years. With state-owned *Doordarshan* itself taking to poll survey based programmes featuring the findings of pre-poll surveys, television channels took to poll surveys like fish taking to water during 1991 to 1998.

Opinion polls, in the context of national elections, are perceived as indicators of not just the dimension of victory or defeat but also the factors for the differences and margins at micro- and macro-levels. Such an exercise reflects at best the trend, mood, and direction at any given point of time. But by using past voting trends from previous elections, one can go much further and that is what psephological exercise is all about - converting vote percentages into seats that a party is likely to get.

News media are not so much interested to sponsor surveys with wider scope, as they are interested more in predicting poll outcome. Tracking trends in public opinion and voting intentions is not always feasible for newspapers to sponsor because of the resource constraints. *India Today* was the first to take to such periodic tracking on a time series basis. Opinion polls sponsored by newspapers were traditionally meant to bring to the fore the mood of the voters with increased competitiveness in contests and rise of regional parties. Statistical accuracy of survey projections in terms of seats has become a concern only after 1990s. The Frontline is perhaps the only other publication that went beyond poll outcome survey by CSDS.

It was during 1989 to 91 that political parties started realising the significance of poll surveys in news media and started to know more about surveys and even commissioned surveys by professional agencies. Both Congress and BJP took to surveys from 1991 with seriousness as an input in their poll strategy.

A poll survey should be clear whether it is meant to capture opinions or preferences or intentions or all. A combination of these, if accommodated, will make the findings more relevant. In the Indian situa-tion, an opinion poll conducted much earlier than the announce-ment of the actual poll schedule would neither elicit the same kind of response nor would it be able to attain the degree of reliability as a poll conducted after the kick start of a poll campaign. Theoretically, an agency engaged in periodic surveys on voting intentions at various critical points would be in a better position to identify the undercurrents and differences before an election to make better projections on the outcome than an agency which has taken to surveys just then.

Pre-poll surveys, started as an academic endeavour by a couple of academicians 40 years ago, have come a long way. Starting from a sample size of 500 voters in the early 1960s and increasing to 10,000 by the 1970s and 1980s, recently samples have grown more from 60,000 to 80,000 during national elections. In fact, with the prime concern shifting to candidate selection, the number of constituencies being covered as sample and the size of voters from each has gone up significantly. A 2009 survey for Andhra Pradesh Assembly elections, for example, sponsored and covered by NTV, covered all assembly constituencies claiming a sample size of 40,

000 voters. One exit poll during 2009 elections claimed 1,60,000 sample.

Today, there are about twenty five agencies across the country which have been conducting pre-poll surveys nationally and regionally with some frequency. Most of them are market research agencies; others include academic bodies, advertising agencies and a couple of professional research bodies which are independent and engaged in ongoing research endeavours to do with one or the other aspect of socio-economic development.

From a budget of less than Rs.10,000 per survey, the budgets for some of recent surveys at the State level is as high as Rs. 10 lakhs (1 million). In 1996, more than a couple of millions was spent in conducting pre-poll opinion surveys before national and state level elections, reflecting how pre-poll surveys have become business propositions for market research agencies. Unlike earlier surveys that were sponsored primarily by the news media, most of today's surveys are commissioned, directly or indirectly by political parties, accounting for two-thirds of the total spending. In the last few general elections, the leading national political parties sponsored more than a couple of rounds of pre-poll surveys. On the eve of Assembly elections in 2009, Congress party in Andhra Pradesh conducted more than a dozen surveys. Even TDP and newly formed PRP of film star Chiranjeevi sponsored nearly a dozen surveys at different points in 2008 – 09. (Prajatantra, March 2009).

This author's estimate of what was spent on poll surveys in the country in 2008 and 2009 is well over Rs.65 crores. A newly launched news channel in Telugu spent more than a couple of crores of rupees for A C Neilson to get poll surveys conducted twice, in less than six months. The budget quoted for one round of national poll in 2009 was more than a crore of rupees.

**Early Pioneers:** Interestingly, political science departments of various Indian universities were more active with election studies in the 1960s than they were after 1990s. Perhaps, because in the earlier years, the Indian Council of Social Science Research (ICSSR) and the Research Programme Committee (RPC) of Planning Commission funded to analyse the results of 4th Lok Sabha election in eight key States at the instance of its member Prof. VKRV Rao, and sponsored academic studies on elections. However, most of these studies, although some of them were based on local field surveys, were in the nature of case studies and only a few of them included projection of a poll outcome in terms of percentage of votes. They did not get coverage in the news media perhaps because they were mostly post-poll surveys. In fact, most of these studies, although they included rural and urban voters, dealt with *unique* constituencies (of former princely State or with considerable minorities) or unique contests (like V.K. Krishna Menon vs. J.B. Kripalani). Most of these election studies were, descriptive, profiling - type, based on secondary data, and academic oriented. Empirical features were elementary.

Rajani Kothari, Rameshray Roy, D.P. Singh and Bashiruddin Ahmed, all from Political Science discipline, were the pioneers of election studies in India. But it was Eric P.W. da Costa, an economic journalist, who was the father of political and Pre-poll sample surveys. Later it was this author, sociologist and political scientist turned public opinion researcher, who took up large scale public opinion surveys at national and state levels, including on voting intentions. He introduced poll surveys as a professional pursuit at Operation Research Group (ORG), India's first market research outfit. The ORG was founded by Vikram Sarabhai as a part of Sarabhai group initially for "store audit". It was this author who expanded its concerns and capabilities to socio-economic issues including pre-poll surveys and media (readership and viewership) surveys (1972 – 1989). Prannoy Roy, however, has made poll surveys popular using graphics as a part of television journalism in India.

The concerns and specialization of IIPO and CSDS, the early pioneers of poll surveys, were different. While concern of the IIPO was limited to public opinion, CSDS has been more specific with electoral trends and voting behaviour. The IIPO pursued its surveys in the context of elections through field surveys, while CSDS initially based its studies mostly on secondary data and qualitative case study approach. While the CSDS's exclusive agenda was political studies, IIPO's was to do with public opinion and public policies to do more with foreign and trade concerns. CSDS's interest to predict poll verdict became serious much later after 1991. Survey research based Pre-poll studies at CSDS started appearing in news media around 1996. The Kerala Assembly study in 1963 – 64 was based on analysis of secondary data on voting. For it took three years or so to get the Assembly constituency wise election results from the Election Commission. IIPO's surveys got recognition at that time because of its association with Gallop, USA. The quantitative orientation to Rajini Kothari's efforts to conceptualize political process and formation of political parties took shape with the involvement of Michigan University's South Asia Studies Unit and with KGK Murthy from Michigan State University joining CSDS project in 1964.

The CSDS scaled up its pre-poll studies after 1996 and further from 2004 with increased visibility in news media and financial support. This is when it realised that poll surveys have acquired prominence, become part of the political process, political communication and campaign strategies of political parties. But market research agencies, because of their relationship with media, were dominating with poll surveys in the media, despite that CSDS pioneered election studies and specialized in election studies. The first National Readership Survey (NRS) with which this author was associated established survey capability of market research agencies into media and public opinion domain. CSDS deserve credit for bringing a discipline of scientific enquiry into electoral behaviour studies. CSDS continue to be a reliable source of time series data and analysis, both at the national and State level. In the process, CSDS has set certain benchmarks for rigor in survey research methodologies.

Despite all those developments, however, over all credibility of pre-poll and exit polls in news media has not gone up after 1996. In fact, it has declined although for several reasons. But the point is that rigor and transparency in CSDS efforts have not bettered the over all standards in the poll surveys, or psephological practices perhaps because of the kind of concerns and priorities that news media tend to pursue.

Research methodology followed for poll surveys has gone through different phases. Until 1991 agencies like IIPO, ORG and MARG, etc used random approach to sampling in the selection of constituencies and respondents. In between, purposive sample was introduced with increased concern for VIP constituencies. The sampling in most cases was not rigid or systematic. CSDS, perhaps, is the only agency which has been particular in its sampling methods and also transparent about study design. In fact, since 2004 CSDS surveys have been undertaken by a network of academic associates. Nevertheless it tried to have the best of both academic and marketing features - speed, visibility and catering to temporal curiosity interests of politicians, news media and their competitive compulsions.

## Media's Concern with Polls

If elections mean democracy-at-work, news media in India have been at its best upholding democratic processes. The Parliament and media are two sides of the same coin in a democracy. Free elections alone are not enough for sustaining democracy. A free and vibrant –news media is as much indispensable for the very relevance of parliamentary democracy. The two are complementary. They sustain and mutually reinforce each other. That is why free and fair elections are as important in a democracy as the freedom of press. Transparency in both is fundamental.

In India, as high as one-third of editorial space of newspapers was being devoted to party politics until recent years. While television has emerged as an entertainment medium, it is increasingly a prime source for news and current affairs. The proliferation of mass media has ensured that opinion-makers constitute a significant and important part of political process. Given the strength of mass media, it should follow that people are actively involved in the electoral process. However, there is no evidence of that especially in terms of voter turnout. In this process public opinion counts and matters a lot more - not just at the time of elections – but in the day-to-day functioning of the government as well as in the realm of policy making and civil society activism. Though elections may come once in five years, government's performance is being monitored, tracked and evaluated by news media on a daily basis. Public opinion surveys have now become a tool for democracy–at–work. Public opinion is a means to enhance and sustain democracy. Pre-poll opinion surveys have become a part of the electoral process and accepted as a democratic practice. With the steady decline in ideology-based party system and the spread of news media, particularly television, the relevance of such public opinion surveys has increased recently and is bound to increase further in the coming years. This aspect further adds to the catalytic role of news media as a pro-active fourth estate. That is why stakeholders concerned with both news media and public opinion surveys should know and understand the processes.

**The 1970s : More Curiosity**

The growth of poll surveys in India over the last 30 years could be broadly traced to three phases. The first phase of 1970s with three national elections to the Parliament, witnessed the first ever national Emergency. In fact, it was the circumstances under which the country went to 1977 general elections soon after the lifting of the Emergency that lead to a major survey in Hindi states by this author. A public opinion survey, with an enquiry on voting intentions, had brought out that voters were angry with the Congress party because of excesses in family planning sterilisations and curbing of civil liberties, that Indira Gandhi was going to lose power, despite this she went ahead with the polls and lost. V.C. Shukla, the then Minister for Information & Broadcasting and a close aide of the then Prime Minister, brushed aside the findings of the pre-poll survey saying that "statistics are a bunch of lies and such surveys are irrelevant in Indian politics". Splinter factor, multiplier effect, division of votes, turnout rate of voters, etc, were the concepts of this period used for explaining the poll outcome.

The first National Readership Survey (NRS) and the first National Family Planning Survey (1970-72) conducted by Operation Research Group with which this author was involved, used the biggest ever (until then) sample of 45,000 households. These two surveys in a way were the turning points in the growth of survey research in India. Selected on multi stage stratified systematic random basis, representing urban and rural India, the two surveys used elaborately developed questionnaires to project the "reach of media" and the extent of "family planning practices" at national level. These two national surveys served as model for sample selection procedures and, importantly, removed the inhibition about covering rural India in large scale surveys in a representative and reliable manner. It was also the beginning of market research agencies getting into survey research in a big way, an arena which until then had been the domain of social science faculties on a much smaller scale and limited to urban and purposive samples.

**The 1980s : Psephological Exercise**

The second phase of poll surveys in the 1980s featured the arrival of new personalities on the political scene like Rajiv Gandhi (Congress Party), N.T. Rama Rao (Telugu Desam) and Jayalalitha (AIADMK). Similarly, this period saw the arrival of Aroon Purie (India Today), N. Ram (The Hindu) and Ramoji Rao (Eenadu)on the media scene and Prannoy Roy on the Indian television scene. The rise and fall of regional parties and decline in the fortunes of Congress Party in the elections to State Assemblies too led to uncertainties which led to more poll surveys, at the national and the state levels. Popular cinema actor N.T. Rama Rao's entry into politics drew unusual crowds and that added to the curiosity as to the impact on the Congress Party's fortunes. In an unprecedented way, in a matter of nine months, NTR's Telugu Desam was swept into power in Andhra Pradesh. The only pre-poll survey under this author's supervision for the prominent Telugu daily, Eenadu, predicted the outcome closely. That was when the first ever write-up in media on a poll survey was published in *India Today* (November, 1979), christening the author as 'Pollster Rao'. This feature identified, the first time by any news media, a personality associated with a poll survey and referred to "survey methodology". Eric P.W. da'Costa's name was the only one, which was known and used in the newspapers until then in this context. The 1982 election to the Haryana State Assembly witnessed keen contest when Times of India (TOI) commissioned this author for the first time for a pre-poll survey. However, it was reluctant to publish the poll findings as it predicted that the Congress was in for a shock. Late Girilal Jain, who was the editor, wanted to meet the author to explain the basis for such a projection. On being satisfied about the methodology, he published it on the front page under by-line of this author. As its prediction was on dot, TOI took to such surveys off and on, both in the context of elections and on other contentious socio-economic issues.

The three elections to the Parliament and the key Assembly elections of Andhra Pradesh and Tamil Nadu States during the period 1980-90 and the kind of political realignments and the suspense involved therein, had ensured a place for poll surveys in the news media. In fact, election analysis programmes on Doordarshan's national network with Prannoy Roy had created a new position for poll surveys on the Indian political scene and have made them a part of the news media since then. 'Swings', 'shifts', 'splits' and turnout factors have become the concerns of poll surveys and bywords and language of politics and basis for forecasting seats/votes.

**The 1990s: Competitive Compulsions**

The spread of Satellite TV channels, increased political uncertainty in the country and increased role of regional parties and personalities have all added to the relevance of poll surveys and significance for their coverage in the news media. Hung outcome of national elections and coalition form of governments with possibility of a next poll to parliament anytime thereafter, has further added to the interest in poll surveys. That is how the media, including television, has begin to sponsor poll surveys nationally for Lok Sabha and even for State Assembly elections and feature their findings prominently and use them to prompt poll eve discussions in the country.

In the 1990s, the priority of poll surveys has shifted to swings and shifts of votes and projection of seats, both at the national and state levels. That is how the exercise has become more psephological. Conversion of vote-intention into seats is what interests the public and hence the news media. This is based mostly on voting pattern in the previous elections and the change in perceptions about parties apart from a host of other considerations to do with the poll scene.

The Election Commission (EC) both at the Centre and in the States has started making available detailed reports soon after the polling on candidates, parties and vote share of parties at micro and macro levels. Constituency wise voter turnout estimates are available now hourly on the polling day and the Election Commission itself puts out turnout figures within a couple of hours after the polling. This has given boost to seat projection oriented poll surveys for psephological exercise. These EC reports have come handy for psephologists to come up with models for converting percentage of votes into seats, and loss and gain explanations. In fact, since 1999 the historical data on polls is available on CD ROMs. Availability of extensive data has helped sampling strategies in selecting constituencies with representative weightages. Anti-incumbency and transferability of votes are the new terminologies of psephology well known today throughout the country.

Proliferation of 24-hour news channels their number more than doubled in 2009 since previous polls at national and regional levels and increased competitiveness among these channels has given fillip to multiple national surveys for each election. Five (DD1, Star, Aaj Tak, Zee TV, Jain TV) television national channels and even State level private TV channels (like Sun, Eenadu, Asianet, NTV, Asianet, Swarna, Gemini) have made poll surveys and voting analysis part of their election coverage. NDTV in fact, had even featured "poll surveys" daily through out the campaign period in the 1998 elections.

After parting ways with Star TV, Prannoy Roy launched NDTV Hindi (1988) and later 24 x 7 news channels in English (2003) and signaled the arrival of news channels in a competitive mode.

While most newspapers were giving news coverage of poll surveys, premier English dailies like the *Times of India* and *Hindustan Times* and popular English periodicals like *India Today*, *Outlook* and *Frontline* even sponsored national surveys. Star TV did two rounds of national poll for 2009 Lok Sabha elections. NTV in Telugu did three rounds of poll surveys for 2009 State Assembly election. Some regional newspapers as well as regional TV channels have also been sponsoring and featuring such exclusive poll surveys. One of them even sponsored exit poll Uttar Pradesh in 2008.

Pre-poll surveys have come a long way in India over the last three decades. What started as post-poll analysis based on secondary data of votes polled by various parties and candidates, surveys have become key inputs for poll preparations. Poll surveys have become quantitative studies based on sample surveys, more to project the outcome of elections in terms of seats and votes than understanding or promoting the process involved in an electoral democracy.

## The 2000s: Surveys to Sway Voters?

"Poll surveys" have come to stay and have become part of politics, election process and poll campaigns. In fact, poll surveys have become the basis for poll campaigns of political parties as well as for their electoral strategies and also for deciding political alliances (as to whether or not to join hands with another party or leader) and the poll plank. These political permutations and combinations are now formulated or decided on the basis of the findings of poll surveys by political parties themselves as well as those by the news media.

Since the 1999 Lok Sabha poll, poll surveys have become part of party campaigns itself as is evident from the fact that political parties are conducting more surveys than the news media. Initially, parties were getting these polls to know the prospects and then to plant or selectively leak the findings to the media. But since 2004, political parties have been depending on surveys to know prospects of sitting candidate and then to identify potential new candidates.

Election studies, pre-poll public opinion surveys, surveys predicting poll outcome, exit polls on voting day and post - poll surveys cater to different societal and media needs. Each one of these depend on different research methodologies. Survey research methodology has been an academic subject practically in most social science disciplines of over 120 Indian universities for several years now. This has ensured adequate trained manpower to conduct countrywide field surveys. All this has facilitated conduct of public opinion surveys quickly. Today, a national public opinion survey with a sample of about 20,000 respondents, covering both urban and rural India, could be completed in a matter of a fortnight. Whereas, a survey with 2000 voters and limited to four metro cities in the 1960s and 1970s took that much time. Today, some of the professional agencies, like CSDS, Neilson- ORG-MARG, IMRB, CMS, DRS, C-Voter, GfK Mode have the expertise and network to conduct public opinion surveys within a matter of a couple of days. Improved communication facilities in the country in terms of cell phones, dedicated phone lines, fax and email have helped this process. For conducting exit polls on poll date for same day broadcast, dedicated phone lines are being made available to field investigators by these premier agencies.

Both newspapers and television channels have of late added regular features with public opinion surveys on issues of current relevance. These include "field based" "sample surveys" or "SMS surveys". The response rate claimed for net surveys range from 500 to 10,000 hits depending on the issue of the day and the newspaper or the news channel involved. With hardly half percent penetration of computers and Internet, the net surveys, SMS polls, with more than 5 percent penetration, are fast catching up. A DMK candidate in South Madras constituency in 2009 claimed receiving 50,000 responses for one lac SMS he had sent to voters. With penetration of cell phones and access to internet beyond urban and privileged sections, net surveys or e-surveys are fast acquiring a place.

Election related field surveys could be broadly of four types with each having different scope and using research methodology.

**Pre-election Surveys:** These could be for two or three different purposes. (a) Once an election preparedness to State Assembly or Lok Sabha sets in, normally 4 to 6 months before a poll schedule is announced and when the Election Commission seizes the situation starting with the process of preparedness of voters lists. This is when news media and political parties would like to know the poll scene and how do parties stand in the perception of voters. The poll surveys conducted at this point obviously would be of less relevance as more voters at this point are undecided, waiting for the scene to get unfolded. Important to know at this point is the percentage of undecided voters who are likely to change their choice closer to the poll date. The enquiry in this phase would be more to identify emerging issues and undercurrents that are likely to matter. A news media may like to rate the performance of sitting MLAs or MPs. (b) A second type of pre-election field survey could be to assess the prospects of a sitting candidate or to identify a potential candidate. Based on projection of seats at this point, electoral strategy about alliances in coalition era are decided, prospects of competing parties or support of important communities would also be assessed. In pre-poll surveys the respondents demographics are more often pre-determined.

Pre-poll surveys are conducted, of late, more for identifying potential candidate for contesting the election. Political parties are taking to surveys to select candidates. News media, on the other hand, are more interested in issues, factors, prospects of parties and poll outcome.

Pre-poll surveys could be qualitative or quantitative. Qualitative ones are to understand the dynamics based on focus group discussions and the like methodologies. Whereas quantitative ones are more to forecast the poll outcome using structured sample surveys. Pre-poll surveys could be combination of both qualitative and quantitative.

**Exit polls:** An exit poll is conducted as voters come out of a polling booth after casting their votes. They are enquired about which party/ candidate they actually voted for. This poll, also based on a sample, is expected to indicate the outcome soon after the close of the voting on the day of polling in the constituency/State/country. The outcome projected in an exit poll is expected to be more accurate than a pre-poll survey and close to the actual outcome on the counting day. The more the time gap between the polling day and the counting day, the more the suspense and relevance of an exit poll.

Unlike in the case of pre-poll surveys, it is not easy to predetermine exact demographics of sample respondents in an exit poll. Secondly, time is limited to go into beyond voting aspects to do with 'why'. Thirdly, the sample size usually is much larger than in the case of a pre-poll survey. Fourthly, exit poll is supposed to be a simulated exercise in voting. That is, a dummy ballot box and a dummy ballot paper with the symbols of candidates contesting the election is supposed to be used in an exit poll. The voter on coming out of the booth, after casting the vote, is requested to perform vote casting exercise. However, in practice not all exit polls use a ballot box or provide the kind of solo atmosphere. The Election Commission rules do not allow such an exercise within a distance of 100 meters from the polling booth. Also, when a dummy ballot box is used, there is tendency of party volunteers sitting outside the booth to influence exit poll process sometimes by putting ballot papers in the box in multiples. Except male and female selection, no other identity or demography is possible in the sample of an exit poll. Also, as some voters, particularly women and minorities, tend to go for voting in a group, exit polls do not always reflect the pattern of actual voting.

**Mid-campaign Surveys :** There have been only a few examples for mid campaign surveys in the last two decades that were featured in the news media. These surveys are conducted in the middle of a campaign or poll schedule. Such surveys are conducted to know the influence of campaigns, manifesto proposals, etc. The relevance of mid campaign surveys no longer exists with the Supreme Court ruling out any such surveys in the media once poll schedule is on course or in between the poll phases same way as in exit polls. Nevertheless, political parties could get such surveys conducted for internal use. And, they do so for mid course correctives in campaign strategies. The methodology involved in such mid course surveys is different and usually tend to be smaller in scope and a combination of survey research methods. News media tend to use findings of such surveys which political parties tend to leak when it is to their advantage.

**Post- poll surveys:** Post poll surveys are the ones conducted usually after results of a poll are known. Since suspense is over with voting, neither political parties nor most news media is interested in post poll surveys and in sponsoring the same. As such it is only the academically oriented and those whose primary agenda is to study electoral behaviour, that conduct post poll surveys. Such surveys based on personal interviews, with emphasis on purposive sample like minorities or dominant communities, try to find out shifts in voting and motivation for voting to a particular candidate / party and the factors that contributed for success or failure. And, more importantly, a post poll survey helps analyze voting by demographics as it is not always possible in an exit poll. A post poll survey need not have large sample as it is not to project an outcome. CSDS perhaps is the only agency which conducts post-poll surveys regularly at national and State level and promptly publishes an analysis based on such polls. In 2009 CSDS presented a post-poll findings on CNN/ IBN while 15 other channels presented exit poll almost at the same time. The significance of a post poll, first time ever presented in such a detailed way, was lost. It is debatable whether these reports deserve media coverage and attention of large sections of citizens. But post-poll analysis rarely get into newspapers. It is limited to EPW or The Hindu. Post poll surveys offer more insights for sharpening methodologies of pre-poll surveys and help understand electoral behaviour and the very processes of democracy at work.

**Insta Surveys :** Insta survey is an ongoing exit poll where instead of projecting the outcome at the end of the polling, it is done

**Lok Sabha and Vidhan Sabha Elections held - Year wise 1991-2009**

| *Year* | *Lok Sabha Polls* | *State Assemblies* | *Number of Elections* |
|---|---|---|---|
| 1991 | 10th Lok Sabha | Assam, Haryana, Kerala, Pondicherry, Tamil Nadu, Uttar Pradesh, West Bengal | 7 |
| 1992 | | Punjab | 1 |
| 1993 | | Delhi, Himachal Pradesh, Madhya Pradesh, Meghalaya, Mizoram, Nagaland, Rajasthan, Tripura, Uttar Pradesh | 9 |
| 1994 | | Andhra Pradesh, Goa, Karnataka, Sikkim | 4 |
| 1995 | | Arunachal Pradesh, Bihar, Gujarat, Maharashtra, Manipur, Orissa | 6 |
| 1996 | 11th Lok Sabha | Assam, Haryana, Jammu & Kashmir, Kerala, Pondicherry, Tamil Nadu, Uttar Pradesh, West Bengal | 8 |
| 1997 | | Punjab | 1 |
| 1998 | 12th Lok Sabha | Delhi, Gujarat, Himachal Pradesh, Madhya Pradesh, Meghalaya, Mizoram, Nagaland, Rajasthan, Tripura | 9 |
| 1999 | 13th Lok Sabha | Andhra Pradesh, Arunachal Pradesh, Goa, Karnataka, Maharashtra, Sikkim | 6 |

*(Contd.)*

*(Contd. Table)*

| *Year* | *Lok Sabha Polls* | *State Assemblies* | *Number of Elections* |
|---|---|---|---|
| 2000 | | Bihar, Haryana, Manipur, Orissa | 4 |
| 2001 | | Assam, Kerala, Pondicherry, Tamil Nadu, West Bengal | 5 |
| 2002 | | Goa, Gujarat, Jammu & Kashmir, Manipur, Punjab, Uttar Pradesh, Uttarakhand | 7 |
| 2003 | | Chhattisgarh, Delhi, Himachal Pradesh, Madhya Pradesh, Meghalaya, Mizoram, Nagaland, Rajasthan, Tripura | 9 |
| 2004 | 14th Lok Sabha | Andhra Pradesh, Arunachal Pradesh, Karnataka, Maharashtra, Orissa, Sikkim | 6 |
| 2005 | | Bihar (Feb. 2005), Bihar (Oct. 2005), Haryana, Jharkhand | 4 |
| 2006 | | Assam, Kerala, Pondicherry, Tamil Nadu, West Bengal | 5 |
| 2007 | | Goa, Gujarat, Himachal Pradesh, Manipur, Punjab, Uttar Pradesh, Uttarakhand | 7 |
| 2008 | | Delhi, Jammu & Kashmir, Karnataka, Madhya Pradesh, Meghalaya, Mizoram, Nagaland, Rajasthan, Tripura, Chhattisgarh | 10 |
| 2009 | 15th Lok Sabha | Andhra Pradesh, Orissa, Sikkim | 3 |
| **Total** | **6** | | **111** |

at different points of voting during the day while the voting is still going on. This is somewhat like a running commentary as voting is going on the polling day. But players in cricket are not listening or seeing radio or TV as voters are in an election. This was done first time in 2007 by a national channel during Punjab Assembly elections. The Election Commission was informed that the channel was giving (repeating) the projections from its "insta poll" from 11.30 a.m. onwards. Having verified the same from CMS Media Lab, the Election Commissions sent a notice to the channel by afternoon to stop the telecast of such a poll.

This "insta poll" could be said was the result of intense competition between news channels to be the first to come out with their prediction – unconcerned of implications of repeat telecast of "prediction" of who is winning and thereby influence the poll process itself. For example, party agents in booths in many places melt away from the booth if they come to a feeling that the party is losing. Such news in the media could also demotivate voters who are yet to vote.

**Rolling Polls:** Rolling polls is conducting periodic surveys to track changes in voters opinion on parties, performance of government, preference of candidates, and voting intentions, etc. The sample frame and the scope of enquiry is ensured in this kind of surveys. Compatibility aspect of sample is critical in such rolling polls. Also, such rolling polls help pre-poll election-eve surveys come up with more reliable findings and projections and also explain the changes among various sections and across the States during the interim period of any two elections. Such polls help mount a strategic poll campaign. Since 1996 CSDS is the only agency which has been conducting series of surveys, systematically both pre-poll and post-poll.

## Changing Electoral Scene

Methodologies of the election surveys meant to project poll outcome in terms of votes and seats depend to some extent or other on the larger political scene. Number of contending political parties

## Lok Sabha Elections in India: A Snapshot

Lok Sabha Elections in India : A Snapshot

| *Parameters* | *1967* | *1977* | *1991* | *1996* | *1998* | *1999* | *2004* | *2009* |
|---|---|---|---|---|---|---|---|---|
| Seats | 520 | 542 | 537 | 543 | 543 | 543 | 543 | 543 |
| Reserved | 114 | 116 | 120 | 120 | 120 | 120 | 120 | 131 |
| Candidates Total | 2369 | 2439 | 8749 | 13952 | 4750 | 4648 | 5435 | 8070 |
| Independent Candidates | 866 | 1224 | 5549 | 10636 | 1915 | 1945 | 2385 | 3823 |
| Number of National Parties contested | 7 | 5 | 9 | 8 | 7 | 7 | 6 | 7 |
| Vote share (%) | 76.1 | 84.7 | 80.6 | 69.1 | 68.0 | 67.1 | 62.9 | 63.6 |
| Number of State Parties contested | 14 | 15 | 28 | 30 | 30 | 40 | 36 | 39 |
| Vote Share (%) | 9.7 | 8.8 | 13.1 | 22.4 | 18.8 | 26.9 | 28.9 | 24.1 |
| Eligible voters (in crores) | 24.9 | 32.2 | 51.2 | 59.3 | 60.6 | 61.9 | 67.2 | 71.0 |
| Poll Percentage | 61.0 | 60.5 | 55.9 | 57.9 | 62.0 | 60.0 | 58.1 | 58.4 |
| Polling Stations | 243693 | 373910 | 591020 | 767462 | 772681 | 774651 | 687473 | 834944 |

*Source: Election Commission*

and their strategies is one such factor. There are about 900 parties registered with the Election Commission in 2008 although only 45 of them are contesting elections at one level or other and at one time or other. However, the number of more visible parties would be about 25. The number of parties that contest in an election obviously influences reliability of survey projections and accuracy could not be similar in the case of each contesting party. State parties (30+) now account for around 30 percent of votes. Against nine percent of candidates who are crorepaties in 2004, there were 16.3 percent in 2009 Lok Sabha poll. On the other hand, percentage of criminals has gone down from 24 percent to 15.1 percent between 2004 and 2009. The phenomenon of independent candidates and rebel candidates is yet another factor. The number of contestants per constituency has not been on decline. Projection of poll outcome could be more accurate with smaller sample if the contest is constantly between the same two parties as in the case of USA, for example. The more the number of constituencies with triangle and multicovered contents, the more challenging is psephological exercise.

Similarly, poll schedule and its spread over a long period of one month as in 2009 in five phases could make a difference. An example of how politicians take advantage of such staggered polls was a controversial statement of Dr. Rajasekhar Reddy at the end of the first phase to influence voters in the second phase belonging to a different region of the state.

The chart given here gives an idea of complexity and magnitude of the challenge for designing poll surveys.

India is one of the very few democratic countries where there are no restrictions of any kind on publishing / broadcasting "poll eve surveys". The Election Commission, constitutionally an independent body assigned with the responsibility of conducting elections "free and fair", never initiated the idea of restraining news media in covering poll surveys until 1998. Perhaps because poll surveys until then had not proliferated so much in news media and become contentious of being criticized for their objectivity.

# 2

# Media Coverage of Elections: Poll Surveys

If elections mean democracy at work, media has been at its best in upholding democratic process. At the end of an election, if the Election Commission is the real winner, media cannot be far behind. Going by extensive coverage of Lok Sabha and Assembly elections, media deserve praise for steering the poll campaign, (reminding the issues and concerns of voters,) and bringing to fore virtues of candidates and leaders in so many different ways interactively and analytically by way of field based discussions and animated studio debates. Since 2004, elections in India have been far more transparent and live.

However, it is time to ponder over the role of the news media. Those who are not interested in politics would say that news channels more or less have gone "beserk with polls". Some others would say it was yet another "festive time" for channels. Preoccupation with politics is well known but not to the extent it has been in the new media scene. Of course, the campaign for the elections in the States and Lok Sabha has been much longer than in the earlier years. That might have been good or bad for the political parties; but it has been definitely good for the media, particularly for TV. Proliferation in the number of news channels, and competitiveness among them, has added to the scope of media coverage of poll campaigns.

Overall, TV's role has been significant as never before. In fact, some of the channels have succeeded in bringing together contending leaders to an "American style-poll-debates". Even in the case of daily newspapers, there has been a spurt in the last couple of years, including in the States that also went to polls for the Assemblies. Newspapers have devoted as much as a quarter of their editorial space to coverage of elections. In the case of TV news channels, it was not less than one-third of time. For 24 hour news channels such occasions are an opportunity to "fill" time and make inroads for adding viewers as well as to attract commercial revenue.

An "incumbent" party had won only where exposure to TV was highest among the States that went to polls recently. For, TV is known more for "negative effects", even in the context of politics. This aspect, of course has nothing to do with individual channels. It is more to do with the very character of television. Unlike in the case of newspapers and radio, TV lends more for negative reporting, personalising, amusing and emotionalising. That is how it holds the viewers. 2009 Lok Sabha poll coverage had once again brought out this character of TV.

### Compulsions of News Media in Poll Surveys

To know why there has been a spurt in the number of poll surveys we need to first understand the news media scenario in the country. Five reasons could be mentioned for news media, particularly television channels, taking to poll surveys as if it is an "opportunity". First, the natural urge of news media to cover power politics of the day better, more extensively and, in the process, consolidate their own political clout. Secondly, it is economics – poll surveys enable channels not only fill good deal of time, also they are a source for generating revenue. Thirdly, competitive scenario among news media in general and television news channels in particular. If one media is taking to surveys, the other has to follow suit as if a domino effect. Fourthly, the urge to play proactive role in electoral politics with elements of drama, suspense, and "reality". Fifth, fast changing character of political scenario in the country with the role of regional parties and complexities of coalition era where political uncertainties have become the order of day.

There are four other reasons that made surveys a regular feature of news media. These include - proliferation in news media, frequent elections in the country, each with increased political significance because of coalition politics, spread of telecom by way of easier phone connectivity and increasing access to email, blogs, websites and internet and miniaturization of desktop computers. And, of course, easy availability of past data for electoral trends in the country and also data on demographics of constituencies.

Proliferation of news media in the country since 1991 has unleashed surveys of all kinds – field surveys, SMS surveys, live phone-in, etc. Surveys have become part of television language and culture. The number of 24-hour news channels has gone up to more than 200 by April 2009. Nearly 40 channels and as many newspapers belong to one or other political party or its candidates or close relative. Most of them are in Tamil Nadu (6), Kerala (3), Karnataka (3), AP (3) and in HP, Maharashtra, Punjab, West Bengal and Chattisgarh.

The credit for making poll surveys a feature of television channels goes to Dr. Prannoy Roy. The format for poll survey based programmes, initiated by Roy - has become a standard feature, with little modification thereafter. Computer graphics and animation were used to explain voting trends and display projections. The only difference is that extent to which hard facts were being dealt with in the discussion has come down. Bytes based coverage has gone up.

An element of uncertainty in the country as to which party or coalition would come to power at the Centre and in the States has added to the relevance and weightage of poll surveys in the news media. Between 1991 and 2009, there were five general elections instead of three that should have been in the normal course. Coalition politics have added to the suspense and political uncertainties. With politicians and parties crisscrossing at the Centre and in the States in their affiliations, field surveys have become a means to know public support or otherwise. Each election to the Assemblies and Lok Sabha in the last decade had acquired added significance also because of role of news media – whether it were polls in Gujarat, Uttar Pradesh, Punjab, Karnataka, or Delhi, Madhya Pradesh, Rajasthan or Chattisgarh. Rise of regional parties and entry of a new set of leaders into competitive politics have further propelled news media coverage of the electoral process and reliance on surveys as a way of reflecting field situation and for projecting electoral outcomes. Environment of competitive politics in a competing news media scenario has led to institutionalisation of poll surveys.

This momentum to use surveys is being facilitated by two other external developments. Newer communication technologies – cell phone connectivity and telecom networks - and access to computer and websites, blogs and internet connectivity. SMS too has become a prime means for routine surveys by newspapers and news channels. Also, on-line and live interactive programmes of news channels have become a regular feature. The trend could eventually lead to lessening of importance of field surveys. Because SMS and online surveys cost less and can be conducted more frequently. Field surveys, on the other hand, could only be periodic as they are expensive and time consuming and require association of an external polling agency. And if such an association is not going to enhance credibility of the survey as well as the user media, alternatives have to be found to fill the vacuum. With restriction on publication of field surveys in 2009 elections between polling phases, the need to find new ways has become a compulsion. That is what Times of India, Dainik Bhaskar, Business Standard and many other dailies and even TV channels tried in 2009 Lok Sabha poll. CMS Academy's review of coverage of polls brings out that urge on the part of news media.

Against these developments, it is but natural for news media to report what people across think on contentious issues and competing politics. To understand this process better, they should know pros and cons of field surveys, and the way news media cover and use such surveys. Only then the positive potential of surveys and news media coverage will be more effective in a parliamentary democracy. One of the factors limiting reliability of field surveys, however well designed they may be, is that only some respondents to such surveys are more active and expressive, while others are not so well disposed of to such enquires and many more are passive in their response pattern. For example, if more people develop suspicion about surveys and refuse to respond when they are approached, what is the relevance of coverage of such surveys in the news media? Or, even when the percentage of people who were sampled for a field survey but could not answer, or respond only partially, the methodology as well as analysis plan has to be different. But such details are rarely indicated while presenting the findings of such surveys. In the case of pre-poll surveys, more specifically, the percentage of voters who were "undecided" or "not sure" or 'not answered" is critical in interpreting the findings of a poll survey, including an exit poll.

News media carries findings of field surveys conducted by an interested political party itself, or by a polling agency, an independent body or it could be by news media itself. If the survey is commissioned or sponsored by a news media, it tends to feature the findings more prominently. Even when not directly sponsored, it does so for reasons of political clout. The glaring example in 2009 was front page features by Telugu daily Sakshi of CNN IBN and NDTV Surveys. As these findings suit the publication's political stand, it went all out. Eenadu, on the other hand, did not carry these surveys at all, presumably because it didn't suit its political stand.

## More a Business Opportunity!

This author estimated a decade ago that about Rs. 10 to 12 crores were being spent by news media and parties for poll surveys.

In 2008 – 2009 it has touched Rs 65 crores both for the Lok Sabha and State Assemblies polls. More than half of this was by political parties, individual candidates and business houses including advertising agencies. A recent trend in the era of coalition governments is big business houses taking to poll surveys and "use them" to decide whom to support to bargain for getting nomination as a candidate. Instances are there of business houses paying to the polling agency for conducting poll surveys on behalf of one or the other party or a leader. This is happening both in the case of general elections to the Lok Sabha and for State Assemblies, (industrial houses got surveys conducted for Chief Ministers of Assam, Delhi, Rajasthan, Madhya Pradesh and Andhra Pradesh in 2009). Then there are polling agencies or pollsters who take money for the same survey from the party as well as the news media claiming that the survey was done for them exclusively. There are polling agencies who have been recycling the "same survey" by giving it to more than one "client" – a party or a candidate and to a news media customizing the presentation some times even with knowledge or consent of the political party / leader. What is important for the credibility of a poll survey published in news media is the source of funding. When it is indicated as "sponsored" by a news media, it does not always mean that the survey was conducted independently or objectively as it is implied.

There is a correlation between the significance of poll surveys and grassroots orientation of political parties / leaders. Political leaders and parties are losing touch with their own functionaries and cadres. That is one reason why they take to field surveys. Taking to surveys in the context of polls by parties reflect declining understanding of needs, aspirations of people and connectivity with grassroots. Some candidates of political parties for Assembly and Lok Sabha are more like visitors to the constituency. Many are crorepaties and business people outside the constituency. They do not reside in the constituency. They stay most of the time with their families away in the State or national capital. Some maintain an office with one or more linkmen on payroll. This has been happening slowly but steadily in the last two decades. As a consequence, political parties / leaders have started depending on "gatekeepers", news media, public relations agents and in recent years, on poll surveys. That is how their interest to get covered in the news media more than ever before and also dependence on news media as a source of information and feedback from their own constituency. This in turn obviously implies pampering or / and manipulation of media establishments for favourable coverage. Field Surveys come handy in this process irrespective of their limitations. That is how surveys of all kind are conducted either at the instance of political parties / leaders directly or at the instance of a public relations agent or a news media directly. Media coverage has become a criterion or a yardstick for assessing popularity of a party / leader or a candidate at a given point of time.

## Glut in Poll Coverage

TV news channels have taken to poll surveys like fish taking to water. New news channels would like to launch the channel with a "political survey". Their understanding is that such survey - based programmes will attract the attention of political leaders, decision

**Issues Covered During Poll Season - 2009**

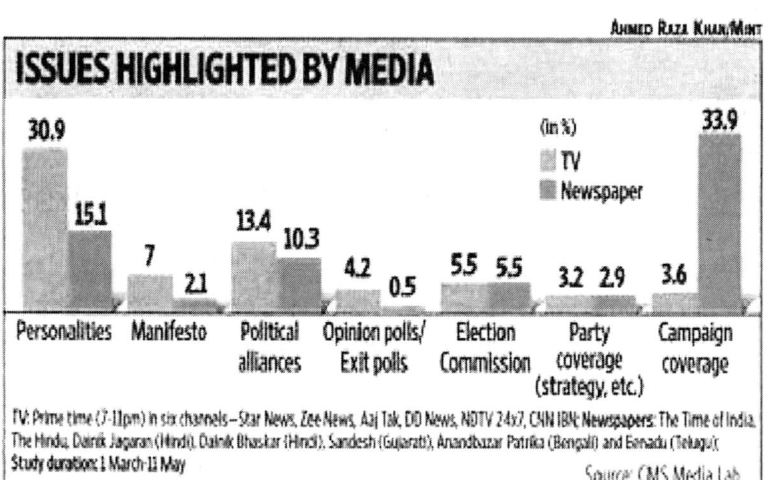


From P.N Vasanti's Column in Mint, June 09

makers and help promote the channel. Having launched with a survey, the channel continues to carry such field surveys as often (including SMS polls and live phone-ins). Having realized that surveys, whether field based or SMS or phone-ins, enable channels as well as newspapers to connect with readers / viewers, news media are taking to surveys not only in the context of elections, but also at other times and in other contexts. Hence we need to understand merits and demerits of news media taking to surveys.

Newspapers and channels devoted one-third (ranging between 25 to 55 percent) percent of their space/time for coverage of poll campaign between February and May 12, 2009 according CMS Media Lab. All that coverage in the media apparently made no difference for the outcome of poll process. For, the final results were more or less same as indicated by the pre-poll surveys at the very outset in January 2009 (unlike in the case of 2004 Lok Sabha poll). There was no dramatic shift in voters' preference. The direction was not reversed because of poll campaign or media coverage. There is no evidence of that. There was no wave, no swing, but news media were flooded with poll campaign coverage. Little over four percent of prime time of news channels was devoted for poll surveys between March and May 2009 against less than one percent of mainline newspapers during the same period.

News media in their coverage of polls were preoccupied with alliance politics from very second phase itself as if the poll was over and the outcome was already known. And then the focus was who the Prime Ministerial candidates were and who was likely to form the Government. What motivating effect such coverage could be expected on voters yet to go and vote on the polling day in subsequent phases?. Because such news media coverage implies that it is not the voter so much but certain individual leaders or journalists who would decide the outcome of the elections. Such a limited view of news and their conclusive view of poll process appears to have demotivating effect on voters.

Over all, media covered 2009 Lok Sabha poll as never before. But also never before poll campaign was so trivialized. "Tu-tu-main-

main" was more evident in media coverage of polls in 2009. That is what a poll campaign ends up as if it is not on issues. Trivialization was at its height in media coverage on the last polling day with exit polls galore. The coverage was personalities dominated and personalized. But more acrimonious and in a negative context. Varun Gandhi was covered more than any other leader as a national hero of BJP although initially all about him was negative.

There was hardly any coverage in the media on basic issues to do with prices, poverty, drinking water, farmers' suicide, free bees in manifesto, etc. But they were echoing Babri, Bofors, Khandlari and such non-relevant issues. LTTE was perhaps the only issue but more in Tamil Nadu media. All through the campaign nuclear deal with USA was no where an issue. The campaign was more about the *past*, not so much about *future* despite hype on young and first time voters. It was preoccupation more in coverage with alliance politics. The coverage was based more on speculative aspects and assumptions.

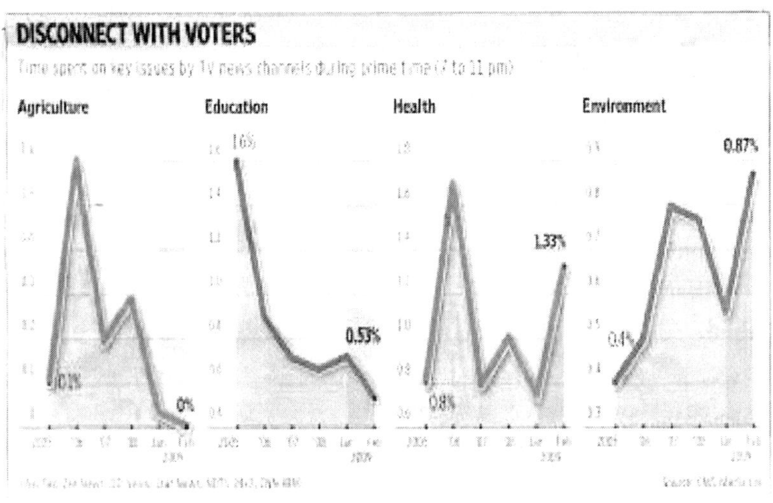


From P.N Vasanti's column at Mini, April 09

**More is not Merrier!**

No wonder why coverage of politics by some 24 hour news channels was so extensive, to the extent of "trivialising" – perhaps because it was presumed that such coverage of electoral process otherwise is "boring" or "too serious" to hold the viewers' attention. That is why channels covered a lot of filmi personalities, TV serial characters and their "dummies" often with funny and filmi dialogues and even puppets/animations. 2009 polls saw ventriloquism in regional language channels. Between animated "notanki" type programmes and studio "jugalbandi" (among pollsters, analysists and journalists) debates, channels had extensive field reports. Repeated visuals within a day (and even within a bulletin) and in so many different ways amounted "more of the same" and an impression of an "over load", particularly the studio based debates.

Poll coverage on AIR (All India Radio) had always been limited in terms of time devoted but far more "informative" and "absolving", particularly its "bridge-programmes", linking capital cities. To the credit of TV channels and competition, it must however be said that their field coverage of campaigns had been much beyond the State capitals and urban centers. The earlier model of reading out on radio and TV by leaders of political parties as part of "poll broadcasts" on AIR and Doordarshan for over two decades, had made no difference to the scope of poll campaign. Nor did those broadcasts have ever expanded listernership / viewership as in the number of contesting candidates/parties. They made no difference to political discourse. AIR and Doordarshan devotes 8 to 9 hours of time in all, in each State that goes for Assembly Poll and similarly in the case of Lok Sabha election. Based on votes polled in the previous election, political parties are allotted free time to broadcast on AIR. The sequence of broadcasts is decided by lottery.

The range of coverage of polls by some newspapers, like The Hindu and Dainik Bhaskar, or Nai Dunia, has been far more. Perhaps because they themselves did not sponsor pre-poll surveys and depended more on their own full time senior staff reporters. Some daily newspapers, even big ones, which covered pre poll surveys of whatever kind, used TV channels as source for their coverage of poll campaign. The Hindu was the only daily which gave post-poll surveys, the importance they deserved in understanding the poll process.

BJP in Delhi and Rajasthan in 2003 State elections, for example, had 10 or more large size advertisements in newspapers. Interestingly, two of those advertisements in Delhi debunked poll surveys (unfavourable ones) and two featured favourable surveys. Late Pramod Mahajan was candid in 2004 when he credited advertising campaign in Rajasthan for BJP turning the table. He said that "things started working for the party" only after the advertising campaign in the media. When Swatantra Party was a key contender several years ago, they relied primarily on such advertisements in newspapers and it was a wash out. The lesson was that media campaign without booth level follow up is unlikely to make much difference. This is also the case with poll surveys.

Nevertheless, no one would say reports in the news media in 2009 Lok Sabha poll was one-sided in their coverage of polls as newspapers were accused three decades ago, when there were no pre-poll surveys. Then newspapers were criticized for their "bias" and staff reporters were accused as being "one sided" or "off the mark" in their coverage of elections. Between 1998 and 2008, the media was accused for their dependence on pre-poll and exit poll surveys. In fact, such surveys have become additional revenue–earners for TV channels. For, that is how poll surveys were hyped and stretched on and on with animated studio discussions – as if they were deliberating on the outcome of an election rather than the process. In fact, in 2004, as never before, BJP had gone all out to publish the so-called findings of such surveys in newspapers as advertisement on the eve of polling day. Findings of poll surveys were discussed in TV studio by rank and file of political parties more than the party manifestos were discussed. A survey is used to generate "cock fight" by channels. They generated more heat than threw light. The discussion was more on how right or wrong a poll survey was. In 2009 a new channel in Andhra Pradesh advertised and based its daily one hour programme on a pre-poll survey highlighting how

**Number of National Poll Surveys - featured in national news media**

| *Year* | *Pre polls* | *Exit Polls* |
|---|---|---|
| 1991 | - | - |
| 1996 | 3 | - |
| 1998 | 4 | 2 |
| 1999 | 8 | 4 |
| 2004 | 9 | 5 |
| 2009 | 12 | 16 |

"famous", "well known", "internationally famous" and "authentic", the polling agency that conducted the survey (AC Neilson – ORG) was. But no individual who did the survey on behalf of that organization was ever discussed. However, it appears that too soon the channel realized that surveys may help draw instant attention, but they do not distinguish the channel from others or even build viewership. This channel quickly shifted and went beyond by taking to "Big fight" type programme. This is only one example.

Against such a dilemma, renowned editors like Girilal Jain, twenty five years ago, had taken to poll surveys as a means to ensure more objective coverage of polls. This author remembers extensive discussions with Jain and the grilling he had put before publishing poll surveys. In fact, he insisted on by-line to identify the one who had projected seats so that there is no ambiguity about responsibility. Jain and Dileep Padgaonkar encouraged use of field surveys not just at election time but for better insights into contentious issues and those of larger national concern. More importantly, they realized at the very outset that a news media should not mix up the survey findings with that of newspaper.

The number of pre-poll surveys published in the media during each election has been increasing, both in the case of Assemblies and Lok Sabha. So also was the number of exit polls between 1991 and

2008. More surveys *ipso facto* mean more variation in the findings and going off the mark of the actual result. Poll surveys have come to stay and will continue to be relied upon by news media. They have become part of our electoral process. Hence we need to better understand their scope, relevance and also limitations. But going by the experience since 1996, one needs to wonder how much sensitivity is there in the news media as to the very character of poll surveys!

**More Media, less voter turnout! ?**

As the daily newspapers and 24-hour news channels have multiplied and mushroomed during 1998 – 2009, one would expect that voters' enthusiasm to participate in the electoral process, the bedrock of any democracy, had gone up. One simple and primary indicator for such an effect is voter turnout. Turnout is generally known to be low among "better off" ones consisting mostly of urban - white collar affluent. Has the news media made any difference in enthusing such sections to come out on the voting day and vote?. A desegregated analysis of voter turnout does not support such expectations. On the contrary, it appears as if more the news media and their coverage of polls, there has been no change in the turnout percentage.

If the outcome of a poll is a foregone conclusion, as news media often tend to make out with the help of poll surveys, where is the motivation for voters to go and caste their vote?. Is there any reason why voter turnout has not been increasing despite dramatic change in the demographics of voters, proliferation of news media and the number of poll surveys recently?. Can one say that media hype of poll surveys and the way they are presented does not enthuse voters to go out and vote?. But may even add to voter apathy. This aspect needs to be pondered over.

The over all voter turn out in 2009 poll has not increased as one would expect with increased media coverage and proliferation of news channels. In fact, in Mumbai it had declined despite all out efforts to promote voter turnout by so many civil society, professional groups and famous personalities. P Sainath, a senior editor of The Hindu, has been writing extensively about the dilemmas to do with the poor. For a change he captured the mood of affluent while explaining the phenomenon of low voter turnout in Mumbai. Which also provides insights about the media priorities.

Voter-turnout however had increased marginally in Delhi, where too media reach was high. But the turnout increased in 2009 far more in Chattisgarh where media reaches hardly one-third of voters. That is to say there is no evidence that hype on polls in the news media has made much difference in voter turnout. In fact, compared to the 1980s, when there was hardly any television coverage of polls, voter turnout since 2003 has been same or even lower. The joke in a post poll analysis by an NDTV comical feature (*Gustakhi Maf*) was that BJP lost in Delhi (2004) because of extensive TV coverage and it won in the other three States because there was not much TV viewership!. In fact, since 1998, voter turnout has increased in MP, Rajasthan and Chattisgarh, than in Mumbai or Delhi where media exposure is more and viewership/readership is high. In fact, media made a negative impact on the voters enthusiasm. Double-edged potential of TV was too obvious in this campaign. It can be termed as a boomerang phenomenon. In Chattisgarh, Aakash Channel in 2003 was supposed to have devoted itself to boost the chances of Ajit Jogi. In 2009 Sakshi TV and daily newspapers went all out as "official campaigner" of the ruling party. In fact, whenever there was blatant "over use" of electronic media by an incumbent, that party's chances to return to power got bleak. There is enough evidence in the last decade to this effect. That was the case in 2004 when TDP lost in Andhra Pradesh; Jayalalitha in Tamil Nadu lost out in 2006. Another blatant example was in AP where the incumbent Congress party was "let down" miserably in 2009! .although it scraped through by a whisker to power – thanks to tactical voting.

News media coverage of polls does not distinguish poll process from poll outcomes. The concern is primarily with outcome in terms of wins and losses of seats or votes. Also, the concern with coverage is limited to parties and candidates and does not deal with social stability or integration aspects as B.G. Verghese wrote in "Polls & pollsters" (The Tribune 27/4/2009) "it does with stability of the govt. or with economic integration as with political coalition". Similarly about participation, involvement or inclusiveness of voices in the media debates. The media coverage is of temporal character, impact and effect aspects hardly get covered and reflected as it requires special skills. The kind of poll surveys, poll debates and analyses that goes on in news media does not provoke or prompt or enthuse voters as media does with consumers about products/ brands.

One might argue that it is not so much the number of news media or their availability or their coverage that matters. Rather it is the content priorities of news media, the structure of programmes and their inclusiveness that matters to motivate readers / viewers. An analysis of contents brings out the excessive preoccupation the news media has for politics. In fact, they consider election season as an opportunity to enter or expand the market, and do "good business" – same way as advertising agencies consider festive season (Dushera - Deepawali period) as the peak period for advertising campaigns.

**Voting Percentage in All General Elections 1952- 2009**

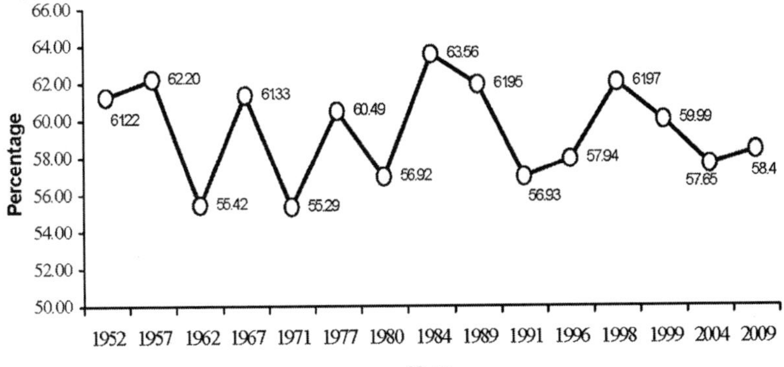


CMS has estimated that advertising budgets through news media during poll periods has increased dramatically. In 2009 it was estimated at Rs 1000 crores, despite down turn in the market, against only a couple of hundreds of crores before 1996. How could we explain this phenomenon. CMS research indicates that while news media covers political parties, including poll campaigns, it does not prompt or activate or engage voters as media does otherwise in the context of negative aspects. And, in fact, that it is more by way of pre-empting than in prompting.

## Pre-emptive coverage of news media

News bulletins in general have gained viewership more than any other niche segments of news channels. But the structure and priority of news bulletins have not changed much during 1996-2009. They continue to be centered around personalities, prejudices, controversies, to which verbosity and platitudes of politicians have been added. Even more repulsive has been the extent such "pre-emptive contents" are hyped and repeated. News bulletins headline poll surveys as if "that is the way it is" (rather than that as a trend or as a possibility) without giving limitations in such an exercises as if trying to "make viewers believe" that the game is over even without their casting vote.

News media in India covers party politics far more than in many developed countries. The coverage is mostly of political leaders, political parties, controversies, conflicts and gossip involving them. This is perhaps partly because politics is relatively easier, less expensive to report, hardly any home work is required and most of it could come without much effort. And, more importantly, such coverage gets them connectivity with political leaders in power, even some influence; in the process journalists even get pampered by politicians and vice-versa.

At the time of elections, journalists and news media rely on gossip, analysis, probe and even "plant" stories involving politicians and goings on in politics. It is in this process that some journalists tend to be pro or against in their reporting about political parties/

leaders. A plant is something which is done by news media to facilitate advantage or disadvantage to a party / leader at a given point. That is how certain informal understanding or wavelength between a journalist and a politician develops. Sometimes this relationship could be adversary rather than cooperative.

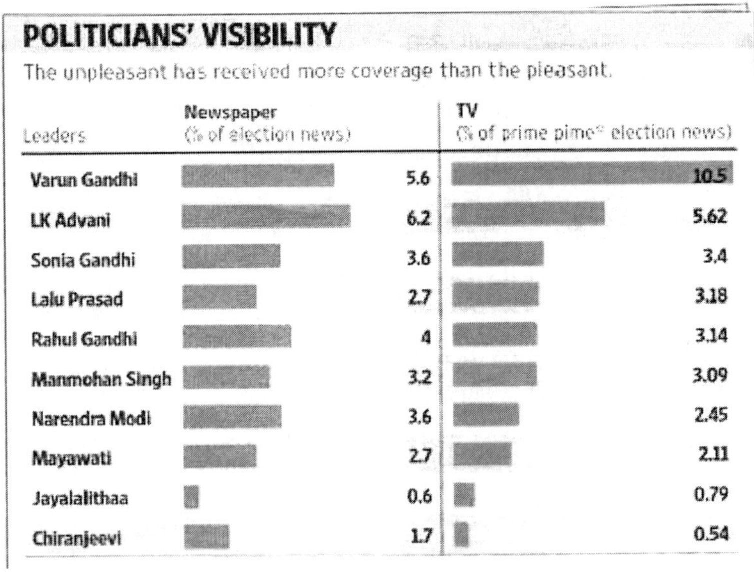


Study period 1 Mar to 30 Apr
(*Prime time is 7-11pm)

*From P.N Vasanti's Column at Mint, May 09*

In the course of "political punditry" or as a part of it, news media sometimes provide platform for competing parties/candidates to clarify their formal positions. After getting into power, a party/leader tends to continue the relationship with journalists individually or with a media house. That is how over the years, government after government has been increasing "facilities" and "favours", formally and informally, to journalists and news media houses.

The way news bulletins feature findings of pre-poll surveys is as if they are gospel truth. This does not enthuse voters to go to booths on the polling day. News media coverage of polls has three possible implications. First, if "so and so" is going to win (as is being hyped by channels) in an election, why bother to go out to caste vote. This view is more among urban, elite and already better informed and media exposed voters. When the news media, on its own or using a survey, gives the impression that one or other party/ candidate had won or was winning with a big margin, some voters are likely not to bother to get out on the polling day. A second effect of poll coverage of TV channels could be if "so and so" is going to win let us as well vote for the same winner that the channel had indicated. This bandwagoning is what parties / candidates push for and try to cause with the help of poll surveys. Such an effect is more likely, particularly among undecided and "floating" voters. A third possibility of news media declaring poll result is to create sympathy for the one projected (in surveys/ news media) as a loser. A few voters are likely to be in this category.

While political parties and leaders like to see that channels give coverage in such a way that it helps them win the election, it might not turnout as expected. It could even be repulsive to viewers and cause a boomerang – not go to vote.

News channels - national or regional, big or small, old or new – all would like to carry surveys. For, a survey also enables them to show support to one or the other party / candidate. A second reason is that surveys give added impression that news media have come a long way with objective coverage of polls. Thirdly, it is a marketing opportunity to woo viewers and to increase advertising revenue. Fourthly, a survey is viewed as a part of competitive strategy. Channels would like to give the impression that they have an expert (a psephologist) in their studio to analyse poll results and tell the poll outcome before hand. While most channels rope in a polling agency for a survey, others take a survey already published or sponsored by one or other political party / candidate. Recent trend is to collaborate with a newspaper to jointly commission a survey and hype the findings and try to create credibility for the survey. Most of them view field survey as a competitive tool to scale up their position.

When there is a convergence in the pursuit of competitive politics with competitive media, readers, voters are likely to be apathetic. On the face of it competition at both ends is good, desirable and help set standards and upgrade quality. But to what extent this is happening?. Or, is it happening at all?. Evidence for any such conclusion, about daunting effects of pre-emptive media coverage of polls, is possible only with controlled – experimental research over time. There is no such study. Neither CSDS nor CMS, which are the potential agencies for such a study in the country, have come up with any evidence. In the absence of any such research, Television Rating Point (TRP) system has become the only yardstick, although such surrogate evidence is inadequate and often even misleading.

In fact, the TRP system by itself is no indicator of viewership or preference for a given programme. In the absence of a culture of "talk back" or active viewership, television set being on at a particular time is presumed as equivalent to viewership. It can only be a first step, essential one though but not a conclusive one. There is no specially designed study on the impact of poll coverage by the news media. This however does not mean poll related coverage has no impact. On the contrary, the political impact of media coverage of poll process could be seen from the anxiety and efforts of political leaders to be visible in the news media. There is ample evidence for that. As a researcher, social activist and having been involved for 40 years, this researcher could say with confidence that leaders, caders and voters alike look for news media for inputs, of course with varied interests. Then, there is ripple effect of what is written or shown in the media. That is, action – reaction of what is covered in the media at various levels and points of poll process. In fact, such coverage often sets the agenda for political discourse, particularly in the context of elections to State Assemblies and Lok Sabha. There are several occasions when news media is the only source to introduce a candidate or party's stand on a contentious issue. More recently, television channels have gone beyond by becoming a forum for contending political parties. By bringing them to a discussion table and making leaders question each other and making the public question the leaders, news channels have become the common platform and, in fact, the only platform and only occasion to assess or appraise contenders. That is how political parties / leaders look forward to avail news media to reach out opinion makers, party cadres and voters. Opinion makers are those who are in active pursuit of talking to, or conversing about an idea or information and in that process influence many others. Opinion makers or/and political cadres are also heavy users of news media. Hence the ripple effect of news media particularly in the context of elections to Assemblies and Lok Sabha. This is because a major part of space in newspapers and TV time is devoted for party politics, politicians, political issues and controversies involving them. However, there was a decline in politics since 2006. One reason for this is increased competition among news media. They are becoming more focused than before in their coverage. Also, they are exploring innovative ways of covering polls rather than limiting to fixed formats and studio based pgorammes. Poll coverage of channels in 2009 has indicated such a trend. They seem to realise the limitation of surveys and look out for alternative ways of covering poll campaign. The Election Commission's curb is expediting this transition from preemptive coverage to proactive or interactive and inclusive coverage. This is good. This trend needs to be sustained. Polls and Politics dominated half of Prime time television channels.

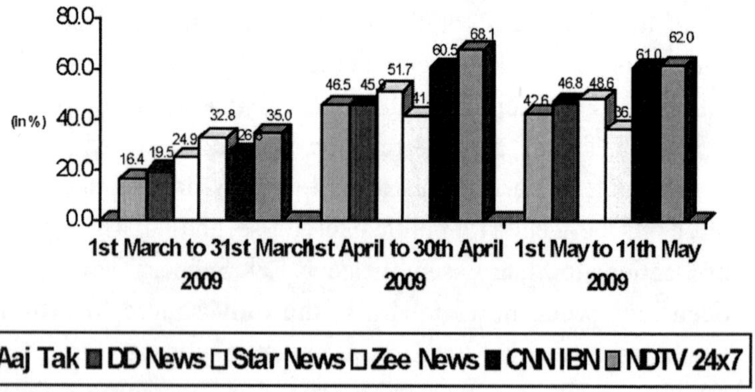


Source: CMS Media Lab

The scope of news media coverage in the context of elections changes from one phase to another in the process. Broadly, this process could be divided into three or four stages. First, guessing phase as to when the elections (Assembly or Lok Sabha) would be held – and whether it is only for Assembly or Lok Sabha or for both. This is because elections could be held before scheduled time if an incumbent fails to hold majority in the House or want to avoid such a situation. The party in power wants to opt for an opportune time to go for polls before the schedule. All parties would like to weigh their chances and gear up instead of getting caught unaware. That is when they look for a survey as a more reliable way of knowing the pulse of the voters and deciding accordingly.

A second phase in the media coverage of electoral process is about *who* will lead the respective parties to polls and *what* could be the main issue on which elections could be fought. Depending on aspirants in each party, they would like to explore and look for inputs as to opportunities including for a coalition arrangement.

Third and fourth phases include candidate selection process, electoral strategy and campaign plan. This phase could be once after poll schedule is announced and the process has set in. Today, every party at State and national level has spokespersons and people for media relations. Their job is to see that news media presents favourable reports. These functionaries are even professionally trained to that effect. Both BJP and Congress party also engage PR experts nationally and regionally to coordinate with news media.

During each one of these phases, there will be suspense, anxiety and feedback requirements which they look for from news media and poll surveys. The more such vacuum the more the opportunity for news media to cover those aspects. The nature and scope of poll surveys and their reliability cannot be the same in each phase of electoral process. 2009 Lok Sabha poll process had surveys conducted by political parties more than once in each of these phases.

## Ripple Effect of Media Coverage

The intense competition among news media being what it is, surveys are being produced by some newspapers over night before the other or along with the other news channel or newspapers. There are a couple of Telugu dailies which pop up with "surveys" and produce a chart with percentages for "Yes" and "No", as if that is good enough proof for that a survey, featured as front page lead story, was actually conducted. A close reading of the story makes it obvious that it was a "dictated survey". Unlike a "doctored survey", this one is totally imagined one to show off support or to rally around to one or the other political party / leader. Because Andhra Jyoti had announced publication in its next day issue of results of a sample survey it carried out on a given political issue, another Telugu daily, front paged a survey on the same issue on the same day claiming that it had "conducted" its own field survey with a bigger sample size than what the other newspaper had. The curious aspect is that results published by the two newspapers differ from each other raising doubt about credibility of such surveys. Such mania for poll surveys for one upmanship is unconcerned about credibility. The news media are already doing this with "SMS polls" – confusing the people and eroding the very relevance of such surveys. And, as if they are doing so more to fill in time / space, raise commercial revenue and lend support (or oppose) to one or other political party - rather than to sustain democracy or to enlighten voters. There is an owner – editor in Andhra Pradesh (never had anything to do with journalism or media directly or indirectly) dictates a "survey" report, sometime on phone, for the front page of the next days issue of the newspaper, including a chart to give it authenticity. (personal discussion with senior news editor). It is not that this newspaper is the only one that indulges in planting surveys. In every State there must be more than one news daily which boasts of such surveys. Now with the number of channels in each State multiplying we will see more such surveys on channels too, sometimes attributing to an unknown source or to a "dummy agency".

A prominent Telugu news channel approached this author in 2006 to help them design a field survey to assess and appraise the performance of party in power in Andhra Pradesh and its future prospects. The field work for the survey was conducted by the field reporters of the channel. The analysis of the field data was also done by its own staff under guidance. The findings were featured in a special programme – but selectively and in such a manner that it could be used for political leverage. Some Telugu news channels organise such surveys. There were nine Telugu 24-hour news channels in January 2009 and the number was likely to be more than a dozen before the year end. And there are 15 daily newspapers in Telugu. One can imagine what it means even if a couple of them take to such surveys as a part of political leverage and for competitive positioning strategy. Surveys are used to stir controversies and to manufacture support. If one channel or newspaper comes up with supporting finding, the other one too will come up with survey findings opposing as if surveys are instruments for manipulation or mobilisation of public opinion.

This was what "media wars" was all about in 2009. In this process media is getting polarised as political parties are without getting distinguished. Now in this scenario how can one expect, the news media to enhance their credibility in the context of elections. That is how Dr Jayaprakash Narayan, made his famous outburst at media at the end of 2009 poll campaign. A well meaning civil servant, took to politics by launching a party and even made a difference in the 2009 Poll campaign. He said that news media was not only misleading voters, but denting the very democracy and their confidence in electoral politics by the way they cover elections.

The news item declaring Rahul Gandhi as the "most liked PM candidate", attributing it to a survey by "Nai Duniya Media Pvt. Ltd", publishers of Nai Duniya, largest circulated Hindi daily, claimed that the exercise involved "550 journalists". It did not say whether these journalists were respondents or they were investigators. For this report, published, as a banner story on the front page, did not give how many people were interviewed, who interviewed them and where they were interviewed and whether any other names were there in the enquiry along with that of Rahul Gandhi. This item was published in most newspapers of India exactly the same way giving the impression that it was a "press release" of Nai Duniya. The newspaper had used the survey to lanch its Delhi edition, same way as some news channels were launched earlier using a survey.

## Domino Effects of Media Coverage

Since the trend now is to use field correspondents / reporters/ stringers of news media for conducting field surveys, it is pertinent to understand the implications of this practice as against investigators of a research agency engaged in conducting field surveys. There are pros and cons. The advantage is that local correspondents are familiar with local settings and could the do the job faster and with the least cost. But, on the other hand, since they are locals, respondents may not like to share whom they intend to vote for or prefer as an MLA or MP. They may even say what is palatable for that particular news media. And when political leanings of news media in the context are known, the findings of such surveys are likely to suffer from such biased responses. If a correspondent of Saakshi (owned by Andhra Pradesh CM's son) goes down to a village and asks a voter whom he / she is likely to vote, how can reliable response be expected. Nevertheless, as a good practice these news media indicate that the survey was conducted by their own reporters – rather than being silent. Sakshi newspaper launched its daily with a survey claiming large sample size conducted by its on "staff" (field and office) but never indicating that. Using own reporters for monitoring ground level implementation of programme (like NREGA, drinking water) could be more reliable than in the case of pre-poll surveys.

Soon after the counting day of the 2009 Lok Sabha polls, this author traced that the first forecast for 2009 Lok Sabha polls was made in August 2008. Arun Nehru started his "2009 Election

Prediction Chart" as a part of his weekly column (Asian Age / Pioneer) in mid August 2008 with certain statewise / party wise numbers, not based on any field survey. No basis was ever explained for the chart. However, most know that it was based on his personal assessment. He was supposed to have been consulting his "old contacts" although he never claimed that in the column. From the very outset he indicated close race between Congress and BJP with neither party any where the number needed but indicated impressive numbers for "third front" parties together. Many in the news media took to Nehru's chart for the next few weeks as the basis or as an input for their news reports.

**Arun Nehru's "2009 Election Prediction Chart"**

| *Date of column/Chart* | *Congress (seats projected)* | *BJP* |
|---|---|---|
| 13.08.08 | 141 | 128 |
| 04.01.09 | 151 | 137 |
| 11.01.09 | 154 | 138 |
| 19.01.09 | 145 | 136 |
| 25.01.09 | 151 | 133 |
| 01.02.09 | 149 | 132 |
| 18.02.09 | 151 | 143 |
| 22.02.09 | 149 | 136 |
| 08.03.09 | 151 | 134 |
| 15.03.09 | 149 | 134 |
| 22.03.09 | 153 | 130 |
| 03.03.09 | 154 | 145 |
| 15.03.09 | 149 | 134 |
| 05.04.09 | 150 | 132 |
| 12.04.09 | 157 | 132 |
| 19.04.09 – after 1st round of polling | 155 | 139 |
| 26.04.09 – after 2nd round of polling | 155 | 142 |
| 10.05.09 – after 4th round of polling | 153 | 147 |
| 17.05.09–(after counting) | 206 | 116 |

*(Asian Age)*

He repeated the same chart with marginal changes in the case of some states or parties in his weekly column between August 2008 to May, 2009. By then that column / chart had become a reference point for other columnists and journalists of English, Hindi and regional language news media across the country. The chart echoed the same scenario with marginal change in numbers as the poll outcome and by November – December 2008 when the talk of the poll schedule got underway, pollsters entered the picture as they were commissioned for poll surveys first by political parties and then by the news media. Pollsters in turn took into account all that the news media was reporting as inputs into their projections. In this process pollsters tended to get influenced by the Nehru column/ charts echoed further in the news media all over as if they were (only?) cross-checking or validating their seat forecasts. That is how the news media and pollsters get into a syndrome. That was how 2009 poll was viewed by journalists, columnists and pollsters alike as "too close" between UPA and NDA or that Jayalalitha stood to benefit from the LTTE issue or that Rajasekhar Reddy's popularity had eroded because of corruption, or that BJP in MP was invincible, etc. This was how, by and large, pollsters got their projection figures despite an undercurrent otherwise significant and spread across a five phased poll over a month, that no sample survey could miss. But it happened not only with pre-poll surveys but even in the case of exit polls in 2009. 2009 was a repeat of 2004 as to such domino effect of one individual's assessment becoming the source for psephological exercises and basis for media coverage.

Going by the figures in Nehru's chart, there was no change in the poll scenario until May 10, 2009. Between January and 10th May 2009, Arun Nehru's chart gave Congress between 151 and 153 seats and BJP between 132 and 147, giving an impression that BJP had improved over the weeks preceding the actual first phase polling on April 13, contrary to what the election results have revealed.

A C Neilson's survey in March 2009 for Star News gave more or less similar numbers (as in Nehru's chart) to Congress and BJP and to some regional parties. This however does not necessarily mean that the agency strictly went by it. Times of India (March 23, 2009) had three column banner "BJP will be close on Congress heals: Survey" and presented a chart similar to that of Nehru's. The "same story" was carried by Dainik Bhaskar on the same day with similar headline on the front page. The numbers were more or less similar to those in Nehru's chart – Congress 144, BJP 137. This was not only in the case of the two contending parties, but even in the case of Paswan's LJP "tipped to increase its tally from 4 to 6" – but also in the case of Orissa. The surveys did not see the wave BJD was making (in the aftermath of its coming out of an alliance with BJP) but concluded no gain and as "losing ground" whereas it swept the polls with a two-thirds majority. This was apparently because of the domino effect of Nehru's chart!. The graph of some pre-poll surveys for 2009 Lok Sabha further indicates this phenomenon.

**Snow balling : "2009 Election Prediction Chart"**

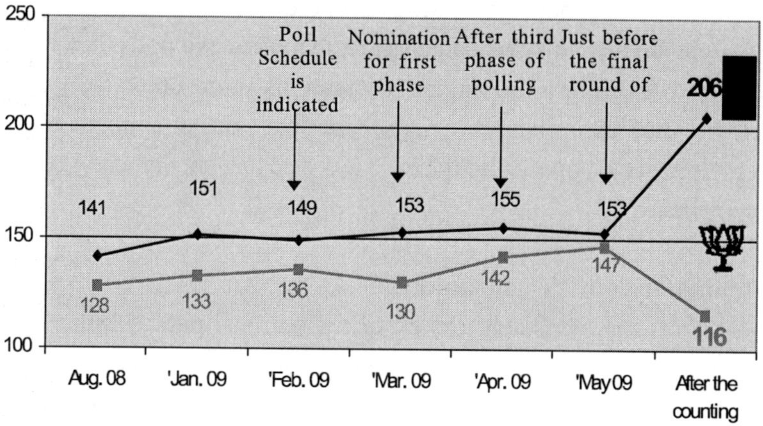


Consider India TV – C-Voter poll. It was conducted, between April 3 and 11 (telecast on 13th April) and projected as a "photo finish" with Congress and BJP getting 143 seats each (against 206 of Congress and BJP's 114 on the counting day). This survey claimed that it "took into account the mood of the people during the uproar over

Varun Gandhi's inflammatory remarks...as also the Jagdish Tytler and Sajjan Kumar's exit" as candidates. In the post-poll analysis both these issues were identified as responsible for Congress party's significant lead. Neither the channel nor the pollster ever cared to explain.

The projection exercise carried by Times of India and the Dainik Bhaskar prominently in the first and second week of March 2009 based on the inputs of their reporters / bureaus was similar – "the race is close", the numbers projected were similar at the national level and in the case of crucial states of Tamil Nadu, Uttar Pradesh, Andhra Pradesh and West Bengal – as in Nehru's charts. Times of India gave a second projection based on the same methodology, showing no change between the 1st week of March and April 2009, same way as Arun Nehru's.

Even exit polls have not gone beyond to reflect an "update" which actually was significant not to get reflected in a sample survey and in an independent psephological exercise.

In the beginning when news media took to exit polls they were expected to bring more angles, projections more objectively and reliably than their own journalists/ reporters. But in a matter of 20 years, the cycle appears complete!. How else this phenomenon could be explained?.

**Manipulation with poll surveys**

Poll surveys conducted by or for political parties cannot get into news media without some tacit understanding between the two. Political parties or leaders choose the timing and specific angle that they like the survey findings to be reported. The understanding may be between the party/leader and an individual journalist or with editor / owner or both.

"Congress sees over 150 seats in own poll" was a front page report in Asian Age on 27 March 2009 when the nominations phase for the first phase polling of the Lok Sabha elections was on. On the same day Times of India had a four column banner story "BJP Survey gives it slight edge in race against Congress" – "saffron party projected to get 160 seats against rival's 135".

Neither of reports mentioned when or where the survey referred to was conducted and whether it was a field sample survey or an assessment of earlier surveys. While Asian Age story was by a news agency (IANS) the one in Times of India attributed the same to "GVL Narasimha Rao who has conducted the survey for BJP". The IANS report claimed that "The findings, revealed to IANS by a trusted party source" and claimed further that survey was "exhaustive and covered all 543 constituencies". Trying to add credibility to the findings, IANS referred in the release that a "similar survey was conducted by the same agency in the Assembly elections" and it "was more or less on the mark". Times of India did not publish IANS report nor the Asian Age carried the Times of India story referred to above. It is obvious from these reports that newspapers know that they were given the "survey story" to influence the poll debate on the eve of nominations phase.

Asian Age published on March 19, 2009 a three column story "survey predicts 20 – 30 for BSP" giving the impression that it was based on a field survey. But on reading the text of the item one could make out that it was based on a "report" "recently submitted to CM Mayawathi" on the "possible outcome" in Uttar Pradesh. The attempt was to show that Mayawathi's BSP is "losing heavily" in Uttar Pradesh. For this "survey" idea was used for the credibility of the planted message although nothing about any such survey was referred to in the text.

A week earlier than the Asian Age report of IANS of 27 March, 2009, Economic Times (March 18, 2009) had a four column story based on the same "leak" or brief by the Congress party. The report "UPA to fall short of majority: survey", "Congress – commissioned survey predicts 150 plus seats for the party". The report sourced to its reporters (C L Manoj and M K Venu) is another example for how "surveys" are used by newspaper and parties to come up with "news stories". The Economic Times, with impressive credentials for its analytical reports, did not mention the name of the agency or where and when the survey was conducted. But it wanted to establish credibility of the story by reporting that "the sample size of around 30,000", to say UPA is "emerging largest block". As in the IANS story, these two senior journalists also reported that "a similar survey done by the same agency during the last round of Assembly polls proved largely accurate". Like Times of India story about BJP survey, this ET report stated that the survey "was submitted to the high command a couple of days back.....".

These cases are mentioned only as an example for many such "plants" by news media using one or the other survey or using "survey" idea for authenticity of the "news". Can we assume that the news agency (IANS) did not know when it released this item on the same "survey plant" reported by Economic Times ten days earlier?. What is that one could make out? Whose credibility was at stake?. Perhaps it was the smartness of a PR agency?. This phenomenon is what this author described a couple of years ago as "jugalbandhi" between "new gatekeepers" of media"!.

Poll surveys, whether conducted by news media or for political parties, directly or through a middle person, get into news media. The news media coverage of poll surveys could be in many ways.

**Polling Agency releasing survey results on its own:** The polling agency releases the findings of a survey it had conducted either on its own or on approach by a news media, mostly as leaks or as press release. It is also done as an opportunity for the agency to come into lime light. This suits both the agency and the media, (the sponsor may or may not like depending on whether the findings are favourable or unfavourable). But the question is why the polling agency did the survey or who had spent the money for the survey?. Research agencies which are engaged in conducting field surveys on various issues using similar frame of respondents as in the case of poll surveys, generate data pertaining to polls by adding questions with no or least additional cost. The most quoted survey of CMS on "note for vote", in 2009, was an example. This was carried out as an "add on" enquiry along with its larger study on "citizen and petty corruption". The MDRA surveys published prominently in Mint in 2009 were also like that. The second type is where a political party underwrites the costs. The third but very rare is where the agency does it on its own as it has manpower available around the time in the field in between two surveys. Once broadband takes roots in the country, more such truly independent surveys could be expected.

**Polling agency going to media at the instance:** Recently the understanding between polling agency and the sponsoring political party / candidate is that the findings of the survey it had commissioned should be released to news media. Some polling agencies, as in the case of CMS and MDRA, do not take such responsibility for media coverage as they think there is a conflict of interest involved. More than a couple of such agencies are active in Delhi and some state capitals.

**Party on its own, as a leak:** A political party on its own leaks the findings at a time when they think newspaper coverage is advantageous. The party does it through a formal press conference or through informal briefs to select media. The Chief Minister of Andhra Pradesh in 2008 and 2009 on the eve of going to polls to Assembly along with Lok Sabha referred to one or other survey finding (without referring to the agency) once a day – as if it were a "mantra" or an unquestionable fact.

**Through a PR by the party:** Some political leaders / candidates as well as major parties have formal or informal arrangement with one or other public relation agency to take on the responsibility of getting poll survey findings covered in news media. Dileep Cherian's PR agency (Perfect Relations) had a formal arrangement more than once with the AICC for such coverage across the country. There are more than one or two individuals, mostly belonging to journalism, who undertake such PR job for political parties including national parties. Their deal includes coming up with dummy surveys and getting the same formally released to media and also to see they are somehow published. One journalist from Rajasthan with no understanding about survey research but with contacts in Delhi political circles claiming a Hindi news agency, has been doing this business for a decade. All that experience he claims for conducting poll surveys was that he translated English into Hindi in slides for a presentation of a poll survey. What should surprise is even the AICC and high level functionaries, formally and informally, used this individual more than a couple of times in the last one decade. The news item, a three column headline "survey predicts 20 – 30 for BSP" in Asian Age (19 March 2009) is a good example for "plants" by PR professionals at the instance of one or other political party. This is not only an example for how "survey" is used to drum up a party but also to plant adverse messages about an opposing party.

**"Should Poll Surveys be Covered in between a Poll Schedule?"**

Do poll surveys in the news media influence voting choice?. Does avoiding media coverage of poll surveys in between polling phases imply curbing fundamental rights?. Since these issues are raised at the time of every election, and since polling for the general election will continue to be a staggered affair over three or more phases, we need to understand the pros and cons of media coverage of poll surveys in between the polling phases. There cannot be any dispute about the fact that for a vibrant democracy both freedom of media and free and fair elections are equally important and neither can be sacrificed for the other.

If poll surveys, both pre-poll and exit poll, have no influence on voters and campaigns, why so many of them are being highlighted in the news media. And why political parties are conducting and sponsoring at various time points of the campaign and getting them covered (by whatever means) and even hyped in the news media. And why political parties are quick to debunk survey findings when they are not in their favour?. The more the gap between the polling phases, the higher the scope for use of surveys for an electoral advantage. To maximize the influence often poll surveys are being presented as if they are independent or objective without even giving minimal information about methodology, sponsorship and giving all relevant findings. That being the case, just before the 2009 Lok Sabha election, there was a rethink on media coverage of poll surveys in between the phases of a staggered poll in the interest of free and fair polls.

This author's analysis of field surveys in the last 38 years, both in the context of elections to the Lok Sabha and the State Assemblies, indicates that 2 to 5 percent of voters eventually end up voting for the "likely winner" notwithstanding their initial intention prior to actual casting of vote. That is what "bandwagon" effect is all about. That is when party workers and voters may change their voting preference from one to another party (or candidate) closer to the voting day. This is based on their perception of the poll scene and about the "likely winner". Such perceptions get accumulated in the minds of voters based on poll campaign and its coverage in the news media. Otherwise why are news media often accused as "trying to influence" the outcome of a poll overtly (by openly endorsing) or covertly (by preferential coverage in terms of time/space), including surveys. Post-poll studies (of CMS in 1996 and 1998) have indicated that the percentage of voters who decide closer to the polling day are on the increase.

In Indian elections, voting choice is not always based on an individual's personal assessment. Family and community often matter equally or even more particularly in the case of relatively well off or close knit communities (as in the case of Jats or Gujjars or Kapus or farmers in some regions). News media, by the extent and nature of their coverage of election campaigns particularly poll surveys, facilitates their voting decision one way or the other.

Also, political parties try to use poll surveys to pep up the morale of their own cadres and demoralize the cadres and campaign of an opposing party. In that process some voters may "migrate" from one party or candidate of initial preference to another one. Survey in one media will have a snow ball effect on other media. Depending upon the nature and keenness of the contests in a given situation, the effect may be good enough to make the difference on the outcome. Another aspect that needs to be taken note of is the increasing competitiveness in the contests in more and more constituencies. That is the margin for win/lose has been on the decline in more constituencies now than ever before. As such a marginal shift of votes is good enough to change the fortunes of a particular candidate/party. About 10 percent of constituencies fall in this category in any given election.

This brings us to another related issue having influence of poll survey forecasts. That is about declining size of cadres of parties. The percent of voters who are activists on behalf of a particular party has been on decline in the recent years in the case of most parties. This has been amply brought out in both pre-poll and post-poll studies. This is one other reason for increase in the size of floating voters from one party to another between two elections to an Assembly or to Lok Sabha.

Pre-poll surveys, nevertheless have good potential to improve the quality of poll campaigns. But have they?. And to what extent?. Campaigns continue to be personality centered, accusation oriented, and increasingly acrimonious. Simultaneously, party manifestos have lost their seriousness and significance. No wonder pre-poll surveys are more concerned in bringing out who wins or loses or the seats they are likely to get rather than the undercurrents and the linkage to voting behaviour. More recently however, some political parties have been using pre-poll surveys to strategize their campaign and make it more focused and localized. But to understand voter behaviour and changing trends in the process, independent field surveys help at various time points before an election. For this, compatible data from time series studies rather than of one time surveys is needed. This is what most news media tend to acquire in their coverage of elections.

Given the peculiar poll and political dynamics in India and fast changing loyalties and shifting stand of leaders and parties, drawing parallels in this regard with other countries is not so relevant. And concluding that any change in voter behaviour is "difficult to prove and in any case (effects) are minimal" is mischievous. For, evidence for any effect or otherwise is possible only when specially designed studies for that are carried out within the country to trace voting behavour at various time points of a poll campaign. A CMS post-poll survey in 1996 has indicated that pre-poll surveys do influence voting preferences of voters, although neither similarly or uniformly across a State or even within a constituency.

The issue is not merely a question of reliability of poll surveys, but about the very intention of surveys whose findings are often presented as if they are independent or objective and as if more the size of sample, the more reliable they are. Or, because the survey was conducted by an "internationally reputed agency", its findings are more reliable?. The issue has to do with media coverage of poll surveys, both pre-poll and exit poll, in between the phases of a staggered schedule and needs to be viewed from the point of view of a free and fair elections.

***Hawa:*** Political parties try to create a *"hawa"* or a "sentiment" in favour or against a coalition. This process involves "creating an impression" among voters, for galvanizing cadres and getting media coverage. The role of news media sets the course and force of such *"hawa"* where the trend and mood at that point is in favour of a party and it enthuses cadres to work with new found confidence. Then of course is the question whether the *hawa* remains until the polling day or it hits a road block from the opposing party/candidate.

**Jugalbandi :** This term was introduced earlier in this chapter. To expand it, poll surveys echo news media coverage of an election campaign and newspapers in turn base their coverage on poll surveys. Such a thing happens not as a coincidence but because players involved in the process are same or have same motivation or have same origins in terms of corporate interests. For example, the nexus of some kind between (PR + MR + Pollsters) public relations, market research, polling and advertising functions. That is when it can be described as a *jugalbandi* phenomenon – coverage of 2004 Lok Sabha and Assembly elections by news channels and newspapers is a good example. Even in 2009 there are certain channels / newspapers who performed *jugalbandi* well.

**Domino effect:** There are instances of pollsters referring to field coverage of campaign by certain newspapers and more specifically to certain columnists or reports of certain senior journalists known for their ground swell. Arun Nehru's column some years ago was one such source for some pollsters at the outset of the campaign. But once a survey gets covered in the news media, prominently or otherwise, columnists and even field reporters of news media echo the trend indicated in the survey. In this process, news media reflect their own inclination. That is depending on their own inclination or bias towards a candidate / party, in a given context, survey findings are highlighted. There are too many examples since 1998 for national channels and newspapers as well as regional ones reflecting such snowballing phenomenon. Once this author got a phone call from an editor of a newspaper asking for the report of a survey. A brief highlight of this survey had appeared in some newspaper and he wanted to feature it prominently in his daily newspaper. He wanted the survey report because the findings were in support of his preferred stand. One reason why pollsters look for news media reports before finalizing their report or /and for coming up with the findings of survey, is that they want to be "safe" or "sure". News media, tend to take quantitative analysis from the sample surveys, to give the impression of authority and objectivity.

What is wrong about it?. Is such a coverage more "authentic" or reliable?. Yes, if the field survey was conducted systematically, independently and with transparency. And, as long as channels in particular do not present the survey as if "that is the way it is" rather than that was only a "possible scenario" at that particular point giving limitations in the exercise. There is nothing wrong in news media endorsing a party/candidate editorially explaining why they are doing so. In fact, that is a better way to contribute to the quality of the campaign than trying to do so in a round about way and with camouflaged coverage or, what CMS describes, as "pre-emptive journalism". In pre-emptive journalism, the tendency is to pre-decide and also preannounce and thereby deflate the significance of and sanctity of vote and movitations/ compulsions of voting on the polling day.

There were hardly any examples in the last decade of news media critically analyzing poll surveys and trying to educate readers / viewers of pros and cons of such surveys – despite several glaring examples of motivated findings of poll surveys being covered in the media. The Hindu and the Frontline made some isolated attempts. On the other hand, news channels and survey agencies keep claiming, by way of advertisements in the media, how accurate their particular survey findings were, even when that was not in fact the exactly the case.

**Celeb crusades & the death of politics**

**P. Sainath**

**The Lok Sabha constituencies of Mumbai averaged over 60 per cent voting between 1957 and 1977. All years of politics, workers' rights, unions, historic policy decisions, rising consciousness and ideological debates.**

The barrage of celebrity propaganda to "get out there to vote" had an impact in Mumbai. Voting fell by 6 per cent.

Corporate media's cutest efforts failed to arrest a decline in voting percentage. Nor did corporate-sponsored events and NGO activism fare any better. The facebook fraternity, and e-activism didn't come out of it too well either (raising questions about real IT penetration even in this wealthy city). That was so even in the constituency that received more space and time than any other – south Mumbai, which saw 40.33 per cent polling (2004:44.22%). Nor did the expected level of "anger over 26/11" materialize much beyond the television studios. There is now a similar trauma over 30/04 (voting day). Many rural constituencies in Maharashtra, despite a relative fall in turnout, saw higher voting than Mumbai.

Even after the polling day, the focus was on how Bollywood stepped up to the challenge of voting. The largest English daily (including its captive tabloid and city supplement) had as many as 11 items across 8 pages on celebrity, mostly Bollywood, voting in Mumbai. These ran

*Contd. on next page*

**More of the same contents**

The scope and structure of contents of news media is "more of the same". That is until recently most channels and most daily newspapers covered polls more or less similarly though with an "angle" or a "tilt" or "focus" in some cases. It was the anxiety of some news media to go beyond such coverage that some newspaper and channels had taken to poll surveys. But the way these survey findings were being presented was also similar. The only difference in presenting survey findings was in terms of "graphics" and studio

*Contd. from previous page*

with heaps of pictures, featuring around 50 film world personae and assorted other celebs, kicking off with the main front-page photograph.

My favourite, though, was the charge of the Lightbulb Brigade on television. On the whole, slumdogs vote in larger numbers than the white-ribbon, candlelight crowds do.

There is even, face it, the apathy of the comfortable. Those who might well explode in drawing-room or television studio outrage about high taxes and 26/11. But who see no real need to fiddle with the status quo. The comfort zone classes exist and are more urban than rural. See the difference between voting in rural Karnataka and Bangalore.

It has much to do with the death of politics. Even the BJP's Hindutva crusade and the Shiv Sena's shrillest campaigns in the1980s and 1990s did not result in Mumbai's best voter turnouts. Has low voting always been the rule here? No. The Lok Sabha constituencies of Mumbai averaged over 60 per cent voting for 20 years between 1957 and 1977.

In the present round, many well-meaning "awareness – raising" groups brought no politics to their voting drive.

At the end of it, voting levels fell in Mumbai. And elsewhere, too. It was curious then, to see one discussion on Maharashtra on television. The panelists wondered if the prospect of Mr. Pawar as Prime Minister would evoke a burst of Maharashtrian pride. And if this would see the NCP-Congress alliance make huge gains. (As the channel's opinion

*Contd. on next page*

format. An over all impression conveyed by 24-hour news channels was to declare the winner – loser and the number of seats that a party was likely to get rather than explaining forces and factors in the poll process.

The participants in studio discussions of survey findings as well as of other poll coverage, are more or less the same leaders from political parties and same pundits from the news media. Participants in some cases were even prompted or made to "fight it out" so that the debate generates a controversy or gets talked about and attracts viewers.

The structure of poll programmes of TV channels earlier was limited to interviews, field coverage of campaign, studio discussions and bytes from field and graphics based on past data or trend in terms of votes polled, margin of wins, candidates, communities, etc. More recently with intensity in competition increasing, channels have expanded debates from being mostly studio based to field based and for live debates from symbolic landmark locations. This recent initiative of channels to bring in citizens, interest groups, experts along with political leaders and activists is a welcome feature of competitive coverage. But even then the number actually taking part in channel circuit would be less than 100. Thanks to competition among news channels, poll coverage has become more inclusive, innovative and

*Contd. from previous page*

poll suggested it would). Now, the alliance could indeed make gains in the state, but would that be the reason? Problem: the decline in voting in Mr. Pawar's bastions in western Maharashtra has been, in relative terms, even grater than that in Mumbai. In Baramati, that decline (compared to 2004) was over six per cent. In Satara, over seven per cent. In Sangli over eight per cent and in Sholapur over 10 per cent. If that is an outburst of pride, it is a very humble pride. Try issues, ideology, politics and decent election schedules. That could bring out for more voters any day. In Mumbai or elsewhere.

broad based in 2009 than only couple of years ego. Between 1998 and 2009 television channels have come a long way in covering elections of State Assemblies and Lok Sabha. In fact, it is this initiative and potential of TV channels that has made newspapers to follow the path of channels and shift over to a more "open – ended" type of coverage.

The open debates started by NDTV a decade ago, have gone much beyond animated studio discussions. Some senior editors anchors like Rajdeep Sardesai and Barkha Dutt deserve praise. Arnab Goswami has acquired his own racing style. They have set examples for channels in other languages. So was Vinod Dua's *"Bus Yatra"* going into markets and communities for a more informal chat-based coverage of the mood of the electorate. Battle ground set by NDTV has enlightened many leaders and voters alike about polls across the county in the last decade and the format is being adopted now by regional language channels. However, this tendency of more of the same of channels often has the chance of over doing or under doing to the extent of going hey-way with poll survey projections.

**Poll Surveys and Media Advertising**

In April 2004, the Supreme Court had expressed its displeasure over acrimonious political advertising on TV and favoured disciplining any mudslinging efforts. This is what the Information and Broadcasting Ministry should have tried at the very outset of 2004 poll campaign, much before the AP High Court hurriedly stayed the ban on political advertising on TV. Instead, the Ministry kept away with an excuse that it had no machinery to monitor TV channels. Since the issue involved is to do with free and fair elections, the government was expected to act promptly and even proactively. The country would have been saved of bitterness in the poll campaigns of 2009 in states like Andhra Pradesh, Orissa and Uttar Pradesh. Nevertheless, since the issue has larger implications, sensitivities need to be understood. If this is done, the issue will not be raked up again as it happened in Andhra Pradesh in 2008–09 three months prior to the announcement of the poll schedule for the State Assembly. It so happened that two leaders (Congress party's Chief Minister YSR Reddy and TDP's Chandrababu Naidu) went berserk with personal accusations against each other through indecent TV and press advertisements, violative of every norm or guideline which Professor Madabhushi Sridhar of Nalsar University of Law, Hyderabad described at length (Bharatiya Pragna, June 2009)

The Indian Broadcasters Federation (IBF) deserve compliments for its decision in 2004 against political ads involving personal acrimonies between political parties/leaders. However, there is no evidence that its advice made any difference. The News Broadcasters Association (NBA) came up with initiatives on election coverage and advertising as it did with coverage of terrorist attacks in the wake of 26/11 attack in Mumabi. Justice J S Verma, under whose stewardship, these guidelines were prepared, should also ensure that at least members of NBA adhere to the guidelines. NDTV should be appreciated for setting an example in this regard. It has taken the initiative by inviting political parties for free telecast on its channels although no information is available whether anyone ever availed of the offer.

There are four basic issues involved in any debate on political advertising on TV. First, differentiation of ads on TV from that of ads in newspapers. Secondly, whether banning political ads on TV amounts to violation of fundamental right to carry on business?. Thirdly, that a ban implies denying access to a powerful media for poll campaigns. And, fourthly, allowing political advertising on TV is nothing but giving fillip to money power in elections. All these questions are also relevant in the context of media converges of poll surveys. But with the lifting of the ban on advertising on TV, 2009 polls have seen a range of advertising although limited mostly to two parties. The Congress party in Andhra Pradesh did maximum advertising on TV for the Assembly polls than ever before with a range of persuasive ads. So also TDP. There was also the example of a new entrant, Lok Satta Party taking to sleek TV advertising in 2009 assembly election in an educative mode and making a dent on the voting in urban areas. Hence we need to understand the larger implications of opening up this route – for crorepati candidates!.

Truly, Television today is a lot more influential than newspapers. It is an instant media and reaches instantly across the nook and corner of the country. There is very little one could do to retrieve a damaging situation once telecast goes on air unlike in the case of newspapers. In the electoral context, where poll campaign is limited to a few weeks, where passions are polarised and emotional animosities sway the campaign, allowing political ads on TV without some norms and discipline, may amount to taking serious risks. Also, advertising on TV is far more expensive than in newspapers and radio to the extent of effecting level playing aspect in a democracy. The argument that cost per contact is lower in the case of TV advertising than print is notional and factually incorrect in the case of poll advertising.

The argument in the AP High Court for lifting the ban was based on the premise that disallowing political ads on TV amounts to fiddling with the fundamental rights of news media and business corporates. However, the fundamental right to do business in the context of broadcasting cannot be unfettered. In this regard it must be understood that as per Supreme Court's landmark judgment (of 1995) airwaves belong to public and any one availing airwaves have to come under certain terms and conditions in the larger public interest. In fact that should be the basis for giving a broadcasting licence. Further, anything on TV that vitiates a free and fair electoral process could be curbed and curtailed under more than one legal provision, including the Cable TV Network Act of 1998. If the government could be empowered to commission private commercial airline services, at times of critical national tasks, why private TV channels can't be roped in at least once in five years for the cause of sustaining democracy, the way AIR and Doordarshan has been for decades?. Section 39(a) of the amended Representation of People Act 2002, empowers the Government to call upon all TV channels to allocate the telecast time freely for debates by registered political parties. In fact, all TV channels and Cable TV should allocate free telecast time for debates by political parties as an obligation. The Election Commission's mandate includes taking reasonable measures to curb activities that go against free and fair conduct of elections. As part of their proactive initiatives, the Election Commission may consult senior editors both in print and electronic media, the same way it frequently interacts with political parties, for their cooperation in implementing poll guidelines.

Third, denying political advertising on TV on an election eve amounts to depriving political parties the most potent medium of mass communication. That is why, in the interest of level playing and fair play, the State should step in and enable political parties to use TV, using the same logic as is being used in allocating time on AIR and Doordarshan free of cost for recognized parties to put forward their position on the eve of an election but in a "non-advertising mode". AIR and Doordarshan, on the other hand, need to reconsider the rules governing actual use of such freely allotted time by parties (instead of allowing them to read out a written script).

Fourth, today there is a realization in the countries, wherever political advertising on TV has been around for some years, to reduce money power in the elections as high expenditure implies distortion of core character of a democracy. In fact, in the USA the concern about this phenomenon is widespread and several national bodies have of late looked for ways of getting out of the trap that political advertising on TV has resulted in distorting the very approach of campaigning and motivating voters. That TV advertising is effecting equal opportunity to political parties and committing parties/candidates to big contributors is too obvious. Affordability to advertise on TV rather aggressively election after election, has become a compulsion to get elected in US politics.

In this regard Sri Lanka has set a good example. Concerned about "misuse of electronic media", on the eve of national elections, the Election Commission of Sri Lanka had appointed an independent authority in 2004 to oversee poll coverage on radio and TV, including Sri Lanka Broadcasting Corporation (counterpart of Doordarshan/ Prasar Bharati). In fact, the Election Commission should lose no time in coming up with norms for political ads and TV coverage of campaigns, as it did on the eve of 2009 Lok Sabha poll, including poll eve surveys.

On the eve of 2009 elections, the Press Council of India also framed guidelines for the media "for free and fair coverage of news relating to the election process". According to them "it will be the duty of the media to give objective reports about the election and the candidates". They are "not expected to indulge in unhealthy election campaigns, exaggerated reports about any candidate or party or incidents during the election". And it reminds that election campaigns on "communal lines are banned under the Representation of the Peoples Act, 1951. Further, that the campaigns "should eschew reports which tend to promote feelings of enmity or hatred between people or hatred between people or hatred between people on grounds of region, religion, race, caste or community".

A close analysis of contents of campaigns of parties/candidates/ leaders and their reporting in news media in 2009 election campaign gives the impression that each of them were competing more to violate all that is there in the codes, guidelines and the Act rather than to comply with.

**Insights from Media Coverage of Polls**

Despite all the expansion, proliferation and the boom in news media recently, the "influence of media" in the context of civic issues seems to be less today than it was some years ago. Even so their credibility. Even in the US in 2004(not so in 2008), the Presidential candidate endorsed by prestigious news media lost out as if such a support made no difference, including "9/11" film presenting President Bush as a villain. How else could one explain, for example, that the voter turnout in India has been static or on decline in clusters where exposure to news media in the country is relatively higher?. Both in 2004 and 2009, the media made all out efforts towards promoting voter turnout. But no difference. Studies have indicated that this was because of limited representative character, priorities and concerns of the news media. So, the disconnect of news media is on account of irrelevance or disconnect with the basic concerns of people and grassroots. No wonder why Journalists organizations themselves maintain that today journalism as a profession has declined despite increased profits of media corporates. This shift in the paradigm needs to be understood in the larger context. (refer to Media Scene as India Globalizes, CMS 2005)

The second is blatant bandwagoning tendency in the news media; This trend of bandwagoning in the media as we witnessed more in 1998, 2004 and 2009 cannot be described as complacency about grassroots; it could be *commerce* and *convenience*. In the author's book in 1968, "Politics of Leadership in an Indian State", he described in one chapter, how news media tend to get *rally around political parties* - journalists by sharing or *pooling their copy* and newspaper managements by *currying favours*. What we have witnessed in recent years is a similar phenomenon – but on a bigger scale. The *difference is, there are more partners and players* competing in this process now. That is how, we see *more of the same,* in the media irrespective of ownership pattern. Such a trend could also be seen in the coverage of corproates and markets.

Media coverage of poll scene in India *took a turn* in the second half of 1960's in the wake of the eclipse of the Swatantra Party in the Lok Sabha poll preceded by an intense media pre-occupation in its favour. That was when media was widely accused of blatant bias and gross disconnect with outside metropolitan India. It was that realization that lead to a wave of expansion – mostly of regional newspapers. Also, it was that experience which lead to great editors of the day looking for *alternate ways of covering election campaigns and more objectively*. That was *how sample surveys* had started to appear and have caught on. Of course it was TV, which opened up this window more than two decades later.

The third is that elections since 1998 have brought out the *inadequacies of poll surveys* and *misleading use* of them by news media as well as by political parties – even in the US polls such was the feeling. This issue alone needs a wider study and debate. Earlier we were not sure of *effects* of poll surveys, but 2004 Lok Sabha poll and subsequent Assembly polls, including Andhra Pradesh Assembly poll of 2009, had brought out certain "double edged" character of poll surveys. The kind of one-upmanship, in the name of competition, even among research agencies and psephologists in 1998 - 2009 was unprecedented. It was as if they operate in tandem. No wonder, why there was no plausible explanation for the "mislead" from neither of the agency *after* April 2004 or after May 16, 2009. US networks on the other hand, tried to give an explanation for their fiasco and were restrained in their coverage to avoid a repeat in 2004 and in 2008.

Methodologies used by research agencies in this context, have by and large remained the same despite significant changes in the political dynamics of the country. For example, using past voting pattern as the basis for projecting seats/votes despite shifts in the very paradigm of politics is one aspect, particularly because of delimitation of constituencies. Going off the mark is nothing unusual in the case of pre-poll surveys. But, not so with exit polls, particularly the way they were in 1998 and 1999. And yet, 2004 and 2009 witnessed further debacle and by the same psephologists – as if we have not learnt or corrected survey and projection methodologies.

Subjectivity based projections of psephologists (implied in exit polls) about something they did not conduct the survey, cannot be expected any better than the specialized working journalists. Exit-polls implied increased weightage to the subjectivity elements. That is how they further eroded the very credibility of such poll surveys. And then the fascination for "larger" and "largest" ever sample size claims (by channels and survey agencies) had ensured *faux pas of exit polls*. Yet, there was hardly any practice of having serious

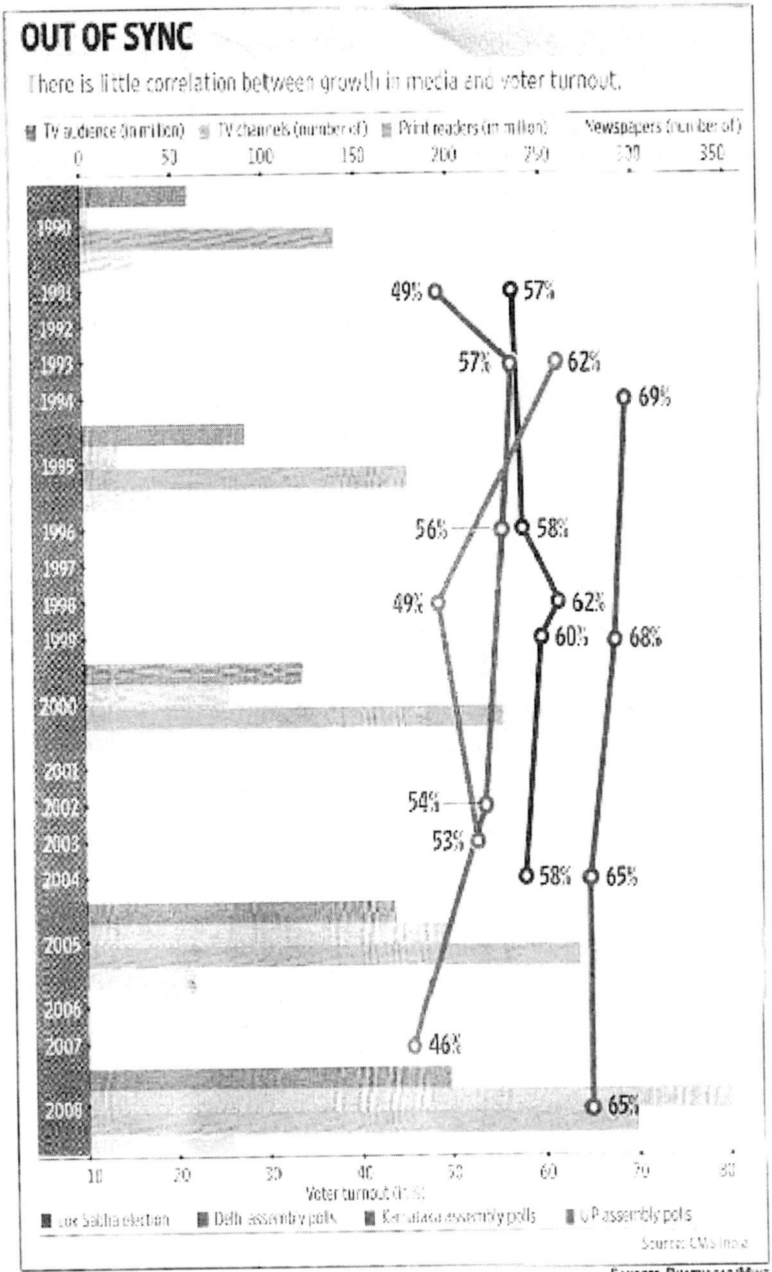


*From P.N Vasanti's column at Mint, November 2008*

interaction between editors/journalists and those who are described as psephologists engaged in the numbers game, before giving out their "results". TV channels have mis-presented exit polls. Lack of sensitivity in the media itself about methodologies too has added to certain "let down" for surveys and psephologists. Invitation to a two day "open house on pre-poll surveys" at CMS Research House, New Delhi, 3 – 4 weeks prior to the poll days in the last couple of Lok Sabha elections, for example, had no New Delhi journalist to come by.

By now everyone knows that poll surveys have become a commercial proposition, a very lucrative one particularly for the one-man surveyors. And yet their presence has been prominent in the media. It has become a "free-for-all" affair. Political parties, parallely, have been using and viewing such poll-eve surveys as part of their election strategies and campaigns. That is how there were so *many plants in the media* in so many different ways, some of them so blatantly. As a result, there is ambiguity on the *four core aspects* of psephological exercises: *(1) Independence, (2) objectivity, (3) reflective or representativeness and in the (4) very transparency of the exercise.*

The fourth observation is as if *all that was because of a "Jugalbandhi phenomenon".* A week to week analysis of coverage in the news media (newspapers and news channels) between January and end of April 2004 and January – April 2009, for example, brings out certain gang up between key players as if it was a Jugalbandhi phenomenon; These include market researchers, public relation firms, advertising agencies and the news media themselves and, of course, the political parties. This phenomenon in was too obvious.

The fifth observation is *politicians pampering media (owners and journalists) and media pampering the political bosses.* How else can one explain some survey researchers becoming overnight rich and resourceful or strategists in the power circles. Despite no guarantee of an incumbent had come back to power, riding on the power of news media, our political parties do not seem to learn lessons. Fear of a boomerang too does not seem to bother our leaders. For, we have examples in India as well as in USA of parties losing despite high pitch media coverage and campaign and reliance on poll surveys. And, in 2004 and 2006 we also had examples of one or two political party scoring impressively - without much coverage in the news media. *That voters* can neither be taken granted or mislead by news media - not every time and not in all contexts is what the lesson is all about. Voters can no longer be viewed as "gullible public". Membership in self-help groups in Andhra Pradesh in 2009, for example, had far more significance on high women voter turnout than of their media exposure although there is no research evidence to present here.

**MAYAWATI DEBUNKS MEDIA-CENTRIC MODEL**

BSP's Mayawati has demonstrated in the landmark Assembly Uttar Pradesh election (2007) how unconventional wisdom could sway voters in the days of hi-tech expensive campaigns. In the process certain myths like that media, money and muscle power determines a poll outcome have been exploded, including poll surveys.

While the other parties in UP were busy with media hype, BSP was busy at the grassroots and, in fact, kept away from the news media. Mayawati did not care what the other contenders were arguing out in the television studios and in the newspapers pages. She also did not waste money on advertising, getting surveys and visibility in the news media. Rather she had gone for localized and personalized campaigns infusing confidence in caders, motivating workers and appealing to those who were not known BSP voters. That is how BSP was able to mobilize its voters when the overall turnout in all the seven phases was an all time low. Unlike other parties, Mayawati had no populist promises, and no poll manifesto. She kept the media at bay because she had no problem of disconnect with different sections of the people.

She had also not wasted her time on commissioning pre-poll surveys or exit polls and had not gone for any animated studio

*Contd. on next page*

**Trivialized poll coverage: 2009 polls**

News channels of the country had gone agog on the evening of the last day of polling of 2009 Lok Sabha election with exit polls galore although the counting day of votes was still two days away. Most of 200 news channels in the country had broadcast one or other "poll survey" estimating partywise/ statewise seats. 16 news channels did their own "commissioned exit polls". In all some 20 surveys must have been conducted (at a cost of over Rs.10 crores – assuming that surveys in fact were conducted as claimed). There must have been as many private exit poll surveys by political parties and lobbyists in the country. The Congress and the BJP also released their "internal exit poll" to the news media. Most local language

*Contd. from previous page*

discussions of channels on poll surveys. All this enabled her to have a proactive campaign from the very outset.

Of about Rs.700 crores spent (as per CMS estimate) by political parties and their candidates in Uttar Pradesh Assembly poll, BSP's share was the least - around ten percent. SP, on the other, spent four times more and conducted more than a couple of poll surveys. BJP and Congress spent about 35 percent and also got poll surveys conducted. Nor did BSP spend to procure votes. She also has not depended on outside the State leaders to campaign for her candidates as the other parties did. BSP cadres and leaders concentrated to their own pockets or constituencies.

In the ultimate analysis, if every party follows the course as BSP did in this UP Assembly poll, the electoral process in India would be far more dispassionate and democratic. The elections would be much less caste and communal based and much less money power driven and more concerned about basic issues of people. The news media too could benefit by deepening their penetration among people.

The coverage of 2008 Presidential election by the US media has some pertinent lessons for India. Similarly, elections to State Assemblies

*Contd. on next page*

news channels carried surveys conducted by one or other national channel. Never before the viewer would have been so confused with the presentation of TV channels as in 2009. In the earlier Lok Sabha polls, not more than 3 or 4 channels carried exit polls.

However, no two surveys matched in their figures and in fact the difference from one survey / channel to another was so much that they could only add to the suspense, curiosity and anxiety and increase political uncertainty and even betting transactions. What was projected for Congress in Andhra Pradesh, for example, was any where between 15 to 29 Lok Sabha seats (out of 42), from one poll to another, for TDP it was between 10 to 19 and for PRP 0 to 3. In the case of Tamil Nadu, one channel showed 20 seats for DMK and others showed highest 24 for AIADMK and 10 for DMK (out of 38). Even national projections varied similarly. The forecasts of exit polls were even vague and confusing. It was 25-35 for BSP in Uttar

*Contd. from previous page*

and for Lok Sabha held since 2003 had several insights in the context of news media coverage of polls in 2009. 2004 polls had exposed news media, survey research agencies even more, and political parties further. In this regard, five observations are worth making.

The first is *the disconnect* of news media. We already know about the *divides* of various kind in the country. But the *disconnect* of the news media, the metro media more specifically, with the main stream India has not been a concern, despite it being a source for some of the divides. Senior Journalists like Nikhil Chakraborthy and H K Dua did write candidly about this phenomenon more than a decade ago. Between the *divide and the disconnect* are the *deep pockets* that media tend to cater to more. That is how media priorities and the popular wavelengths are at such a variance. We are being reminded of this at the end of every election.

*From Transparency Review, May-June 2007, by Dr N Bhaskara Rao*

Pradesh, 30-40 for Left and the like. According to Times Now, AIADMK piped DMK, but according NDTV, DMK was far ahead.

Channels/agencies claimed that their exit poll was "largest ever" or "most authentic" or "definitive" or "most trusted" or "most credible poll survey", etc. They claimed sample of anywhere between 70,000 to 1,60,000 voters spread across the five phases. Some channels released their findings to news agencies by noon itself with a 5 p.m. embargo. Sample size claimed was several times more than what it was for similar exit polls in 2004 and earlier Lok Sabha elections.

The glut was the result of "channel war fare syndrome". That was how a political leader described the poll surveys. But, curiously as in 2004 and earlier, in 2009 too political parties were quick to publicly debunk exit polls, including the ones who themselves, had conducted one or more exit polls. Exit polls have been criticized by most political leaders as "biased", "speculative", "politically inspired" and so on. In 2009 TDP and Congress party in Andhra Pradesh got exit polls conducted by more than one external agency and also internally.

And yet exit polls have proved wrong more often. Not only all exit polls of 2004 Lok Sabha had gone wrong, but the ones conducted for Assembly polls since also had gone wrong, including the classic case of Narendra Modi in Gujarat, Chandrababu Naidu in Andhra Pradesh in 2004, Ajit Jogi in 2008, Veerabhadra Singh in Himahcal Pradesh in 2007, and of course, of Samajwadi Party in Uttar Pradesh in 2002.

**Predictions and Results**

An analysis of surveys conducted by news media over the last couple of rounds of national and state elections brings out how survey projections have been off the mark, not only in 2009 and 2004 but also earlier. Many pre-poll surveys were however correct in indicating the direction and even the trend. But is it good enough to justify such an expensive and intensely discussed exercise. Proliferation of poll surveys started in 1991 and more visibly from 1996 Lok Sabha Poll.

As long as poll surveys were limited to newspapers, their number was limited and also generally were more considerate.

The increase in the number of poll surveys and in the number of channels taking to poll surveys however does not indicate any competitiveness as to their reliability and relevance or concerns in their presentation. There is more evidence for one to say the opposite. A review of the projections of poll surveys and actual results indicate such a trend. No wonder why columnists from outside politics and journalism in more and more numbers are becoming critical. Dhirendra Kumar's column in the Hindustan Times in the wake of 2009 Lok Sabha polls (May 18, 2009) sums up that phenomenon.

One can make out from a comparison of both the projected figures and the news write up with the actual results that those news media who did the exercise internally were off the mark. While the idea of using staff reporters and bureau to do a survey is good, it requires considerable preparations and networking with professionals. The fact that they (TOI, Dainik Bhaskar are given here only as an example) were off the mark, even more than the poll surveys of course with large samples, should not get discouraged. Such experimentation should continue notwithstanding the accuracy aspect. What should be of far more importance for the "fourth effects" in covering the poll is the process view and reminding every one concerned that means (of winning) are as relevant as the outcome in electoral politics.

**Lok Sabha 2009:**
**Pre Poll Surveys and Actual Results**

| *News Media* | *Survey Agency* | *Sample size* | *Date of Publication/ Telecast* | *NDA* | *UPA* | *LEFT* | *Forth Front* | *Others* |
|---|---|---|---|---|---|---|---|---|
| CNN-IBN | CSDS | 16569 | Feb. 22 | 165-185 | 215-235 | 35-45 | 90-110 | |
| Star News | AC Nielsen | 50402 | Mar. 22 | 184 | 210 | 96 | 47 | 6 |
| India Today | ORG-AC | 12374 | Apr. 3 | 195-200 | 150-170 | 85-100 | 110-125 | |
| India TV | C Voter | 30000 | Apr. 13 | 189 | 187 | 115 | 41 | 11 |
| NDTV | GfK-MODE | 51390 | Apr. 14 | 160-170 | 205-215 | 120-130 | 30-35 | 6-10 |
| The Week | C Voter | 30318 | Apr 19 | 186 | 198 | | 159 | |
| Times of India | Own | | May 6 | 187 | 195 | 111 | 50 | |
| Business Standard | Own | | | 184 | 176 | | 93 | |
| DNA | Own | | | 177 | 184 | | 182 | |
| | **Actual Result (May 16, 2009)** | | | **157** | **262** | **80** | **27** | **17** |

## WHAT THEY PROJECTED

Lok Sabha 2009: exit polls and actual results

Telecast on 13 May 2009

| News media | NDA | UPA | Third Front | Others |
| --- | --- | --- | --- | --- |
| CNN-IBN | 165-180 (135-150) | 185-205 (145-160) | 110-130 | 20-30 |
| Times Now | 183 | 198 | 112 | 50 |
| Headlines Today | 180 | 191 | 38 | 134 |
| India TV-C voter | 189 (143) | 195 (152) | 113 | 14 |
| News X | 191 | 199 | 104 | 49 |
| Star News-Nielsen | 198 (154) | 202 (157) | 97 | 12 |
| Zee Business | 208 (157) | 182 (145) | 109 | 14 |
| UTVI | 195 | 183-195 | 105-121 | |
| News 24 | 194 | 218 | 101 | |
| NDTV | 177 | 216 | 105 | 45 |
| **Actual results** (16 May 2009) | **157 (116)** | **262 (206)** | **80** | **44** |

*Figures in bracket are for Congress and BJP on their own

Compiled by CMS Media Lab

SANDEEP BHATNAGAR/MINT

*From P.N Vasanti's column at Mint, June 2009*

**The Hindustan Times** **May 18, 2009**

# Perils of non-linear predictions show up

TO LOOSELY paraphrase Danny DeVito in some movie, 'No one can foretell the future. That's why it's called the future."

That's a lesson that's always been there for all manner of soothsayers and their followers to learn. You couldn't tell this from watching the news channels, but the electorate has made an even bigger joke of psephologists and pollsters than it has of Lalu Yadav, Paswan and the Left.

I feel this rather strongly as an investment analyst and advisor. Election pollsters may crawl out of the woodwork only once in a while, but their investment equivalents are in business all the time, even though they have been wrong almost all the time. Over the last two years, they've been wrong first on the way down, and then on the way up.

The basic problem is not that this or that psephologists or analyst doesn't know how to do his job, but that this job cannot be done, at least in any useful way. Almost by definition.

Indian elections are what would be called a non-linear system in science or maths. In such systems, small changes in inputs produce large changes in the output. These changes are neither proportional to, nor even necessarily in the same direction as the changes in input.

A first-past-the-post parliamentary election with a huge number of fragmented battlefields is severely non-linear. At any reasonable sample size, perfectly reasonable sampling errors would magnify to such huge deviations in the final results that the entire exercise will be meaningless. There's no hope of making a correct prediction, except a fluke once in a while. As the results of the past many elections prove, this is an exercise that can't succeed.

Or maybe not. Whether this exercise was a success or not actually depends on what its goal was. I'm just naively assuming that the goal was to make correct predictions.

However, there should be no such ambiguity about the purpose of predictions about stock markets. Those should have a precisely-defined goal—to help people make more money, or at the very least, to help them lose less money. Unfortunately, the stock markets are an even more non-linear system. Besides having a wide variety of poorly-knowable inputs, it is a system in which its own outputs are continuously becoming further inputs, like a vicious circle.

Interestingly, while both systems seem immune to systematic analysis, in my experience they both yield to the instinctive understanding of people.

In these elections, practically every experienced journalist who had traveled across the country would privately say that the Congress was likely to sweep the polls. Once upon a time, this would have been the view that the media would have carried. Unfortunately, we have developed a mindset where we would rather trust half-baked systems with a veneer of science and ignore the instincts of the experienced.

dhirendra@valueresearch.com

**Lok Sabha Poll 2009**

**How Poll Surveys Projected over the weeks**

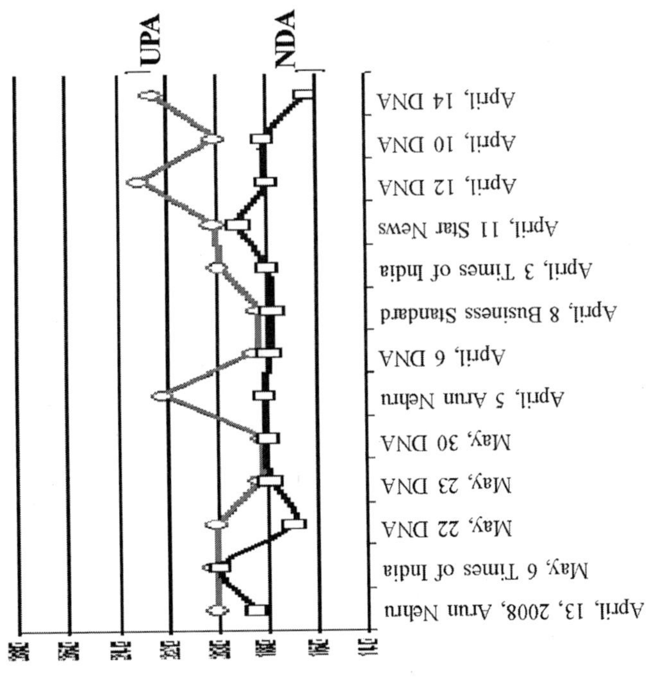


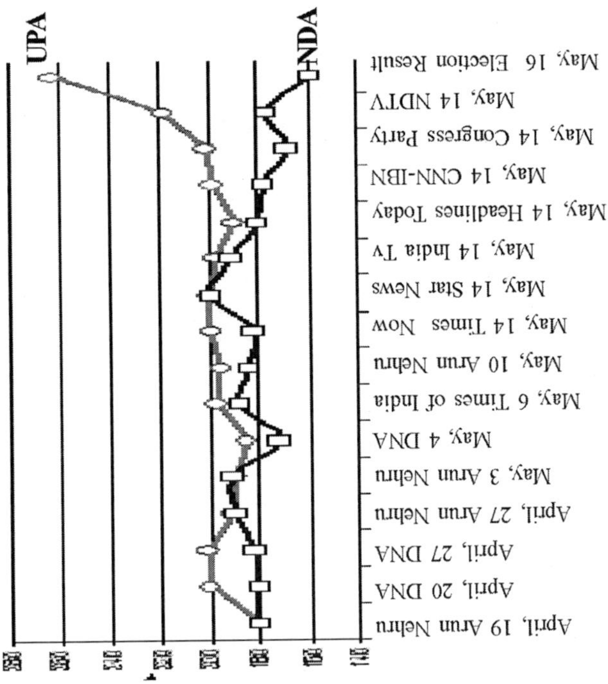

**Lok Sabha 2004:**
**Pre Poll Surveys and Actual Results**

| *News Media* | *Survey Agency* | *Sample size* | *NDA* | *Cong+* | *Others* |
|---|---|---|---|---|---|
| Outlook | MDRA | 12,249 | 280-290 | 105-115 | 89-99 |
| Sahara TV | DRS | 65,089 | 271 | 168 | 104 |
| The Week | TNS | 17,513 | 230-265 | 170-200 | 95-110 |
| India Today | ORG Marg | 51,000 | 282 | 165 | 96 |
| NDTV-Indian Express | AC Nielsen | 16,393 | 260-280 | 165-180 | 97-105 |
| Star News | C-Voter | 12,000 | 272-286 | 154-170 | 95-11 |
| **Actual Result (May 25, 2004)** | | | **185** | **220** | **137** |

**Lok Sabha 1999:**
**Pre Poll Surveys and Actual Results**

| *News Media* | *Survey Agency* | *Sample size* | *Date of Publication/ Telecast* | *BJP+ NDA* | *Congress+* | *Others* |
|---|---|---|---|---|---|---|
| India Today | INSIGHT | 20640 | 13 Aug. 1999 | 322-336 | 132-146 | 70-80 |
| Outlook | CMS | 14220 | 19 Aug. 1999 | 319-329 | 135-145 | 78-83 |
| Hindustan Times | Lokmat-CMCR-IMS | 15199 | 30 Aug. 1999 | 265-270 | 210-215 | 60-65 |
| Hindustan Times | AC Nielsen | 13959 | 1 Sep. 1999 | 300 | 146 | 97 |
| Pioneer | DRI | 14850 | 3 Sep. 1999 | 313-318 | 140-145 | 84-89 |
| Times of India | DRS | 23098 | 1 Oct. 1999 | 284 | 179 | 80 |
| | **Actual Result (October 5, 1999)** | | | **296** | **134** | **107** |

**Delhi Assembly Election 2008:**
**Pre Poll Surveys and Actual Results**

| *News Media* | *Survey Agency* | *BJP* | *INC* | *BSP* | *Others* |
|---|---|---|---|---|---|
| Star News (November 8, 2008) | AC Nielsen | 29 | 38 | | 3 |
| The Week (November 21, 2008) | C Voter | 36-42 | 28-34 | 1-5 | |
| Star News (November 26, 2008) | AC Nielsen | 27 | 39 | 3 | |
| **Actual Result 2008** | | **23** | **42** | **2** | **2** |

## Delhi Assembly Election 2003:
## Pre Poll Surveys and Actual Results

| *News Media* | *Survey Agency* | *BJP* | *Congress* | *Others* |
|---|---|---|---|---|
| Zee News (Nov 28, 2003) | C-Voter | 14-22 | 43-51 | 7-11 |
| Times of India (Nov. 22-24, 2003) | DRS | 28 | 37 | 5 |
| Hindustan Times (Nov 28, 2003) | CSDS | 10 | 58 | 2 |
| Sahara Samay | DRS | 26 | 40 | 4 |
| (Nov 29, 2003) | TNS Mode | 11-20 | 46-54 | 5-8 |
| The Week (Nov 30, 2003) | AC Nielsen | 11 | 56 | 3 |
| Outlook-Zee News (Dec 1, 2003) | ORG-Marg[4] | 10-20 | 50-65 | 0-5 |
| India Today – Aaj Tak (Dec 1, 2003) | C Voter[3] | 21-29 | 40-48 | 1-4 |
| Zee News (Nov 14, 2003) | DRS | - | - | - |
| Times of India (Nov. 13, 2003) | ORG-MARG[1] | 10-20 | 45-55 | 0-5 |
| India Today – Aaj Tak (Nov. 3, 2003) | CSDS[2] | - | - | - |
| Hindustan Times | CINS | 18 | 42-46 | |
| **Actual Result** | | 20 | 47 | 3 |

[1] ORG-MARG has not provided sample size state wise. Over all in the four states the agency has sampled **17413** respondents spread across **115** assembly constituencies.

[2] At the time forecast was made only 55 assembly constituencies were covered. How ever subsequently CSDS has sampled 14000 voters spread across all 70 constituencies in Delhi.

[3] ZEE - C Voter Poll Methodology (November 14, 2003)

1. Phase I: Qualitative study of all 590 seats in the four states.
2. Phase II: 12000 voters were covered across 245 seats
3. Phase III: 4000 voters across the 40 seats in the last 7 days

[4] ORG-MARG second round of opinion poll covered 21,773 respondents across 142 assembly constituencies in four states

## Madhya Pradesh Assembly Election 2008: Pre Poll Survey and Actual Result

| News Media | Survey Agency | BJP | INC | Others |
|---|---|---|---|---|
| The Week (November 21, 2008) | C Voter | 118-128 | 100-110 | 5-15 |
| **Actual Result** | | **144** | **70** | **16** |

## Madhya Pradesh Assembly Election 2003: Pre Poll Surveys and Actual Results

| News Media | Survey Agency | BJP | Congress | BSP | Others |
|---|---|---|---|---|---|
| Zee News (Nov 28, 2003) | C-Voter | 133-141 | 62-70 | -- | 25-29 |
| Sahara Samay (Nov 29, 2003) | DRS | 160 | 55 | 5 | 10 |
| The Week (Nov. 30, 2003) | TNS Mode | 165-195 | 19-33 | - | 14-34 |
| Outlook-Zee News (Dec 1, 2003) | AC Neilsen | 147 | 58 | - | 25 |
| India Today – Aaj Tak (Dec 1, 2003) | ORG MARG[3] | 140-150 | 55-65 | - | 15-25 |
| Zee News (Nov 14, 2003) | C. Voter[2] | 122-130 | 77-85 | - | 19-27 |
| India Today – Aaj Tak (Nov 3, 2003) | ORG-MARG[1] | 115-135 | 75-95 | 20-25 | - |
| Indian Express (Sept 18, 2003) | Internal Cangress Survey | 114-145 | 108 | - | |
| **Actual Result** | | **173** | **38** | **2** | **17** |

[1] ORG-MARG has not provided sample size state wise. Over all in the four states the agency has sampled **17413** respondents spread across **115** assembly constituencies.

[2] ZEE - C Voter Poll Methodology (November 14, 2003)

1. Phase I: Qualitative study of all 590 seats in the four states. 2. Phase II: 12000 voters were covered across 245 seats 3. Phase III: 4000 voters across the 40 seats in the last 7 days

[3] ORG-MARG second round of opinion poll covered 21,773 respondents across 142 assembly constituencies in four states

### Rajasthan Assembly Election 2008: Pre Poll Survey and Actual Result

| News Media | Survey Agency | BJP | INC | Others |
|---|---|---|---|---|
| The Week (November 21, 2008) | C Voter | 94-106 | 94-106 | 4-14 |
| **Actual Result** | | **78** | **96** | **32** |

### Rajasthan Assembly Election 2003: Pre Poll Surveys and Actual Results

| News Media | Survey Agency | BJP | Congress | Others |
|---|---|---|---|---|
| Zee News (Nov 28, 2003) | C-Voter | 80-96 | 96-112 | 11-27 |
| Sahara Samay (Nov 29, 2003) | DRS | 95 | 85 | 20 |
| The Week (Nov 30, 2003) | TNS MODE | 55-60 | 125-135 | 10-14 |
| Outlook-Zee News (Dec 1, 2003) | AC NEILSEN | 67 | 113 | 20 |
| India Today-Aaj Tak (Dec 1, 2003) | ORG-MARG[3] | 55-65 | 120-130 | 15-20 |
| Zee News (Nov 14, 2003) | C Voter[2] | 77-85 | 107-115 | 5-13 |
| India Today – Aaj Tak (Nov 3, 2003) | ORG-MARG[1] | 73-83 | 110-120 | 5-15 |
| Hindustan Times (Aug 30, 2003) | MMR | 105 | 89 | - |
| **Actual Result** | | **120** | **56** | **24** |

[1] ORG-MARG has not provided sample size state wise. Over all in the four states the agency has sampled **17413** respondents spread across **115** assembly constituencies.

[2] ZEE - C Voter Poll Methodology (November 14, 2003)

1. Phase I: Qualitative study of all 590 seats in the four states.
2. Phase II: 12000 voters were covered across 245 seats
3. Phase III: 4000 voters across the 40 seats in the last 7 days

[3] ORG-MARG second round of opinion poll covered 21,773 respondents across 142 assembly constituencies in four states

## Chhattisgarh Assembly Election 2008: Pre Poll Surveys and Actual Results

| *Media Agency* | *Survey Agency* | *BJP* | *INC* | *Others* |
|---|---|---|---|---|
| Star News (November 8, 2008) | AC Nielsen | 55 | 33 | 2 |
| The Week (November 21, 2008) | C Voter | 44-52 | 38-46 | 3-7 |
| **Actual Result** | | **50** | **38** | **2** |

## Chhattisgarh Assembly Election 2003: Pre Poll Surveys and Actual Results

| *News Media* | *Survey Agency* | *BJP* | *Congress* | *NCP* | *Others* |
|---|---|---|---|---|---|
| Zee News (Nov 28, 2003) | C-Voter | **30-38** | **41-49** | **5-9** | **2-6** |
| Sahara Samay (Nov 29, 2003) | DRS | **33** | **49** | - | **8** |
| Outlook-Zee News (Dec 1, 2003) | AC Nielsen | **43** | **43** | - | **4** |
| India Today-Aaj Tak (Dec 1, 2003) | ORG-MARG[3] | **30-40** | **46-56** | - | **2-10** |
| Zee News (Nov 14, 2003) | C Voter[2] | **34-42** | **40-48** | **4-9** | **2-6** |
| India Today – Aaj Tak (Nov. 3, 2003) | ORG-MARG[1] | **38-48** | **38-48** | - | - |
| Indian Express (September 29, 2003) | Jabalpur Agency | **48** | **34** | | |
| Sahara Samay Sahara Times (Sep 27, 2003) | DRS | - | - | - | |
| **Actual Result** | | **50** | **37** | **1** | **2** |

[1] ORG-MARG has not provided sample size state wise. Over all in the four states the agency has sampled **17413** respondents spread across **115** assembly constituencies.

[2] ZEE - C Voter Poll Methodology (November 14, 2003)

1. Phase I: Qualitative study of all 590 seats in the four states.
2. Phase II: 12000 voters were covered across 245 seats
3. Phase III: 4000 voters across the 40 seats in the last 7 days

[3] ORG-MARG second round of opinion poll covered 21,773 respondents across 142 assembly constituencies in four states

**Lok Sabha Poll Surveys - a comparison 1998-2009: some examples**

| *Year* | *Alliance* | *Actual Results* | *Projection By* | | |
|---|---|---|---|---|---|
| | | | *Star News* | *India Today* | *Outlook* |
| 2009 | NDA | **157** | 198 | 195-200 | - |
| | UPA | **262** | 202 | 150-170 | - |
| | LEFT+ | **80** | 97 | 85-100 | - |
| | Others | **44** | 46 | 110-125 | - |
| 2004 | NDA | **185** | 263-275 | 330-340 | 280-290 |
| | Cong+ | **220** | 174-186 | 105-115 | 105-115 |
| | Others | **137** | 86-98 | 95-105 | 89-99 |
| 1999 | BJP+ | **296** | 295-305 | 322-336 | 279-289 |
| | Cong+ | **134** | 145-155 | 132-146 | 152-162 |
| | Others | **107** | 85-95 | 70-80 | 97-107 |
| 1998 | BJP+ | **254** | - | 234-249 | - |
| | Cong+ | **144** | - | 150-165 | - |
| | Others | **147** | - | 120-135 | - |

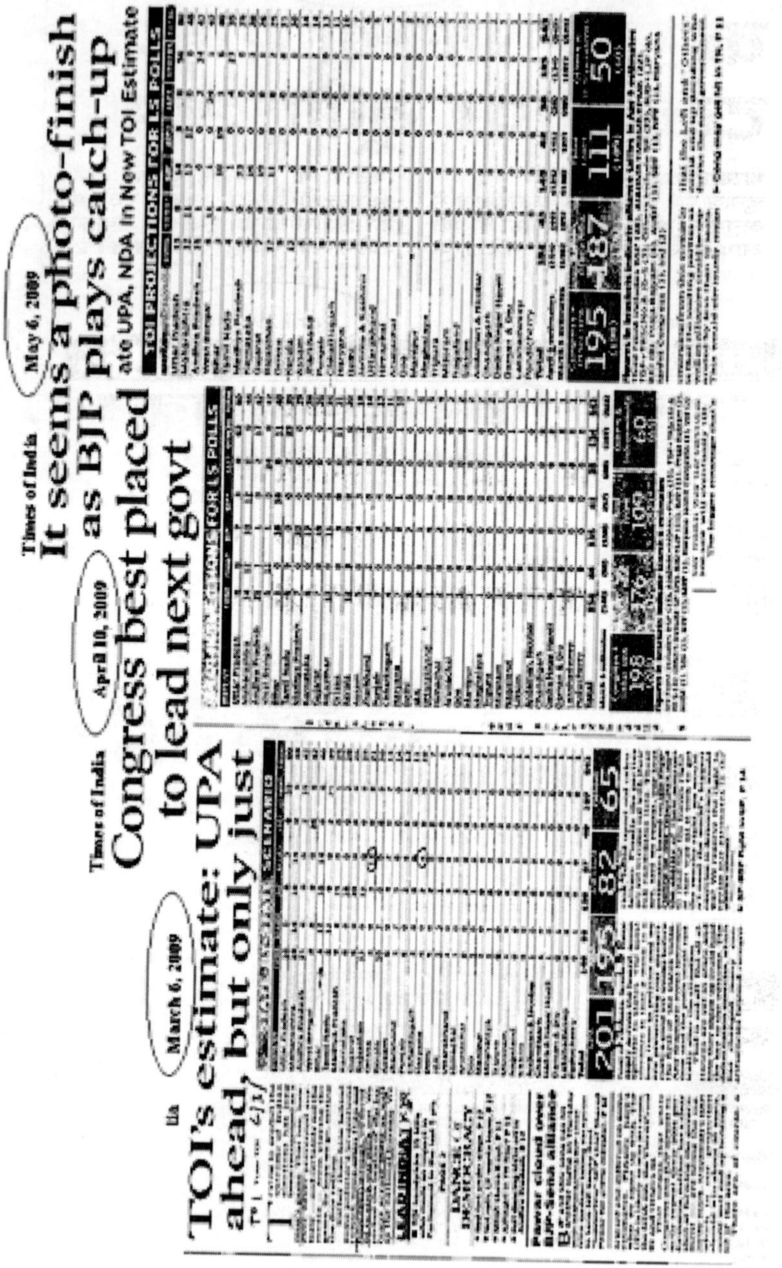
Times of India
May 6, 2009
It seems a photo-finish as BJP plays catch-up
ate UPA, NDA In New TOI Estimate
TOI PROJECTIONS FOR LS POLLS
195 187 111 50

Times of India
April 10, 2009
Congress best placed to lead next govt
FOR LS POLLS
198 176 109 60

March 6, 2009
TOI's estimate: UPA ahead, but only just
201 195 82 65

**Dainik Bhaskar** March 23, 2009

# कांग्रेस-भाजपा में कड़ी टक्कर, पर यूपीए आगे

**भास्कर नेटवर्क. नई दिल्ली**
चुनाव पूर्व किए गए एक सर्वेक्षण में अनुमान व्यक्त किया गया है कि आगामी आम चुनाव में कांग्रेस के मिलेंगी जो शिवसेना से एक सीट अधिक होगी। सेना-भाजपा गठबंधन की 22 सीटों के मुकाबले राकांपा-कांग्रेस-आरपीआई गठबंधन को 26

**Dainik Bhaskar** April 29, 2009

साप्ताहिक पोल मीटर

# 'अन्य' फिर हुए मजबूत

**कांग्रेस : 188 भाजपा : 183 अन्य : 172**

भास्कर/डीएनए के संपादकों द्वारा किए गए ताजा आकलन में कांग्रेस और भाजपा के बीच कांटे की टक्कर बनी हुई है, वहीं तीसरा मोर्चा फिर मजबूत हो गया है।

| राज्य/यूटी | मैदानी स्थिति | अनुमानित परिणाम-09 | | | कुल सीटें |
|---|---|---|---|---|---|
| | | कांग्रेस व घटक दल | भाजपा व घटक दल | अन्य | |
| आंध्रप्रदेश | टीआरएस, टीडीपी व लेफ्ट के बीच सीट बंटवारे के विवाद से कांग्रेस को हो सकता है फायदा | 18 | – | 24 | 42 |
| असम | अंदरूनी लड़ाई के बावजूद बीजेपी-एजीपी मजबूत | 4 | 9 | 1 | 14 |
| बिहार | सीट बंटवारा समझौता न होने से यूपीए को नुकसान | 2 | 28 | 10 | 40 |

**Dainik Bhaskar** April 21, 2009

साप्ताहिक पोल मीटर

# तीसरा मोर्चा पिछड़ा

**कांग्रेस : 202 भाजपा : 185 अन्य : 156**

भास्कर/डीएनए के संपादकों द्वारा किए गए ताजा आकलन में कांग्रेस और भाजपा की ताकत बढ़ती नजर आ रही है, जबकि तीसरा मोर्चा कमजोर पड़ रहा है।

| राज्य/यूटी | मैदानी स्थिति | अनुमानित परिणाम-09 | | | कुल सीटें |
|---|---|---|---|---|---|
| | | कांग्रेस व घटक दल | भाजपा व घटक दल | अन्य | |
| आंध्रप्रदेश | टीआरएस, टीडीपी व लेफ्ट के बीच सीट बंटवारे के विवाद से कांग्रेस को हो सकता है फायदा | 22 | – | 20 | 42 |
| असम | अंदरूनी लड़ाई के बावजूद बीजेपी-एजीपी मजबूत | 4 | 9 | 1 | 14 |
| बिहार | सीट बंटवारा समझौता न होने से यूपीए को नुकसान | 2 | 28 | 10 | 40 |

**Dainik Bhaskar** April 5, 2009

साप्ताहिक पोल मीटर

# भाजपा खेमे को मामूली बढ़त

**कांग्रेस : 174 भाजपा : 188 अन्य : 181**

भास्कर/डीएनए के संपादकों द्वारा किए गए ताजा आकलन से पता चलता है कि भाजपा खेमे को कांग्रेस खेमे से मामूली बढ़त मिल गई है। हालांकि अंतिम चुनाव परिणाम किसी के भी पक्ष में जा सकते हैं।

| राज्य/यूटी | मैदानी स्थिति | अनुमानित परिणाम-09 | | | कुल सीटें |
|---|---|---|---|---|---|
| | | कांग्रेस व घटक दल | भाजपा व घटक दल | अन्य | |
| आंध्रप्रदेश | टीआरएस, टीडीपी व लेफ्ट के बीच सीट बंटवारे के विवाद से कांग्रेस को हो सकता है फायदा | 18 | – | 24 | 42 |
| असम | अंदरूनी लड़ाई के बावजूद बीजेपी-एजीपी मजबूत | 4 | 9 | 1 | 14 |
| बिहार | सीट बंटवारा समझौता न होने से यूपीए को नुकसान | 2 | 28 | 10 | 40 |
| छत्तीसगढ़ | भाजपा का दबदबा रहेगा, कांग्रेस को थोड़ा लाभ संभव | 2 | 9 | – | 11 |
| गुजरात | कांग्रेस के पास मोदी का जवाब नहीं | 8 | 18 | – | 26 |
| हरियाणा | बसपा, कांग्रेस के वोट काट सकती है, इससे भाजपा-इनेलो गठबंधन को फायदा | 7 | 2 | 1 | 10 |
| हिमाचल | विधानसभा चुनाव में जीत से भाजपा ड्राइवर सीट पर | 1 | 3 | – | 4 |

Times of India April 10, 2009

# With 150-plus, Cong could be back at helm

- Continued from Page 1

So, compared to our first assessment, UPA is down by three seats, NDA by 19 seats and Left by five eats. The non-UPA-NDA-Left bloc is up: s per our estimates, it could account or as many as 134 seats. Out of these, vhat's referred to as Third Front partners — Mayawati's BSP, Chandrababu Naidu's TDP, Jayalalithaa's AIADMK, Vaiko's MDMK, Ramadoss's PMK and Deve Gowda's JD(S) — could account or a bloc of nearly 110 MPs, Left included. Others and independents, including the SP, RJD, LJP and some smaller parties, could be close to 60 seats.

The final tally for Congress of 154 nay not be startlingly different from vhat we estimated in early March, but

STRONG CONTENDER?

what it has gained in some states has been largely offset by losses in others. For instance, the Congress stands to gain in Orissa as a result of the break-up of the BJP-BJD alliance. It also seems to be better placed in Kerala, Punjab and Haryana than what we had rashtra than earlier estimated. However, it seems to have lost some ground in Karnataka, UP, Bihar and Assam, so that our total tally for the party is up by only eight seats. The tally for the BJP has also not changed significantly, going down by just three, largely because most of the changed equations in the last month have taken place in states where the saffron party is a relatively minor player. Thus, while Nitish Kumar's JD-U will hope to gain significantly from the split of UPA in Bihar, the BJP may gain little or nothing.

Similarly, the failure of SP and Congress to tie up in UP is unlikely to add much to BJP's kitty. The Congress-Trinamool alliance too makes no difference to the BJP, though the party has reason to believe that it just might win

There are some states where alliances are just as they were a month ago, but our assessment has changed as the campaigns have rolled out and so have our reporters. West Bengal and Tamil Nadu are both worth mentioning in this context. In Bengal, while we had earlier estimated that both Congress and Trinamool would gain from their alliance, it now appears that Congress would be lucky if it can repeat its 2004 performance and Mamata Banerjee may be the bigger gainer from the alliance.

In Tamil Nadu, our March forecast had taken into account the possibility of the PMK switching sides, but now that the switch has happened and Vijayakant's DMDK has also made it clear that it will not align with the DMK or Congress, the momentum clearly

Times of India Marey 27, 2009

# BJP survey gives it slight edge in race against Cong

## Saffron Party Projected To Get 160 Seats Against Rival's 135

TIMES NEWS NETWORK

**New Delhi:** A shrinking UPA offers opportunities to BJP, but the saffron party has considerable ground to cover before it can seize a clear lead in the 2009 elections lending

which are now likely to split between Mulayam Singh and Mayawati.

Similarly, an absence of an RJD-LJP-Congress alliance could help BJP in Bihar. Surveys showed a Muslim preference for Congress which might

**DNA** — **May 4, 2009**

## DNA Poll Shows Congress Inching Ahead

DNA weekly poll meter swings again and it is Congress gaining as many as 9 seats, largely because of problems that the opposition alliances are facing in AP and Haryana -- exactly the same states that cost NDA the elections in 2004.

**DNA WEEKLY POLL METER**

# ADVANTAGE CONG AGAIN

**Cong: 184 BJP: 177 Others: 182**

**In the latest assessment by *DNA* editors, Congress, after slipping behind [cut off] last week, regains edge on account of hiccups in rival camps in AP, Harya[cut off]**

| State/UT | Ground zero | Projection for '09 Cong & allies | BJP & allies | Others | Total seats |
|---|---|---|---|---|---|
| Andhra Pradesh | TRS, TDP, Left seat-sharing troubles may [cut off] | 20 | – | 22 | 42 |

**Business Standard** — **April 8, 2009**

## What Will The Prez Do If BJP Is The Single Largest Party?

Srikant Sambrani in the Business Standard:

**GENERAL ELECTIONS 2009**

| State | BJP | Allies | NDA | Congress | Allies | UPA | Others | Total |
|---|---|---|---|---|---|---|---|---|
| UP | 9 | 4 | 13 | 4 | - | 4 | 63 | 80 |
| Maharashtra | 13 | 12 | 25 | 11 | 12 | 23 | - | 48 |
| AP | - | - | - | 10 | 2 | 12 | 30 | 42 |
| WB | - | - | - | 4 | 12 | 16 | 26 | 42 |
| Bihar | 10 | 16 | 26 | 1 | 13 | 14 | - | 40 |
| TN | - | - | - | 4 | 7 | 11 | 28 | 39 |

**Economic Times** — **March 18, 2009**

# UPA to fall short of majority: Survey

## Congress-Commissioned Survey Predicts 150-Plus Seats For The Party

**DOWN for the COUNT**

C L Manoj & M K Venu

asses the emerging mood on the ground just when campaign for the April 16 phase of the Lok Sabha polls is picking up.

Incidentally, the Congress leadership has set an ambitious target of winning over 170 seats on [cut off]

premacy in Jharkhand.

While Congress is shown as losing seats in Gujarat, the party may not improve in Maharashtra, either, because of compatibility problems with alliance partner NCP.

**The Pioneer** — **May 11, 2009**

# Keep mum till votes are in

Only a few days remain for the coalition games to begin and the political horizon is indeed very blurred. We will see many a twist and turn in the process of Government formation. So far, the way things are shaping up, there is going to be only a marginal difference in numbers between the BJP-led NDA and the Congress-led UPA.

On the other hand, the Left and the regional parties seem to have consolidated as a 'viable' group and will pose a serious challenge to both the dominant coalitions. I had said previously that the best policy for all political parties was to keep quiet till May 16. The 'winners' in this election will be those who are able to maintain or improve upon their seat share.

The difference between the Congress and the BJP is going to be wafer thin and there is no doubt that [cut off]

the world that will witness a [cut off] turn but will still manage to gen[cut off] a growth in GDP. In recent wee[cut off] have witnessed greater market [cut off] dence and I think this will cont[cut off] The confusion in Government fo[cut off] tion and the influence of the [cut off] could cause more than a ripple [cut off] May 16, but this will only be te[cut off] rary as few political parties or [cut off]

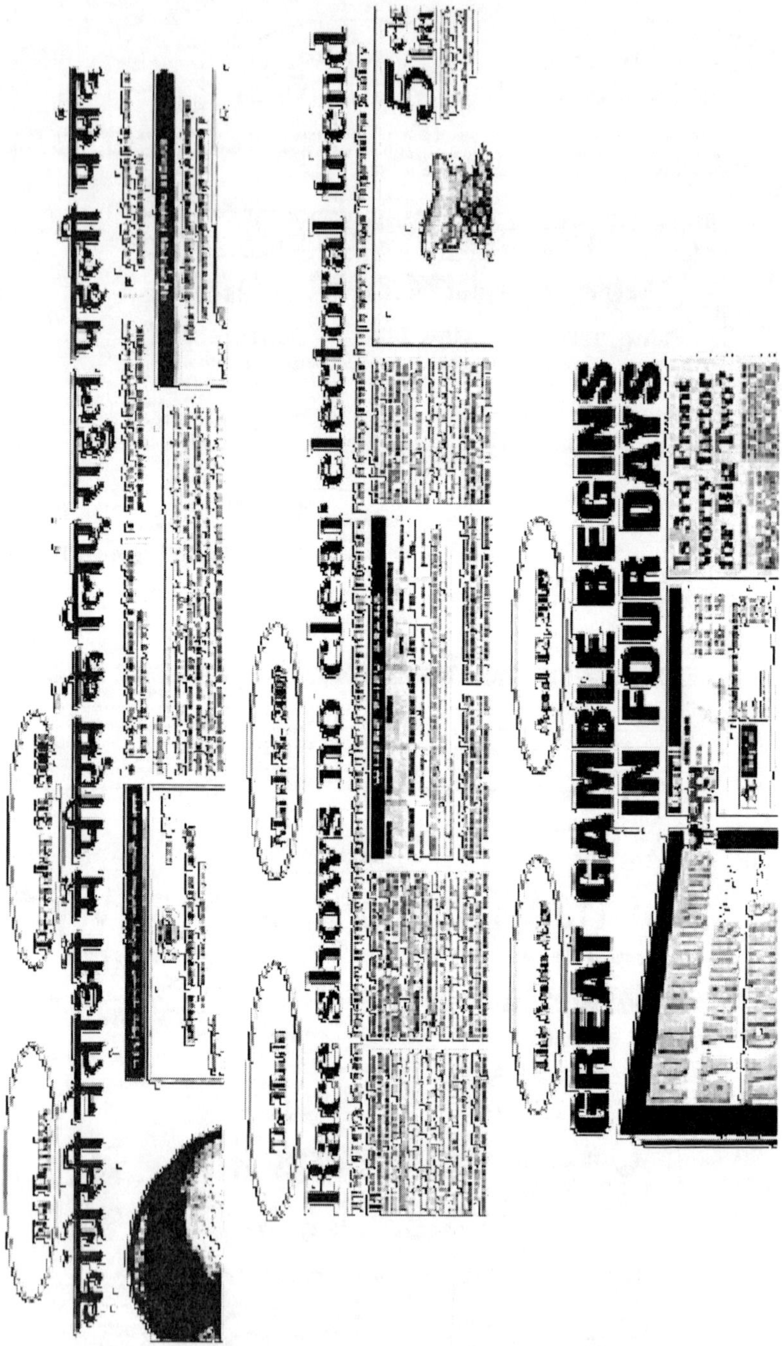
Race shows no clear electoral trend
GREAT GAMBLE BEGINS IN FOUR DAYS
Is 3rd Front worry factor for Big Two?

# 3

# Anatomy of Poll Surveys

### What is a Survey?

"Survey" has now come to denote a number of things. In this chapter we take a look at them. Survey has become a popular term frequently used by political leaders, news media and advertisers alike in the context of electoral politics. Channels also use the term poll to mean a survey of opinions. News media take to surveys to mean and claim objectivity or authenticity of their findings and as a way to reflect views or opinions of a large section of people. News media use the term survey or poll in a general sense as well as in a specific way based on survey research methodology. Surveys on who wins or how many seats or votes a party or candidate is likely to get in an election involves a forecast or Projection with a certain degree of probability. It may or may not be a direct outcome of a survey as the conversion of opinions and voting intentions often requires additional inputs. The extent to which people take to such surveys in the media seriously depends on the credibility of the news media itself and the way the survey findings are covered or reported. Times of India front page banner news based on the assessment of their own field reporters (in April 2009) was described as a "survey", "Star News –

A.C. Neilson's" poll projections were also described as a "survey", CMS's content analysis of poll coverage by media was covered in Asian Age with headline "survey", Finance Minister's economic report is also headlined as a "survey".

A poll-eve survey that the news media uses could be a "sample survey" or an ad hoc survey based on a review of literature or discussions. A sample survey, as it implies, should be based on a selection procedure of respondents and specifying the number of respondents out of the total it is trying to represent and the scope of inquiry. An ad hoc survey may or may not be based on any sampling system but implies reaching out to "random" respondents irrespective of its representative character. An "on-line" survey, as many news media use these days, is neither ad hoc nor based on a (predetermined) sample. Such polls are limited in their scope invariably to readers / viewers and that too the self – motivated ones. It may reflect some "broad or general" trend on a given question at a given point but does not reflect the larger phenomenon. Most such online surveys have to be "then or there" or within specified period (usually during a programme period of a channel or before the next issue of the publication) and with limited responses, mostly by way of "yes" - "no", agree or not agree or vote or not vote type of responses.

What is the difference between a "study" and a "survey". A study is going beyond "top of the mind" opinion at a given moment. A study goes into the pros and cons of related aspects in which a survey may be a part. Polls are limited in their relevance and reflect a transitory phenomenon. A study may include "past" and "future" of a phenomenon beyond those reflected in a survey. A study may use a combination of methodologies. And, more often, a study is explanatory and involves linkages by way of experimentation or by implication. A survey should yield quantitative picture for a particular point of time?. "Brain Study shows how junk food tempts us" was a two column headline in Times of India on April 22, 2009, "Every 40 seconds, one suicide, says Lancit Study" was a three column headline in Indian Express on April 22, 2009. These are just examples.

"Analysis" is yet another term often used in the context of news media's coverage of a poll scene. An analysis is a mode of examination of linkages involved in a phenomenon. It deals with more than one set of figures and involves comparing or contrasting with another set of observations or findings. An analysis could be in quantitative or qualitative terms. Compatibility in parameters used is important in an analysis. More often it takes into account a survey finding or is based on the conclusion flowing out of a filed survey.

"Survey research" is a discipline in methods of inquiry in a structured manner. This expertise is required for those engaged in poll surveys. Such a background however is not sufficient for doing poll surveys objectively.

Surveys have triggered populism in the country. Now even the very urge for "good governance" appears bugged with "survey mantra" to convey or establish such a phenomenon. Populism is something that interests or caters to or lures the immediate instincts of individuals. Both media and politics should be more concerned about basic interests of people although they tend to chase more often basal interests or instincts. Surveys on news media and on poll scene often ignore the subtle difference between the two – top of the mind and substance.

## Market Surveys and Poll Surveys

Election-eve surveys are different from those conducted to assess markets or public opinion surveys on contentious contemporary issues of the day– in the scope of methodology and reliability aspects of the outcome. Poll surveys have to be far more reliable and their credibility eventually depends on accuracy on the counting day. In market research and opinion surveys, there is no exercise regarding "conversion" of responses into seats and votes. And yet it was market research agencies which dominated the business of poll surveys until a few years ago. One particular reason why Dr. Prannoy Roy, Dr. N Bhaskara Rao and Yogendra Yadav were successful in grasping the dynamics and coming up with better explanations in the news media is that individually they have not come from "market research" business. The main reasons for pollsters from market research stream going way off the mark more often in their projection of poll outcome and lack of transparency is their "markets" orientation and lack of understanding of political dynamics. Market research agencies sustain themselves with their ongoing work to do with markets. The "business" from poll surveys is only a small part of their turnovers. Except CSDS which gets grant from ICSSR and other (foreign and Indian) bodies for one or other type of research related to electoral politics in India, other agencies have to sustain themselves by taking to other type of research assignments involving surveys. It is interesting to know that only two large market research agencies (A C Neilson – ORG – MARG and IMRB) have full time field investigators and supervisors. Most others engage the same floating (freelancers) investigators / supervisors for field work of poll surveys. Additionally a number of investigators are locally recruited from time to time.

A survey, irrespective of the methodology, aims to assess or yields summative statement of opinions and preferences of a given set of respondents in a given context and at a given point of time. A survey implies arriving at certain findings with certain reliability and represent a larger set of people. A primary survey is supposed to be based on certain methodology of enquiry with a set of people or events which if repeated should yield similar kind of result. The reliability or sanctity of a field survey is only when the methodology followed for arriving a set of conclusions is indicated. The methodology in turn should be based on certain theories as in the case of "sampling", "perceptions", or "attitudes". A field survey could be based on a sample when the area or population to be covered is wide and large or over a longer period. It could also be in the form of collecting observations from field visits on a systematic basis or it could be by way of discussions. It could be individual level or group level depending on what the basis of enquiry is. In a poll-eve survey an individual who is qualified to vote at that point in that election is the basic unit of enquiry.

A survey finding derives its relevance only when all such criteria are relied upon and indicated. For example, a weather forecast is given in the news media every day based on certain field observations and giving the source for such observations.

A survey of poll scene in a State or constituency could be by way of analyzing past voting trends, it could be by having discussions with certain specific people like party leaders, experts or civil society groups or voters themselves – with or without a method in selecting the respondents. The enquiry could be by way of discussions or interview in a general way or with the help of a structured interview schedule or questionnaire, which is used the same way for all interviews.

When a survey is among certain specific experts or voters at one location and without a uniform and structured guide, it is more likely in the form of a discussion. But when the number of experts or voters are scattered across a state or constituency and their number is large, it could be by way of a sample of them. When the selection of sample of respondents is based on some criteria or with certain stated assumptions, it becomes a sample survey. Similarly, it is not only the number of people covered but the nature or structure of enquiry, which determines whether it is a primary survey or not. A survey however could also use a combination of methods of enquiry – in-depth discussion, a structured questionnaire and a sample of respondents. A survey could be qualitative and quantitative. A sample survey is viewed "scientific" when it states these various methods for arriving at a set of conclusions or findings and expresses its findings in quantitative terms. The most important clarity needed in a sample survey is the "universe" which it tries to represent or reflect with certain reliability. The universe in the case of a poll survey is voters. In the case of opinion survey, in a deferent context, the universe would be different – depending on the subject of enquiry.

Since "survey" has become a most commonly used term, one needs to understand in what way a structured sample survey is different from any other type of "survey". Most often surveys on elections covered in news media are presumed as structured sample surveys reflecting or representing a scattered and large "voter universe" with certain reliability. This is often expressed by way of "margin of error" or chances of the finding being right.

For unleashing this power of "influencing public opinion", the news media, avail of opinion surveys by way of SMS polls, on-line (internet or phone) polls, field surveys and sample surveys. Based on such surveys, lengthy discussion programmes are being mounted by television channels, sometimes as if the "findings" of such surveys are "final" or "conclusive" of the process. In the course of discussions based on such survey findings in the news media, the basic premise of reliability of such findings should be indicated at the outset.

There is neither transparency about these poll eve surveys published or broadcast by the news media nor an understanding of the scope of surveys is provided. For appreciating such surveys requires better understanding and sensitivity among all sections – politicians, news media and viewers / readers and more importantly, the voting public.

**A Sample "Survey" should be known by:**

Transparency in every aspect of a sample survey is more critical and determines its weightage. Transparency as to the following aspects should particularly be known.

**Methodology, core of surveys:** The sponsor is not always the one who has paid for the cost of the survey. Nevertheless, indicating the identity of the sponsor adds to it credibility. If a news media is the sponsor, then obviously it could ensure that all vital details are presented. But even when a news media publishes a report of a field survey done by someone else, it should ensure that sponsorship is indicated in the news story.

**How Representative.** Who were the respondents in the field survey. Were they eligible voters or general public or party workers or opinion leaders?. Are they representative of local voter demographics? Equally important is whether they were interviewed individually or in a group situation or by phone or internet?.

**Sample Size. Its Spread and Selection procedures** are critical features of a field sample survey for credibility of its projections.

Another aspect one needs to indicate is whether projection is "as of the day" or "if poll is held today" or for as and when an election takes place even though voting intention is normally enquired into for 'as of now" or "if an election takes place today".

A news media should be concerned about conflict of interest, if any, before publication of findings of a poll survey irrespective of who had sponsored the survey or who had released the findings of the survey, particularly when it is being published as exclusive.

While the approach to sampling has, of late, become more systematic and more or less uniform among market research agencies, the actual selection practices of respondents vary considerably. Some agencies have not given up street corner interviews, some others select the sample respondent going by physical setting or based on economic-criteria. Very few go strictly by updated voters list of location. CSDS invariably uses voters list. Street corner interviews, cannot be expected to possess the same attributes and degree of reliability as interviews which are conducted at the household level with a selected member.

Opinion polls often suffer on account of unexpected developments once the electoral process starts, such as the death of a political leader (as in the case of late Shri Rajiv Gandhi). This author remembers some years ago when a poll survey went haywire with boycott of essential supplies under PDS to many areas just prior to the poll dates for a State assembly. Split in a political party between any two elections or changed alliances between parties (formal and informal), and the role of dissident candidates, and delimitation of constituencies are other factors which contribute to the accuracy level of opinion surveys conducted on the eve of a state or national election.

**Interdisciplinary approach:** Some recent poll surveys declared a sample of 40 to 50 thousand voters as if the agencies were in competition to claim larger sample size. The challenge lies in doing with as small a sample as possible (as in USA). For a second time in a row (1998 and 1999), for example, CMS was able to forecast accurate results for Lok Sabha poll with a sample of around 3,000 voters, better than the surveys with ten- to twenty-times bigger sample size. Furthermore, an analysis of such poll surveys conducted during recent years shows that market-research-based and commercially-oriented polls which tend to go for larger samples, (implying higher volume of business) do not necessarily have more accurate results. The performance of different research agencies shows that market research background alone is not enough for more reliable and insightful poll surveys and psephological exercises. The analytical skills needed for such an exercise have to be interdisciplinary in the light of the constantly changing political scene and voter priorities. Since market research agencies have dedicated field investigators, they are being commissioned for poll surveys.

**Techniques of investigation:** The time gap between the field work of a survey and the actual voting day determines the accuracy of the survey. The shorter the number of days of fieldwork, analysis and publication, the more relevant the results are likely. Also, when surveys are conducted in various parts of the country, the questions may carry different connotations in local languages and dialects. This is a problem that is peculiar to India. The manner in which questions are posed to different sections of voters by investigators, therefore, is important. CSDS perhaps is the only agency which is very particular about these aspects.

A good interaction of the person analyzing the field data with field investigators can prove to be an additional advantage. But this does not always happen. If the analyst himself is involved in the field work, it greatly enhances the accuracy of the analysis and avoids mistakes like ignoring the significance of "no *response*". In some agencies there is no connection between the field investigators and analysts and the one who does psephological exercise using such analysis. Of late this is how it is with most agencies engaged in conducting poll-eve surveys. One could say that this practice also has something to do with accuracy level of projections.

**Sample Size:**

The size of voters being 714 million (2009), doubts are always expressed about the relevance and reliability of sample surveys as the sample size involved could never be as massive. Thirty years ago when Eric P.W. da'Costa started election surveys the sample size was 2000 or less voters and limited to urban areas. In fact, he advocated 1500 sample size for national level prediction at 5 per cent margin of error. In the middle of 1970s the pre-poll survey of this author using the countrywide field set-up of a market research agency (ORG), the sample size was 7000 voters. In the 1990s the sample size of pre-poll surveys was between 10,000 to 20,000. However, the sample size used by different agencies for exit polls in 1999 varied between 30,000 to 1,50,000 voters. In 1998, 1999 and 2004 it appeared as if the higher the sample size of an exit poll, the more it went off the mark. Sampling has been on the basis of number of Parliament seats (out of 543) and Assembly segments (out of over 5000) covered. The selection procedures have been such that sample is reflective of certain key voter segments (known in the earlier years as "vote banks") like rural and urban, Muslim or certain castes or occupation who are likely to make a difference for the poll outcome at that time point.

The selection procedure of voters is not always based on "voters' list", which as a rule is the basis for voting on the voting day. Earlier, opinion surveys conducted for a leading magazine were based on "street corner" interviews. "Clustered random interviews" was another easy approach followed. Despite the fact that relatively smaller sample surveys have proved no less accurate than the large sample surveys, "the more the merrier" tendency prevails in the country. An analysis of 1998, 1999 and 2004 opinion surveys convincingly brings out that spread of sample and the selection procedures of respondents is far more critical than the overall size of sample and that a bigger sample does not necessarily ensure more reliable projection as deviation is likely to increase in the representative character of the sample. There are several examples where the "universe" for selection was "public" rather than "voters". The fact that a significant percent of voters in the voters list are invalid, or dead, the use of voters list may not be good enough even assuming the voters list used is the latest. Similarly, many of those eligible to vote do not figure in the "voters list". In fact, in 1999 Lok Sabha elections, an independent "poll watch" agency (Lok Satta) brought out a range of deficiencies in the voters lists. As such research agencies need to be aware of such deficiencies and use alternate methods with consistency.

## Limitations of Sample Surveys:

All poll surveys use a questionnaire, with most of the questions being structured and even pre-coded thereby limiting the scope of the large scale sample surveys for a quantitative analysis. Surveys have been accused as having "loaded" or "leading" questions, which are bound to come up with certain subjective findings. The way a

**About Sampling**

Opinion polls are surveys using a sampling methodology. The methodology is designed to enable surveys to represent the opinions of a particular segment population by asking questions to a sampled number of people of that segment and then extrapolating the answers to the larger population. To be valid, an opinion poll should satisfy certain criteria such as sample size, systemic process of selection of the sample and their representative character.

Opinion polls using SMSs are being widely practised by the news media. These types of polls have both advantages and disadvantages. However, practitioners as well as users should be aware that many of the online polls conducted by SMS or Web sites or phone-ins by channels or newspapers have no scientific validity. They could at best only be indicative.

Respondents to SMS polls in media are usually self-selected people who may not be necessarily representative of the particular universe. In other cases, the sample may miss out on predominant

*Contd. on next page*

question is framed and asked obviously determines the response pattern, both in the case of open-ended and pre-coded questions. While CSDS and CMS surveys are based on an extensive enquiry, in such a way that respondent fatigue as well as "lying" (about voting preference or intention) and investigator bias is minimized, most agencies use simple and short cut questionnaires with no political sensitivities in the field. More importantly, most agencies compensate their investigators on "per questionnaire" basis with scope for rushing in the selection procedures for respondents as well as in the very process of interview. Also, in a national election, questions have to be in local languages and the issues that need to be understood have to be specific to the State. All this requires State specific questionnaires rather than a uniform one for the entire country. CMS always used "state-specific" questionnaires for any national survey.

Rate of "non-response" in field surveys and percentage of "undecided" or "do not know" is important for a better understanding

*Contd. from previous page*

opinion in the context. Doubts can be raised about SMS poll on: affordability to SMS. Then there is the issue of unlawfulness to make unwanted calls to cell phone owners who may be charged for taking a call while roaming. Moreover, such polls lack transparency and are open to manipulation by the respondents.

Although ad-hoc sampling may be sufficient for opinion polls on issues of general public interest, to be able to forecast an outcome, systematic sampling is required based on population profiles (age, sex, employment status, income levels etc). Poll surveys about the outcome of an election should, however, cover respondents from a widely spread area from all age groups and strata of the society.

**Advantages:** Since participants in an SMS opinion poll are volunteers rather than units in a random sample, such polls represent the relatively more interested individuals who can afford cost and time.

**Disadvantages:** Due to various kinds of bias in selection procedures, opinions polls may not have participants that represent

*Contd. on next page*

of poll surveys findings and for a psephological exercise. But very often this is not indicated in the media reporting of the findings. All survey research is bound to have some limitation(s) either at design level or in the field in executing the surveys or in analyzing the field data. And yet seldom are these limitations or certain abnormalities referred to in the media coverage even when it has significance. There are no systematic studies to go into "non-response" or "non-corperation" of voters to poll surveys. Similarly, how differences in articulation and comprehension levels of respondents to certain specific aspects or issues such as secularism, coalition, stability, etc., should also be highlighted.

As a consequence of wide media interest in covering poll-eve field surveys, news media has taken to public opinion surveys on issues of current controversies and public interest. In fact, this author started fortnightly public opinion surveys for the Times of India in 1984 on a wide range of issues. It was at the initiative of

*Contd. from previous page*

certain section of concerned population. The results of such a poll cannot be generalized as they are valid only for the participants in the poll. The drawback is that such surveys are inaccurate, as anyone can participate in the survey, irrespective of whether they are voters or not.

**Non response bias:** Some people do not reply to SMSs coming from strangers or respond to interviews even by person or telephone. Because of this selection bias, the characteristics of those who reply or respond may be markedly different from those who do not respond. In this way the actual sample is a biased version of the intended universe. Moreover, this error cannot be overcome with larger sample sizes.

**Potential inaccuracies**

**Sampling error:** All sample surveys are subject to sampling error which reflects the effects of chance in the sampling process. The error due to chance is often expressed as margin of error. As a general

*Contd. on next page*

Dileep Padgaonkar and Girilal Jain. It revived the idea in 1999 and continues to do so as often – both field based and SMS based. Some mainline newspapers and TV channels have been using telephone surveys, Net surveys as well as field surveys on a wide range of issues in their endeavour to set the agenda for a public discourse. With limited telephone and PC penetration at the household level, telephone and PC are yet to become the reliable channels for ascertaining public opinion, particularly in rural India. However, metro based newspapers are increasingly covering phone, SMS and PC based surveys.

In the Indian context, predicting the results of elections precisely can only be a coincidence. Like the contents of a boiling pot, election-time dynamics change continuously until the actual poll hours, unlike in more politically stable countries such as the United Kingdom or the United States. But opinion polls in India are not entirely futile if they can identify the trend, the mood, and the direction of the outcome

*Contd. from previous page*

but also as practical rule, for a survey with a random sample of 1,000 people a margin of sampling error of 3% means that using the same methodology, 95% of the time a repeat survey would give the same estimate within ± 3%.

**Coverage bias:** Another source of error is the use of samples that are not representative of the population or particular universe as a consequence of the methodology or design. In the case of a sample of **mobile phone** users, a built-in error may also occur because many times and in many places, those with telephones may be different than those without. Similarly, a respondent may be of voting age, but not yet a voter or not a voter in that particular constituency sample.

**The sample size in polls:** To calculate required sample size for a poll one must consider (1) the current status of indicator to be studied, (2) the precision of the estimate (how much variability from sample to sample can be allowed), and (3) the statistical confidence level. In the absence of any information of current level

*Contd. on next page*

more accurately. Poll surveys over time should facilitate issue based poll discourse, enthuse voters to go out and vote, better their discriminative outlook and concern for good governance.

How much is spent on poll surveys?. The total expenditure on poll surveys was estimated by CMS as Rs.6 crores for 1996 Lok Sabha poll which in 2004 went beyond Rs. 20 crores, with more than half of it by political parties and candidates. Four national channels which sponsored surveys (pre-poll and exit polls), were able to rake in twice the amount as advertising revenue than what they spent on serveys.

Opinion surveys are expected to improve the quality of poll campaigns by providing insights for a more focused and issue based electioneering. But there is no evidence. Also there is no increase in voter turnout at the polls with proliferation of poll surveys and competitiveness in the contests. The overall voter turnout continues to be less than 55 per cent even in metro cities. Nevertheless, it

*Contd. from previous page*

of indicator, a 50% level is used to optimize the margin of error. (Margin of error is generally kept for an opinion poll as 3%). A 95% statistical confidence level is required for validating the results within a desired margin of error. But the big caution is: sample selection needs to be done based on random sampling i.e., every intended respondent should get equal chance of being selected in the sample. Deviation from this condition will increase the margin of error.

For general information it should be remembered that no matter how large the population, be it 5,000 or 5,000,000, size of sample required for obtaining desired level of margin of error and for specified level of significance will not increase. Depending on accuracy required, time and resources available for conducting a survey, one decides the size of the sample. (of constituencies or booths and voters).

All SMS and the like polls, based mostly on self-selected sample, suffer from serious limitations and produce an enormous margin of error than in the case of a survey among systematically selected sample.

could be said that pre-poll surveys have, over the last 15 years, facilitated certain level playing in the understanding of the political process and raised public awareness of opinions and views of various sections of society on political parties, their leadership and sometimes on issues.

Poll-eve surveys have now become a part of the Indian electoral process and democratic practice. With recent decline in the party system and the spread of mass media, particularly news channels and the competitive initiatives between various news media, poll surveys will be relied on even more in the coming years, for the national elections as well as for the state elections. Hence, the need to improve their methodologies, ensure transparency in conducting the poll surveys and their over all credibility.

**Who Sponsors Surveys?**

There is a difference between "commissioning" and "sponsoring" a poll survey. Commissioning implies conducting the survey "at the instance of someone" whereas 'sponsored' does not necessarily imply such a position. A survey covered by a news media could be its own sponsorship for exclusive coverage or in collaboration with another news media. Quite often, this aspect is not clear even where a news channel and a newspaper claims the survey conducted by a polling agency. This clarity and transparency is paramount for the credibility of news media and also for freedom and fairness of electoral process. Who actually paid to the poll agency for conducting the particular field survey covered in the news media?. It should be declared. For example, The Hindu clearly states whenever it carries any poll survey as a feature whether it commissioned or sponsored it and if so to what extent.

A practice in vogue in the last decade has been that a polling agency gets "commissioned" by one or other business group usually at the instance of one or other political party. The agency then "offers" the findings of that survey to one or other news media for featuring it as a sponsored survey and release the findings to the news media formally or as a "leak" or "scoop" depending upon the relationships between the two. Such examples have been many between 1999 and 2009, both in assembly and Lok Sabha elections. Business houses even pay a polling agency on their own first and, then use the same to "deal with" a political party, mostly the party in power. In this process such surveys cannot be expected to be truly reflective of the findings. The particular survey nevertheless ends up getting covered in the news media without any indication of its origin. This however does not mean that all surveys appearing in news media are like that. But the number of such surveys has been on increase. Further, how the findings of a survey are actually presented by a news media? This is another factor that determines the role or influence of a pre-poll survey at that point of electoral process. The 2009 poll scene had good examples, e.g. in Andhra Pradesh and in 2008 in Rajasthan and Delhi.

Another interesting trend is that political parties might have agreed with the Election Commission on the need to curb poll surveys but most of them or their leaders and candidates have been commissioning poll surveys directly or clandestinely. More surveys covered in the news media in 2008 and 2009 were of this category. They do so to assess opportunities, to strategize election campaign and decide the candidates. In this process, poll surveys have become a solid business proposition for polling agencies. Today we have some psephologists who individually and informally work for one or other political party or leader but use a research agency to get into a sponsorship arrangement.

### Who does a Survey? What is Psephology?

Psephology is a sociological study of election results and trends. It requires an understanding of group dynamics, grass root political processes, significance of alliance between parties. It also requires experience in survey research methods and interpretation of response and non response and past voting trends. Psephology is neither an academic discipline by itself nor does it qualify to be described as "scientific". Psephological exercises avail disciplines of social psychology, social anthropology, sociology and political science apart from statistics. In fact, some ideas could even be picked up from biological phenomena as in the case "honey-bee" or "migration of birds" for interpretation of "undecided" and "indecisive" voters and patterns of opinion. Psephology at best could be described as an evolving subject of study of the outcome of elections. In his article in The Hindu in 1999, this author first clarified the distinction between a pollster and psephologist.

If someone has benefited most from poll surveys recently, it has been the pollsters and the news channels. During the 1999 poll about Rs.10 to 15 crores was spent for conducting pre-poll surveys and exit polls at the national level. On the eve of 2009 polls there were 7 to 8 surveys at the national level and as many at the state level that were covered in the news media. And several more surveys were conducted privately by political parties and leaders only some of them were "leaked to" media. (Hardly any two surveys covered in the media tallied in their predictions except by way of direction).

In 1999, for example, there were four exit polls at the national level, including one with deceptivity described as being "sponsored by Doordarshan" and discussion was as if the "results" were being presented "officially". These exit polls helped television channels to generate well over Rs. 8 cores as advertising revenue and, even more, helped private poll companies launch and promote themselves.

Those who conduct or present these pre-poll and exit poll surveys are often described as "psephologist" and, as if psephology is a "science". The news media too, often echoed such an impression. To what extent is psephology a "science"?. Psephology is a field of interest, not a discipline by itself. It is a field which takes help from different disciplinary positions. Sampling is only one of the determinants of reliability of such surveys. Sampling practice are based often on fairly well established sampling methods. The core of psephology, is based on converting voting intention percentages into number of seats at various levels. This conversion process is full of pitfalls e.g., subjective assumptions. Political environment is not static and has frequent surprises.

Being "scientific" implies a rigorous and systematic method of acquiring knowledge in such a way that it is verifiable, replicable and could be validated. That is why transparency in the procedures followed is important. The claim of psephological analysis being presented on news media is in fact never explained. Instead, what is provided or offered is survey findings. But the basis for conversion, which is what psephology is all about, is never indicated to the reader / viewer. As a result, the very credibility of such survey research based exercise in the news media becomes doubtful.

Reliability of the exit polls has to be far more than that of pre-poll surveys. Reliability has to do with replicability. Reliability is considered high if two or more researchers, trying to assess the same situation with same or similar methodology, come up with the same or very nearly similar results. In a complex electoral context, however, such statistical confidence level happens to be irrelevant, since such criteria apply more in controlled experiments. In a dynamic electoral context as in India, what is more pertinent is "margin of error" in the projections. The margin of error, expected and allowed in such surveys, should be within the limits of 3 percent plus or minus.

Featuring poll surveys in the news media has been in vogue for more than two decades now. Neither those in the media or viewers/ readers are ever told how pollsters / psephologists estimate / forecast the seats / votes that political parties are likely to get in an election. Yogendra Yadav made a brief attempt to explain psephology but that was only in 2009. Prannoy Roy who promoted use of the term in media in India in early 1980s explained more about sample surveys.

Forecast of seats that different parties are likely to get is made at various points of an election process and by individuals / agencies having different background. What are the assumptions and calculations that go into such an exercise? And, why some surveys are closer to the actual poll result than other surveys or why all of them sometime are off the mark?. Pollsters/ psephologists too make claims of superiority of their methodologies. What are the variables that go into such an exercise? More than two decades old CMS model, which MDRA continue to use as do some others, comprises five or six elements which with different weightages go into projection of seats/ votes in an election. Together they provide inputs for forecasting seats/ votes, some weeks or months prior to the polling day.

## Interpreting Poll Surveys

The news media themselves and citizen groups should be sensitive about the relevance and reliability of field surveys and about their coverage in the news media. Readers/ viewers should look for some basic details before believing surveys that appear in the news media. Even more, those in the news media who are responsible for contents, should be familiar with basics about surveys, particularly that in the context of elections. In fact, news media organizations should declare the kind of concerns they observe while covering poll surveys with their own guidelines – same way as they cover judicial matters or violence or pornography.

**Six most critical ones that one should look for:** First, whether the "survey", covered in the news media was a sample survey, giving sample base or whether it was a "focus group" based field survey among a select few, or, was it a survey based on an analysis of secondary data – particularly past election results. Second, who sponsored or at whose instance the survey was designed and conducted. Third, who constituted the universe of the sample survey or to whom the percentages given represent. Four, if it was sample survey what was the sample size and its distribution and when exactly the field work was conducted. Fifth, what was the percentage of non response, non availability and even refusal. Six, what was the percentage of undecided voters at the time of field work for the survey.

Sometimes it is also important to know whether the field survey was based on structured questions with options given or whether it was an open ended one for spontaneous responses. For example, in December 2008 a news item appeared prominently giving that a survey "found Rahul Gandhi as most suitable as Prime Minister". The significance or otherwise of this "news item" is all the more if it was the finding of a sample survey conducted nationally not just in Uttar Pradesh, and was based on a open ended enquiry. Without such a disclosure, such finding could be viewed as a political statement or a biased interpretation of a field survey giving no other option along with Rahul Gandhi's name. Similarly, for the news item in *Mint* in January 2009 reporting a survey by MDRA on L K Advani and Dr. Manmohan Singh as Prime Ministerial candidates.

The other aspects that one need to be sensitive about is whether the particular story is that of news media or by the agency which conducted or analysed the field survey. For example, a front page story featuring prominently in the *Mint* on November 28, 2008 (about State Assembly) headlined 24-hours before the Delhi election that the poll was "too close a race" between two contending parties whereas the text of the story has no reference or backup for such a conclusion. In fact, the particular weekly column which appears regularly on an inside page, published this particular one as a front page lead. What does this imply?. One can say the priority or emphasis was a matter of judgment of the Editor. Fine. But, then there has to be some basis for such "headline –conclusion"?. This is not an isolated example for news media's "biased coverage", intentionally or unintentionally or knowingly or unknowingly.

Who is responsible for what appears in a news media. Morally and legally it is the Editor. But these days when Editor is not known or least known, it is the responsibility of the news media itself and also the agency which is credited with the particular survey. The problem these days is the way electronic media features a poll survey by involving representatives of political parties to discuss the findings – or/and by reporting or hyping the findings. Quite often without the presence of the agency or the individual who conducted the field survey in the studio discussion.

Results of poll surveys published with a byline for the survey reflect a higher degree of confidence. This practice also ensures greater responsibility by both the news media and the researcher and helps achieve improvement in subsequent surveys.

In 1987 when this article was written, there were neither 24-hour news channels nor there was the kind of competition between media as we see now in 2009. It was after this article was published, that the first major poll survey based programme was telecast by Doordarshan with Dr.Prannoy Roy and Dr Ashok Lahari, both from Delhi School of Economics then

**Reliability of sample surveys:**

The criteria to do with accuracy and relevance require to be viewed in specific context of a survey. Nevertheless an attempt is

**Influence and Relevance**

**Rights and wrongs of pre-election opinion polls**

Opinion polls are increasingly becoming part of our public affairs. More and more newspapers are carrying reports of such polls. It is time we understand the complexities that are involved.

The impact of opinion polls on campaigning and even on actual voting needs to be examined. Research in the U.S., for example, shows that poll results shape the voting behaviour of many citizens. The sudden decision of Telugu Desam leader N.T. Rama Rao to jump into the campaigning in Haryana on the eve of assembly elections was attributed to the opinion polls of a leading daily.

As opinion polls become professional in their methodology and acquire credibility, they are bound to make greater impact on the campaign and even on the actual voting trend.

Hence, the urgency for professional ethics and *Media Monitor* continues the initiative towards such a debate.

N. Bhaskara Rao, with his experience of conducting opinion polls

*Contd. on next page*

made here to outline the concepts for the benefit of those with no statistical background.

**Margin of error or precision:** "Margin of error" is least understood or most misunderstood aspect both among the general public as well as by those in the news media. The survey agency itself does not often indicate the margin of error in the projections. And when sometimes given, it is hardly mentioned in the media reports. When mentioned, it is not clear whether "margin of error" is for the percentage of votes or seats or both. And, whether such a margin of error applies equally for all parties? and, for all States in the case of Lok Sabha poll?.

Most often, the projection of seats is indicated in a range (between 30 – 35; 100 – 110, etc), as if that is indicative of margin of the error. The range of seats projected often is vague, too wide and general. In fact, the range projected is so wide that it does not justify

*Contd. from previous page*

over the last 16 years confirms, the increasing tendency "to vote for a winning candidate or party" rather than for the "preferred or favoured". **He calls for formulation of basic guidelines as safeguards to prevent distortion of opinion polls.** This would serve the interests of newspapers which have faced accusations on poll reporting. Readers should also be made conscious of the pitfalls of poll methodologies and results.

Shreesh Choudhary's article (March/April1987) on the, subject of reporting opinion polls was timely, relevant and raised significant issues. Opinion polls conducted in the context of State and national elections are often remembered more than the ones conducted in other contexts. It would be useful to examine the phenomenon of opinion polls in such contexts separately, since the criteria for evaluation have to be different.

Opinion polls sponsored by newspapers are meant more to bring to the fore the mood of the people, constituting mainly the reading

*Contd. on next page*

an expensive and time taking field survey. There are instances where projection of seats was "30 – 50" or 190 – 220 (*some examples).* Even in the case of exit polls, projections are given with such a wide margin. For example, exit poll for Andhra Pradesh Assembly in 2004 was given as 120 – 150. Close to polling day, as also in the case of exit polls, such a range should be smaller. And, more often the reasoning for the wide range in projection is never explained.

**Accuracy:** Accuracy, sometimes called precision, of a sample generally relates to the size of sample. Generally larger the universe (population), larger should be the sample size. But statisticians also point out that the size of sample is not invariably the sole basis for ensuring accuracy. Accuracy of a sample survey is measured and expressed in two different ways. One is in terms of "margin of error" and the other is in terms of Confidence Interval. "Confidents Interval is an interval within which the population value will lie with a certain

*Contd. from previous page*

public. There are a systematic effort to supplement news and source of views in specific contexts as snap-shots. Capturing a trend more objectively other than merely the accuracy level of prediction is often the primary concern.

A poll should indicate at the outset whether it is meant to capture opinions and beliefs, or preferences and practices, or values and perceptions. A combination of these, if capable of being accommodated, will make better sense and be more relevant. But such a comprehensive poll often leads to confusion.

Opinion polls in the context of elections are often perceived as indicators of not just the dimensions of victory or defeat, but also differences and margins at micro-and macro-levels. Opinion polls, in general, reflect at best the trend, the mood and direction at a given time limit. Of course, using past voting trends in similar or related sections, one could go much beyond. But then opinion polls are not conducted by newspapers in such a large context although it is more relevant.

*Contd. on next page*

assurance of being so". *(Presenting Survey Information. J. Chalmers and W. Lutz. 1989)*. A "90 percent level of confidence" does not mean that a survey prediction could be plus or minus 10 percent of the projected vote percentage. Rather, it implies that the *probability of being proved wrong* is not more than 10 percent. That such a survey would yield same result 90 times if it is repeated. Nearly thirty years ago, Eric P.W. da'Costa talked of 4 to 5 percent margin of error in national level survey. CSDS is the only agency which gives an idea of this for most of its poll surveys. Most poll surveys more often do not indicate the margin of error and those which do, are not clear as to whether margin of error is on the percentage of votes or seats projected. That is, if the projected number of seats of a party by an exit poll is 100, "it is ok" even if the final result is between 97 and 103. Here again, the larger the spread and more the regional distinctions, as in the case of Madhya Pradesh or Andhra

*Contd. from previous page*

Nevertheless, the relative correctness of the results of opinion polls would depend on the kind of methodology that has gone into the campaign and the methods followed for field-work. Several distinct factors that matter in this process relate to: a) the very electoral process, b) methodology, and c) publication-specific policies.

**I. Election – specific considerations:**

Whether the elections in context are for the state assembly or for Parliament or for both:

How well in advance the election schedules were known;

Whether the distinction between candidates was sharp enough. Against what background or specific context elections are being held.

And opinion poll conducted much prior to the actual poll schedule, or even irrespective of such a schedule, would not elicit the same kind of response and reliability as the one conducted after a formal announcement was made.

*Contd. on next page*

Pradesh or Uttar Pradesh, the margin of error could be within plus or minus five percent. Obviously, the margin of error cannot be same for national level outcome and state level outcome. In electoral context in India, however, such statistical confidence level is not so relevant, since such criteria apply more in controlled experiments/situations. In an electoral context what is more pertinent is "margin of error" in the projections. The margin of error expected and allowed in pre-poll surveys should be within 3 percent plus or minus.

However, an exit poll is expected to have even a smaller margin of error than in the case of pre-poll surveys. Similarly, sequential or tracking pre-poll surveys, are futile and misleading if they do not bring out the changing phenomena and the undercurrents over time during the campaign period

**Relevance:** Relevance of an exit-poll exists only when there is a time gap between the exit poll date and the counting dates. Exit

*Contd. from previous page*

Considering the campaign – related complexities in the Indian electoral system, opinion polls conducted at different time points as Times of India (TOI) did recently in Haryana, soon after the announcement of the election schedule and during the course of the campaign, would add to the predictability of the outcome. But then such "rolling polls" are not always possible for newspapers because of resource constraint.

**II. Methodological Issues:**

In any opinion poll conducted amongst a sample of individuals, from a universe of such vocal diversities as is there in every party of India, sampling strategy and method of interpretation are of crucial importance. Some of the components which are vital to the methodology of opinion polls are referred here.

- Sample selection – representativeness of the universe;

*Contd. on next page*

polls by their very nature prolong and even intensify speculation and guessing about poll outcome. Anxiety of voters, candidates, leaders and of news media to know the outcome on the same polling day would of courses be there. The time gap between the last polling day and counting day (as in the case of 2009 Orissa and Andhra Pradesh Assembly elections) was more than three weeks. As such the significance of an exit poll, although this gap in the case of Lok Sabha poll 2009 was less than a week (the last phase of polling was May 13 and the counting day was May 16)

An exit poll has the potential of vitiating the voting pattern of "re-poll" at some booths or in some constituencies, particularly when the number of booths involved in the "re-poll" the next day or the following day is large. The "band-wagon effect" in such cases could be detrimental for the final outcome when the contests are too keen as in some constituencies in most States. Pre-poll surveys on the other hand could be relevant both to the parties, candidates and the

*Contd. from previous page*

- Techniques of investigation – tools to capture an elusive trend, mood, perception or behaviour.
- Analysis of data and estimation – vital link between the sample and the universe; and
- Method of interpretation – attributing meaning to bare statistics.

**(a) Sample Selection:**

An important aspect of sample selection is representativeness of the universe. The method of sample selection and the sample size should have ample room to accommodate attributes of heterogeneous dimensions. The sampling plan should also capture temporal attributes like political affiliations, campaign phenomenon and other configurations. Such selection procedures have to be uniform and consistent across homogeneous clusters/states.

*Contd. on next page*

voters. The Parties could get to the pulse of voter and select the right 'winning' candidates and take up the issues bothering the voter. The voter too will feel comfortable that he or she had been enlightened about the dynamics of political options. The candidates could strategize their local specific campaign and make mid course corrections in that process. (The author had written on these aspects in *Politics India* in 1999 and in *Indian Express, New Delhi* in December 1998)

**How Seats are Estimated?**

The dimensions that go into forecasting a poll outcome based on field survey data include psephological, sociological, political and psychological. These aspects are enquired into in different ways. The psychological dimensions include perceptions and preferences and phenomenon to do with bandwagoning or sympathy in the context of a given election.

*Contd. from previous page*

The prevailing sample selection procedures include street corner interviews, voters list, physical settings and broad economic criteria based divisions. Street – corner interviews obviously cannot be expected to possess the above attributes and reliability as the household level interviews.

Any election time phenomenon is continuously changing like the contents of a boiling pot. At each time point the attributes of the universe (contents) itself are changing.

However, it should also be pointed out that, the fact that TOI (1987) poll was right in the case of 13 out of 16 assembly constituencies covered in the survey was more a coincidence, the sample size and selection was not meant for predicting at individual constituency level. Of course, an opinion survey which fails to bring out glaring trends in the electoral scene, as in the case of Haryana, cannot be considered systematic particularly when such a poll was conducted more than once.

*Contd. on next page*

Second is sociological. Which community or functional group a voter belongs to and whether that is in majority or minority locally. The assumption here is that people of a social group tend to vote similarly and network each other. The third is economic. How do voters weigh advantage or disadvantage of voting to certain party or candidate at a given point? How do they perceive and prefer opportunities by way of employment or immediate gratification, etc. A fourth element is political. Whether one is an activist in political activities and what has been the past voting preference. Similarly, where does one stand on critical issues that parties stand for example secularism or nuclear agreement or independent statehood, etc.

A fifth is the demographic and geographic aspects. The assumption here is that voters of similar demographic (age, gender, income, employment), background tend to vote similarly in a given situation. "Push and pull" weightage of these various aspects,

*Contd. from previous page*

**(b) Techniques of investigation:**

Different methods of investigation are required to arrive at the actual and considered opinion of the respondents rather than their momentary reactions to questions. The techniques of investigation range from cross-checking of answers by direct and indirect reference to important questions in the questionnaire.

Procedures followed in conducting the field-work include the content of checks and counter-checks on the investigators' work and watching of field-work between different locations in terms of interviews obtained. Uniformity in the mode of enquiry, given the language differences and interviewer characteristics, is also very critical. Most agencies engage part-time investigators on a piecemeal basis, although reliability level of the results would certainly be better when full-time experienced investigators are deployed.

The gap between the field-work period and the actual voting day also determines the actual results; particularly the last few days of

*Contd. on next page*

individually and together, is what contributes and determines the outcome of an election. Then there are external variables like the number of candidates in a given poll and how voters are likely to be divided or polarized and how these parties/ candidates reach out with their appeal. Each of these elements is quantified from the responses in a field survey. The weightage of each element may be different from one election to another and one State to another. To supplement these responses from a one-to-one interviews, sometime "focus group" discussions are conducted to identify the logics, linkages, motivations and trends that contribute to voting behaviour. The focus group discussion could be with local experts or opinion makers or typical voter groups, depending upon the pollsters own understanding of a poll scene and past experience in the state / constituency.

Yet another important aspect in this process of estimating seats based on a field survey is at what time such an exercise was conducted

*Contd. from previous page*

campaign in Indian elections are more crucial. The shorter the process of field-work, analysis and publication, the better the relevance of results of a survey. Only an agency with a network of permanent investigators can afford to do such a task when the poll is at the national or state level.

Equally important is the kind of questionnaire that is used to elicit voter intentions and images. A questionnaire with both open ended and pre-structured questions will yield better results than the one with only Yes-No type questions. A questionnaire should invariably have built-in checks to detect inconsistencies in the response pattern. Quite often, the questionnaire canvassed is Yes-No type and with no built-in checks. When results appear too close such checks come to risk.

The interaction of the person who writes about the likely poll results with field investigators and his involvement in the design greatly enhance the relevance and reliability of results. The mood prevailing

*Contd. on next page*

from the actual day of voting. The intervening variables could be who was the candidate, what does the manifesto have to offer, how effective the campaign is, and of course, the last minute lures or pulls and pressures.

Some agencies, like CMS or MDRA, do claim certain model in their methodology for estimating the outcome of an election based on their primary field surveys. There are of course some, either senior journalists or former politicians (like Arun Nehru), who also project the numbers as political analysts, but not based on field survey. But most professional agencies use some approach or method based on a field survey among voters. Yogendra Yadav of CSDS conducts field surveys for a news channels based CSDS's experience and extensive data base, depends on a model developed by a Professor of Statistics - this Professor after using his model with mixed results has now moved into a software consulting agency. Despite claims

*Contd. from previous page*

before the Haryana elections could never be missed even from a class-room exercise-type survey. To the extent the author himself is involved in the field work as in the case of TOI Haryana poll, to that extent the (news item) story will acquire credibility and accuracy.

Also, when surveys are so often undertaken in different parts of the country, the concepts being enquired about may have different connotation in local languages or dialects. Therefore, the way the questions are formulated and posed by investigators is important.

**(c) Data analysis and estimation:**

Any statement about the attributes of the universe has to be checked by sample data. In statistical sense, ultimately it is the extent of the error margin and the percentage confidence that speaks of the representative character of the sample and hence the accuracy with which it predicts the attributes of the universe. The error margin and the confidence level would vary for different questions or attributes of

*Contd. on next page*

of a sophisticated statistical model for estimating / projecting the outcome of elections and build up given to it in the news channel over the last decade, the model has neither added to the credibility of pollsters or psephologists nor of the news media. This model was never explained or written about except that the anchor of the TV channel attributes the forecast to the particular model and the professor, Dr. Rajiv Karandhikar. But his impressive software comes handy for TV channels to graphically intervene and keep updating even on the counting day. None of the other polling agencies or psephologists have ever referred to any model or ever bothered to explain. But the forecasts made by market research agencies like A C Neilson – ORG – MARG are based more on "sales forecast models" in vogue (personal discoveries of another). There are others who do not believe in any model as they think that "Indian politics is beyond

*Contd. from previous page*

the universe even in the same survey. Most of the opinion polls neglect to indicate these aspects.

**(d) Methods of interpretation:**

This is probably an area which requires utmost care and high level skill to convert dumb data into articulate characteristics. Specifically, for an opinion poll on elections, one should be able to grasp both the numbers and the political mood in the context of issues dominating a given scene. To give an example, TOI survey of 14 June, 1987 revealed that the Lok Dal – BJP alliance had improved by about 7 per cent in urban and 5 percent in rural votes as compared to the previous round at the end of May, while the Congress (I) position had deteriorated by 10 percent in urban and 8 percent in rural votes. Although the results were quite matching, these figures by themselves do not suggest that changes in voting intentions would proportionately reflect on the number of seats won/lost. This is an area where the expertise required goes

*Contd. on next page*

patterns" and right or wrong of their seats projection was a matter of chance. And, they continue to take chances !

Five elements are considered to provide insights for selecting or choosing those intervening factors for the confidence level of prediction of either or both the seats and the votes. Taking these different elements together, either from a field survey or from focus group discussions, or both, the pollster first assesses the shifts in voting intentions against the background of a previous election or a benchmark data if available. In and out migration of voters between two poll periods are assessed to influence the outcome of an election along with other factors that contribute in that process. The five elements referred to are supposed to provide insights for taking these intervening factors into account for the confidence level of prediction in terms of seats / votes. The CMS model also included taking into account the percentage of undecided voters and percent of those who are "likely to change" their preference close to the polling day. One might call them fence sitting voters. The higher this percentage,

*Contd. from previous page*

beyond the specific poll and statistics and calls for an understanding of the political scenario and campaigning.

"An exact tally between the actual outcome of an election and the opinion poll could only be a coincidence. But an opinion poll is futile if it cannot bring out the trend, the mood and the direction of outcome. A poll which fails to bring out glaring and sustained trends, as in Haryana, cannot be considered reliable or systematic".

**Newspaper – specific aspects:**

Some newspapers publish only hard results in percentage, some others leave it totally to the pollster; in a few cases the final version is a collaborative output between the newspaper and the researcher.

The actual date of publication after the field-work has been done also reflects the velocity of poll findings as such. If the newspaper

*Contd. on next page*

more the need of "sensitivity analysis" of each of the elements and their weightage in the over all forecasting.

**Factors that go into forecast models:**

What goes into various poll forecast models that come up with seats/votes? Some indicative examples for the factors that go into psephological exercise from out of field surveys include:

- Related to response pattern of sample
    - Over / under claim of voting intentions, preference for candidate or party.
    - Past voting and present voting intention and shifts
    - Likeliness of last minute change in voting.
- Related to perceptions about parties
    - How well various factions of the party are campaigning / united in efforts
    - Dissenting elements (walk-outs/walk-ins)
    - Perceptions about who is likely to win, etc.

*Contd. from previous page*

does not publish the poll story promptly and in the meantime there are new turns in the campaign, then obviously the relevance of poll survey findings will be less.

Poll survey results when published in a newspaper with a clear by-line reflect a higher degree of confidence in the project. This practice also ensures higher responsibility, both on the part of the publication and the researcher, and helps achieve improvements in subsequent efforts.

Quite often, newspaper policies determine the fate of opinion polls. While some of our mainline dailies like TOI, The Hindu, and The Hindustan Times are innovative and enterprising in this respect, even prominent periodicals tend to adopt a "let-loose-as-it-suits" approach despite their lack of time constraint for sponsoring a more systematic poll. India Today deserves credit for going beyond a mere poll approach in some of its election – time polls.

*Contd. on next page*

- Related to candidate(s)
    - Matching with local demographics
    - Past (performance) track record – positive/ negative
- Related to "if and but" aspects in a poll scene
    - Factors or issues of consequence that are likely to sway voters (like LTTE in Tamil Nadu in 2004 or 2009).
    - Undecided voters, indecisive voters

These models imply considerable subjective element. Using a computer model, psepholgists come up with projections. The weightage given to these aspects differs from one election to another and even from one State to another in the case of Lok Sabha election. Scores are assigned by someone who is familiar with the process. There may be more than one individual's subjective consideration in arriving at an overall weightage.

More than a couple of news media in 2009 Lok Sabha poll used subjective element based on "journalistic experience" to come up with projection of seats party/state wise. (Times of India, Dainik

*Contd. from previous page*

Knowledge of trends in the response pattern in the earlier field-surveys would help avoid embarrassment as in the one during Haryana election, particularly when the poll in context is for scattered locations and variations in the response are glaring and inconsistent. Several examples of this could be seen in various magazines for many recent polls.

The Times of India opinion poll conducted in Haryana perhaps was a good example of a somewhat better conceived, coordinated and executed opinion poll.

These are some of the added complexities of an opinion poll in the specific context of elections.

Note : This was an article by Dr N Bhaskara Rao in 1987 in India Today's Media Monitor magazine. This magazine is no longer published. This article was written in response to another article in this magazine in its earlier edition by one Shreesh Chaudhary.

Bhaskar, etc). The fact that the number of such projection and their prominence in the news media have been on the increase (from only one of Arun Nehru a decade ago), obviously reflect declining credibility of field survey based projections by commercial polling agencies.

# 4

# Role of Surveys

## Introduction

Given the kind of complexities of Indian elections, concluding direct effect of poll surveys on the outcome of an election could only be an exception at the most. The phenomenon of "last mile glitches" as the Chief Election Commissioner of India Navin B. Chawla (Pioneer, June 24, 2009) would like to describe the imponderables at the booth level, is something which eventually determines the actual exercise of franchise. The recent "micro management" strategies further increase uncertainty in the relations. In any case, no one single factor could be attributed for the outcome of an election to the Assembly or Lok Sabha. It is always a combination of factors, poll surveys being only one, that go into the outcome of an election. The weightage of these factors however changes from constituency to constituency and from one voter demographics to another. The significance or weightage of poll surveys in such a complex process depends on the timing of the survey and the way the news media covers and hypes or otherwise of the survey findings.

Just because pre-poll surveys have gone wrong on the day of counting, it should not mean they were incorrect at the time they were conducted. Irrespective of that, if they were widely covered in the media they could have direct as well indirect effect on the voting pattern. If the polling was held a couple of days later with a different expose to candidate or campaign, a survey could yield a different finding which could have been closer. Such a possibility can never be ruled out. This dimension is what psephological exercise is expected to consider and take into account. There are no experimental or empirical and time series studies to establish cause and effect relationship of poll surveys in the Indian context. It is more by the strength of inferences of responses that one could talk of the role of poll surveys. This author from his own involvement in poll campaigns, personal observations and discussions with those who have steered campaigns over the years, could say quite affirmatively that poll surveys have their impact on the very nature of poll campaign and voting behaviour patterns.

**What Role do Surveys Play?**

The number of pre-poll surveys has more than doubled in the country in the last decade. On the eve of the six phased 2004 general election, for example, there were almost two dozen surveys most of them forecasting the outcome of Lok Sabha poll in terms of party wise seats/ votes. Most of them were published or broadcast in news media prominently, either as a news item or as a prime time special programme. There must be as many or more field surveys conducted in the country by political parties and resourceful candidates as part of their internal exercise. The purpose of these surveys ranges from identifying issues factors to assess winning chances of candidates and to assess and project poll outcome. The outlook to these surveys varies from poll to poll and party to party. There are parties / candidates who get surveys sponsored to get them covered in news media directly or indirectly, to help/facilitate poll campaign and electoral strategy. More than half a dozen exit polls were broadcast by television channels. What is even more curious is that many of those surveys, including the exit polls, were off the mark in their desegregated projections. What is more interesting is that it was not only the pollsters who had egg on their face, but even the news media including prominent television channels. In 2008 too, most news media had gone off the mark in their projections of Karnataka Assembly polls, including CNN-IBN survey by CSDS, for a second time in a row both with respect to pre-poll surveys and exit polls. A new entrant in 2008 into psephology – Cfore – whose pre-poll and exit poll for a news channel in Kannada, (Swarna TV), was the only one on the dot, perhaps by chance. But this has demolished a myth with the media, political parties and the public that surveys by already well known agencies are more reliable. In fact, Indian psyche is full of craze for foreign agencies notwithstanding their track record in forecasts. Often, these agencies work for competing media, competing parties and also candidates at the same time.

**Number of National Poll Surveys - featured in national news media**

| *Year* | *Pre polls* | *Exit Polls* |
|---|---|---|
| 1991 | - | - |
| 1996 | 3 | - |
| 1998 | 4 | 2 |
| 1999 | 8 | 4 |
| 2004 | 9 | 5 |
| 2009 | 12 | 16 |

Despite proliferation of poll surveys and their use and coverage in the news media, so little is known about them, pollsters, and polling agencies, the methodologies used by them and their reliability. Survey findings are covered by news media as if it is a public service and in support of free and fair elections. Most news channels have been featuring pre-poll surveys election after election until 2009. Even major newspapers have been doing so either on their own or in collaboration with a television channel. A more recent trend in the case of State election is a two or three-way collaboration between a news channel, a national news daily and a regional daily – to sponsor collective surveys. This was more to infuse confidence or credibility in the survey itself. Not only because of ban on surveys in media during polls but also as a realisation of limits of field surveys, the number of pre-poll surveys had come down for 2009 Lok Sabha polls. There were hardly a couple of pre-poll surveys three months before the national polls against many more before 2004 polls. But not in the case of one month long 2009 Lok Sabha elections, when 16 channels had telecast exit polls on the last day of polling.

**Impact of Opinion Surveys:** Results of barely one-third of two dozen pre- poll surveys conducted before Lok Sabha polls across the country get into the news media. One of the reasons for this trend is the reluctance of newspapers to sponsor, or even to publish, survey findings. Some surveys are not published because the results are not favorable to the sponsors or not consistent with the political stand of the newspaper. However, there is no evidence that pre-poll surveys have made a qualitative difference to the pre-poll scene in terms of character of the campaign or the process of selecting candidates. Pre-poll surveys have not earned reputation for influencing poll agenda setting, nor is there any evidence that any political party has benefited from such surveys. An exception publicly acknowledged was the isolated case of M. Karunanidhi of DMK who had a landslide victory in the 1996 elections for the Tamil Nadu Assembly. He publicly credited CMS's pre-poll survey as one of factors that contributed to his party's sweep (Front Page of The Hindu, 1996).

## What difference Surveys Make?

Despite proliferation of news media and their reach in recent years and efforts made by some of them to motivate voters to go out and caste their vote, what difference have they made on the percentage of voter turnout?. Curiously, voter turn out has remained more or less at the same level in the last couple of decades. In fact, it is either static or there is a marginal decline in some pockets. These pockets are the ones where a high percentage of voters are exposed to news media more intensely with multiple options of news media available to them. While covering pre-poll surveys prominently in 2004 and 2009, some channels maintained that their poll was "definitive" and claimed that voters "see today the results of next months election" as if they pre-empting the very essence of an election in a democracy.

If the outcome of an election, where voters are yet to vote, is presented as if it is a "foregone conclusion", as news media often tend to make out with poll surveys, where is the motivation for voters to go out and cast their vote on the polling day?. Frankly, this aspect had not occurred to this author until eminent editor Girilal Jain and Dileep Padgaonkar posed it more than 20 years ago. Is there any reason why voter turnout has not been increasing despite dramatic change in the demographics of voters, proliferation of news media, efforts of the Election Commission and in the number of poll surveys recently?. Even when it is known which section of voters by and large are unlikely to take part. And to what extent poll surveys in media motivate or empower voters?. And enrich the electoral process?. Can one say that media hype of poll surveys do not enthuse voters to go out and vote?. This aspect needs to be pondered very seriously over as news media are being inundated with pre poll surveys of all kinds.

Given the peculiar poll and political dynamics in India and the fast changing loyalties and stand of leaders and parties, drawing parallels with other countries as to the relevance of poll surveys may not be pertinent. But, in such a scenario, to conclude that any change in voter behaviour is "difficult to prove and in any case (effects) are minimal" amounts to deferring a problem or ignoring insights. For, more specific and quantified evidence for any effect or otherwise of poll surveys is possible only when specially designed studies for that are carried out within the country to trace voting intentions at various time points of a poll campaign. A CMS post-poll survey in 1996 and 1998 has indicated that pre-poll surveys do influence voting preferences of voters, although neither similarly or uniformly across a State or even within a constituency. Even post-poll surveys carried out by CSDS had indications to that effect. We of course need more experimental research in this regard.

The issue is not merely a question of relevance or reliability of poll surveys, but about the very intention of surveys whose findings are often hyped in the prime time news media as if they are independent or objective and as if larger the size of the sample, the more reliable they are. The issue of media coverage of poll surveys needs to be viewed from the point of view of a free and fair election. We need to reposition poll surveys in the media much beyond the who wins or loses aspect. The processes should be more relevant, than the outcome. Sometimes they are hyped by news media beyond a point to sustain themselves in the competitive media scenario, vitiating the freedom and fairness aspect and preempting voters' choice to the extent of marking them passive. This is what this author described as "preemptive journalism" as against "proactive journalism" that they are more often engaged in.

**Do Poll Surveys Make a Difference?**

Over the years CMS, had maintained that pre-poll surveys appearing in the media influence poll process. Based on the insights from conducting election studies for over 35 years, this author had written that pre-poll surveys and even exit polls (when conducted prior to completion of the poll process), do make a difference to the poll process and even the poll outcome. Realising such potential, as early as in 1987, this author wrote on Rights & Wrongs of pre-poll surveys in the then Media Monitor of India Today and suggested the need for Dos & Don'ts for pre-poll surveys being covered in the news media. He also advocated that editors should be the first ones to understand pros and cons of pre-poll surveys.

With the over all reach of media being far more today than it was two decades ago, such a concern for the impact of media coverage of poll surveys has to be more. The implications however cannot be expected to be uniform. Depending upon the demographics of the electorate and at the stage of a poll campaign, the findings of a pre-poll survey get covered in the news media and how prominently 3 or 4 distinct influences of coverage could be traced. The same could be said about coverage of a poll campaign by media even without surveys. These are:

(1) *Band-wagon effect.* Where the tendency on the part of undecided voters is to go along with the party/candidate projected in the surveys as a probable winner or as leading or having higher chance of winning.

(2) *Underdog phenomenon.* Where the tendency, particularly on the part of disloyal voters, all other factors being the same, is to sympathies with the candidate projected to lose in the survey. Fortunes of Sheila Dikshit in 2008 changed with media reports of how she was going to be 'dumped by her party', after poll surveys showed BJP's edge.

(3) *Complacency factor.* Where leaders and cadres become complacent with multiple pre-poll surveys projecting pretty much similar outcome with safe margins, as if underwriting the victory of the party or candidate in context. TDP loss in 2004 Assembly and Ashok Gehlot Government's in 2003 Assembly are two such examples. Even AIADMK's performance, much below what was projected by the survey, with an undercurrent of LTTE, could be another example.

(4) *Tactical Voting:* Going by talk as to who is likely to win some voters are likely to change their initial intention or choice and vote for the other party / candidate. Such a talk gains momentum by pre poll survey or findings of an exit poll in the initial phase and voters in the second or subsequent phases of polling are likely to vote differently than without such a talk about who the likely winner.

For example in the 2009 poll, Andhra Pradesh had two phased polling. The first phase poll covered all Telengana constituencies and on completion of that the talk or the rumor mill going by "private exit polls" or/and assessments of news media, that the TDP or Mahakutami alliance had done better, a significant percent or voters in the coastal districts, who voted a few days later in the second and final phase, assessed the consequences of TDP or Mahakutami winning and voted otherwise for Congress party in the assembly, contrary to what the poll surveys had indicated earlier. Had this election been in one phase, the outcome perhaps would have been different for the assembly. A second example for tactical voting is that a significantly high percent of voters in Andhra Pradesh voted differently for assembly and Lok Sabha in the simultaneous poll of 2009. Where they assessed the choice for the two polls and voted differently, to one party for the Lok Sabha and for another party for Assembly. This phenomenon was not indicated by the pre poll surveys. The voters voted tactfully. The difference between underdog and tactical voting is subtle. In the latter, it is the consequence of a likely outcome which drives voters. Whereas in the former, it is not such reasoning but sympathy or as an opportunity to show the power of vote.

The higher the percentage of undecided voters or higher the number of keenly fought constituencies, the more likely the implications of poll surveys in the news media. The least the pre-poll surveys covered in the media do is to enthuse or dampen cadres and influence fence sitters directly. And coverage of poll surveys in media facilitates shift of local leaders to a likely winner or otherwise. No wonder why pre-poll surveys have become yet another instrument in the armory of political parties. The editors should be the ones to discriminate pre-poll surveys which are part of a party campaign and ensure transparency in the interest of their own credibility as well as of the media. When a new survey agency - crops up with a poll survey, the news media should indicate its credentials. In the four States that went to Assembly polls in 2008, we can find some evidence for all the three types of influence of poll surveys in the media to some extent or the other – Bandwagoning in MP, complacency in Rajasthan and underdog phenomenon in Delhi. So also in the 2009

Lok Sabha polls. Poll surveys appear to have influenced differently in West Bengal, Andhra Pradesh, Maharashtra and Tamil Nadu. It is however, generally believed. It is generally believed that it is the last couple of days before the polling day that make the difference to the poll outcome. Should that be attributed to media coverage or poll management, including "note for vote" and other modification has to be established.

**Do they Influence the Outcome?**

Do poll surveys influence voting choice?. This question is quite relevant to pursue. Since this issue is raised at every election time and since poll schedule of the general elections for the Lok Sabha and some State Assemblies will continue to be a staggered affair over two or more phases, we need to understand the pros and cons of media coverage of poll surveys, particularly in between the phases. If poll surveys have no influence on voters and campaigns, why so many of them are being commissioned and highlighted in the news media?. What other purpose they serve?. Are they enlightening the voters in any way?. Why political parties are conducting or sponsoring at various time points and getting them covered (by whatever means) and even hyped in the news media. And why political parties are quick to debunk survey findings when not in their favour?. The more the gap between the phases of polling dates, the higher the scope of their use for an electoral advantage of one or the other. As if to maximize the influence poll surveys are often presented as if they are independent or objective without even giving minimal information about the methodology used, and/or who sponsored the survey. That being the case a rethink on media coverage of poll surveys in between the phases of a staggered poll is appropriate and necessary in the interest of free and fair polls. For, the role and standing of news media is much bigger and long ranging than one individual election.

An analysis of field surveys for over 35 years by this author, both for the Lok Sabha and the Assemblies, amply indicates that voters more (particularly the undecided and indecisive voters) eventually end up voting for the "likely winner" notwithstanding their initial intention prior to actual casting of vote. That is what "bandwagon" effect is all about. That is when party workers and voters may change their voting preference from one party / candidate to another closer to the voting day. Whether such votes are less than two percent or more depends on and differs from election to election and constituency to constituency. But the phenomenon is based on voters' perception of the poll scene and about "likely winner". Such perceptions get accumulated in the minds of voters based on poll campaign and its coverage in the news media. Why else are news media often accused of "trying to influence" the outcome of an election overtly (by openly endorsing) or covertly (by preferential coverage in terms of time/space) including by poll surveys. Post-poll studies

**How surveys could help poll process**

One of the observations resulting from a review of poll surveys has been that they did not contribute to better the quality of poll campaigns or in making the poll process free and fair. As an example of how surveys can help the poll process, a CMS "note for vote" survey is briefly described. Having realized from its annual surveys of Citizen and Corruption, that a significant percent of voters are given cash on the eve of polls for Assembly and Lok Sabha, CMS did a survey in 2007 among 23,000 BPL households. Alarmed with the outcome, CMS did another round of survey in 2008 across the country, this time among 18000 voters across demographics. This round of survey confirmed that cash for vote prevailed not only among the poor or in rural areas only but across and irrespective of location, age, education and occupation. Both the surveys were undertaken when there was no poll fever. Concerned at the alarming implications of this trend, CMS decided that it should sensitize larger public and opinion leaders about this large scale phenomenon of note for vote statewide by releasing its

*Contd. on next page*

by CMS have indicated that over all percentage of voters who decide their voting choice closer to the polling day are on the increase. But one by CSDS indicate otherwise. This author had written nearly two decades ago how in such situations poll surveys, covered prominently in news media, influence voters in different ways.

Outcome of elections to the Lok Sabha and the State Assemblies eventually depend on voter's assessment of the options, particularly when the contests are keenly fought and margins are expected to be narrow. News media by the extent and nature of their coverage of election campaigns, and based on their own credibility in relation to the reader / viewer, facilitates voting decision one way or other. That unique function of news media cannot be questioned - as long as objectivity and transparency is ensured in that process.

*Contd. from previous page*

finding to news index. Later, in December 2008, CMS did yet another round of enquiry and analysis of cash distribution in the by-elections for eight Assembly constituencies in Karnataka. It was found that the phenomenon of cash for vote was rampant and that all parties were involved, and, in fact, such a practice had become as if it is a necessary condition to fight polls.

CMS had decided to generate a debate on the phenomenon and its serious repercussions to the very electoral process and its potential to dampen the democratic culture itself. This phenomena was brought out first at the Lok Sabha Speaker's roundtable three months before the 2009 poll process with eminent personalities and was televised nationally more than a couple of times. CMS sent out to news media first with its estimation of expenditure involved in the Lok Sabha poll (Rs.10,000 crores) which was extensively covered all over in print and electronic media. Most news channels in fact had one or more discussion programmes on the subject. As a follow-up, CMS had put out what

*Contd. on next page*

**Whose Interests Poll Surveys Cater to?**

Poll surveys are expected to sustain and substantiate objective coverage of polls by news media. That is why they have come into being and have become part of news media. News media expect that by covering poll surveys their own share and role in the "market" improves, their own political clout increases and stands out in the competition. News media always try to increase their revenue and market share or advantage by taking to coverage of polls in a big way. Then, of course, there are many instances where news media support or oppose a party or candidate and use a "survey" for that purpose.

Political parties try to use poll surveys to pep up the morale of their own cadres and demoralize the cadres and campaign of the opposing party/ candidate. In that process they expect some voters to "migrate" from one party or candidate of initial preference to

*Contd. from previous page*

note for vote meant to citizens as the source of all corruption in the country. This linkage dimension of accepting cash for vote once in five years is to perpetuate bribe that a citizen ends up paying in availing (II) public services to which he / she is entitled otherwise.

The Hindu daily newspaper published an article "How 'notes for votes' dampen democracy" by Dr. N Bhaskara Rao prominently (on 6th April 2009) in its op-edit page describing the phenomenon. This article attracted attention and evoked wide spread response. As a follow up the Ennicala Nigha Samithi (AP Election Watch) has taken up a two pronged campaign appealing voters not to accept money for votes. It also pursued with the State Election Commission and the Police Commissioner to take measures to curb the flow of money. The news media coverage had brought out that cash for vote phenomenon was going to be highest ever anywhere. The survey helped news media create awareness which in turn led to initiatives on the part of civil

*Contd. on next page*

another *(Contd. Box)* Depending upon the keenness of the contest between contenders in a given situation, the effect of media coverage of the situation may be good enough when the difference between winning or losing is likely to be minimal. Another aspect that needs to be taken note of is increasing competitiveness in the contests in more and more constituencies. That is the margin for win/lose has been on the decline in more (Assembly / Lok Sabha) constituencies now than ever before. As such a marginal shift of votes is good enough to change the fortunes of a particular candidate/party. The issue here is about "deceptive" or "innocent" coverage of poll surveys in the media without revealing all about and their methodology. Obviously, this is also to do with credibility of media, individually and collectively.

Pre-poll surveys, nevertheless have the potential to improve the quality of poll campaigns. Have they?. Do they?. What has been the recent experience?. Poll campaigns continue to be personality centered, accusation oriented and acrimonious. Simultaneously, and

*Contd. from previous page*

society groups at the grassroots, and election officials to take preemptive measures. Together, these efforts have made a dent on the practice of cash being distributed. All party leaders too were made to condemn such a practice.

The survey, having identified a critical ground level reality, brought the issue to fore. This enabled civil society groups to take campaign against accepting money for vote. Over Rs. 40 crores cash in bundles was seized between March 15 and April 15 2009 practically in all districts of Andhra Pradesh as in Karnataka Assembly election in 2008. But without the exposure and initiatives, several times more cash might have been distributed on the eve of 2009 poll.

That some voters are paid money for their vote is known even before CMS survey had brought it out. But the survey had helped to systematically bring out that phenomenon, establish its magnitude and helped formulate an action plan to curb the phenomenon in specific contexts. (www.cmsindia.org).

also as a result, party manifestos have lost their seriousness and significance. But pre-poll surveys are more concerned in bringing out who wins or loses or the seats they are likely to get rather than the processes aspect of electoral system and undercurrents and the linkage to voting behaviour. Coverage tends as if coercive measures work more than reasoning. Some political parties avail pre-poll surveys to strategize their campaign and make it more focused. This is fine. The problem is when findings of such surveys designed for internal use are presented or covered in the news media as if they are independent, stand alone and objectively conducted.

**Election Commission's Concerns**

At the height of 2009 poll campaign, a website (www.mediavisfot.com) had reported with examples how prominent newspapers (three Hindi newspapers were specially named) were offering "package deals" with different levels of coverage for a price. Formal complaints were also made with Election Commission and Press Council of India at more than a couple of places/states. Reports about some news media indulging in such practice had come to this author's notice in 1998 Lok Sabha poll when a journalist went about promising publication of a survey for a fees. His services were used even by a national party, more than a couple of times, both for Lok Sabha and State elections. This person first had a letter head – news-agency and then a poll survey agency. He was offering "two in one" (for one price he would come up with a "survey report" and also get it covered in the media). A former minister and veteran who contesed for sixth time for Lok Sabha, had gone on record much after 2009 polls about his experience with news media's "package deals" for covering poll campaign. His was not a general observation but with specifies (mohallalive.com - archive 2009/07/05). There are known Public relation firms offering such services to political parties and individual candidates. Most of the rich MPs and MLAs have availed such services and even sustained such agencies.

Despite instances of newspapers and news channels indulging in surrogate advertising in the form of "news" in the context of Assembly or Lok Sabha election, there is nothing that the Election Commission could do. There has been no action even when news media or candidates themselves complain about such blatantly distorted coverage of poll campaign, including by way of "surveys". While admitting the practice, one Election Commissioner himself narrated (to this author) instance of a candidate in the 2008 Assembly poll in Rajasthan complaining about how local news media took money from candidates / parties for supportive news coverage and for suppressing the campaign of the opposing candidate. All that the Election Commission did was to advise the candidate to file a complaint with the Press Council of India. There is no instance of the Press Council of India doing anything proactively or in response to any complaint on the eve of poll campaign although it is widely known and also talked about that news media were indulging in such a practice – and that such practice is no longer isolated or limited to small sized local media. Neither Editor's Guild of India or IBF or News Broadcasting Association had seized with the problem having implications to the very credibility of news media. The Election Commission does not appear to have grasped the implications of the character of such a fraud on free and fair means of polls.

In the middle of the 2009 campaign, the Press Council of India issued an advice to news media to be fair in reporting, give equal opportunity and that they should differentiate paid news from the rest. And that media should "eschew reports which tried to promote feelings of enmity or hatred between people on grounds of region, religion, race, cast or community". Media is "not expected to indulge in unhealthy election campaign, exaggerated reports about any candidate or party or incidents during the election". Such guidelines are too general, and even vague. These guidelines have not made any difference at any level and among any - so far. And in any case there have been no serious efforts to even independently monitor such trends and debate.

**Poll Surveys Empower Voters?**

It took a decade for the Supreme Court of India to realize that poll surveys, when published in news media in certain ways can influence or interfere with free and fairness of elections. This was the stand of the Election Commission notwithstanding the provision of "freedom of press". Soli Sorabjee, former Attorney General of India, should be credited for poll surveys galore (over two dozen) in 2004. By advising the Government that banning exit polls and pre – poll surveys amounts to violation of Article 19 (a), he facilitated a free for all polls in the news media. But Sorabjee had rightly argued earlier in the Supreme Court that allowing political advertisements (acrimonious/surrogate) on TV amounts to "distorting the electoral process". How can the poll surveys, when covered in news media, be viewed differently?. The all - party meeting held in April 2004 at the instance of the Election Commission reached a consensus to the effect that exit polls could be broadcast only after all the phases of voting were over. While there was no ambiguity in this regard on exit polls, the decisions on pre- poll surveys was not clear. One view was that pre - poll surveys should not be carried by the media once the Election Commission had issued its notification on elections. However, it is not clear whether it is from the time of the first notification announcing the elections or the second notification with actual schedule of polling. The other view was that pre-poll surveys should not be carried in the media once campaigning comes to an end 48 hours before the polling. But in a staggered poll schedule across 4 or 5 phases, which should be the cut off point for stopping media use of pre - poll surveys the 2004 elections has new insights.

Going by its experience of 1999 in trying to restrain poll surveys in media, the Election Commission (EC) did not take any chance towards bringing some order. It felt that consensus at an all-party meeting does not amount to a legal sanction to curb poll surveys in the media. That is how the EC wanted the Government to promulgate an ordinance immediately empowering the Commission to restrain exit polls. But even after that, the Ordinance would have been questioned on the same lines as in 1999. That would not have put an end to the controversy on media coverage of poll surveys. The applicability under Section 126 and 132 of Representation of People's Act in this regard is yet to be pursued by the Election Commission. However, it should have atleast come up with some guidelines before the first phase of 2004 poll – this was what the Delhi High Court in 2008 had suggested.

**Poll Surveys are here to Stay!**

Certain innocence in media reporting election surveys, both pre-poll and exit polls, deserves to be understood better now since they have come to stay and become part of our electoral process. As such those in the news media should know how to evaluate or appraise a pre-poll survey before covering it. Also, they should explore different and alternative ways of availing such surveys to enhance the quality of poll campaigns, increase voter turn out and make voter, understand the linkage of proposals of contending parties. Those in the news media should be explicit why they cover and sponsor poll-related surveys.

An exit-poll is expected to be more reliable than a pre-poll survey. An exit-poll result is not expected to be in the reverse direction of the actual result, as happened in the case of Madhya Pradesh Assembly poll in 1998, Maharashtra and Tamil Nadu in 1996 and in Andhra Pradesh in 2004. An exit-poll should become news for the media not when it is right, but when it goes off the mark. If a pre-poll survey, which is expected to indicate the direction of the likely outcome, ends up closest to the election result on the counting day; could make news. More so when such a pre-poll survey is conducted at the very outset of the poll process, several weeks prior to the announcement of poll dates. For an exit-poll the primary criterion for evaluation is its accuracy more in terms of seats. In the case of pre-poll surveys, the criteria would be multiple, including: (a) how well ahead of the polling day was the likely overall outcome indicated, (b) how close predictions were to the final outcome, (c) what was the sample size of the constituencies and voters used for conducting the pre-poll survey, and, (d) equally importantly, how well the factors and issues involved in the context of the election were brought out.

Presenting findings of exit poll and even pre-poll surveys in the midst of a staggered poll schedule could be misleading. Certain hype in the coverage of exit polls by TV channels even before the completion of all phases of polling may influence the poll process by influencing undecided voters in the remaining phases in whichever direction and extent that may be.

Attorney-General's idea of a "regulatory mechanism" in this regard is interesting, but it cannot be outside the perview of Election Commission. The proposal was never intended to be a ban on poll surveys altogether but one of restraining on media coverage of the results of exit polls even before voting is complete everywhere and in all phases. The need for such a restraint should be understood – for four reasons–one, proliferation of television news channels across the country and in every language; second, increased competitiveness in the very contests of political parties; third, such poll surveys are not necessarily and always objective but could be part of party campaigns as seen recently in 1999, 2004 and 2009 and who is accountable or responsible for poll surveys is not clear in the absence of transparency.

In the interest of free and fair elections, some guidelines, more by way of self- discipline are desirable, both for the news media and polling agencies. For, both "freedom of speech and expression" as well as holding of "free and fair polls" are paramount for a vibrant democracy. Realizing proliferation of poll surveys of all kinds, the same way as surrogate ads., this author had written as early as in 1986, that research agencies as well as news media themselves should evolve certain guidelines for themselves and what such guideline should be like also was indicated.

## Why Media Coverage of Poll Surveys be Viewed Differently ?

Notwithstanding all this, pre-poll surveys have become part of poll process and they are here to stay. In fact, they could help

**Reader/viewer Views about Poll Surveys in Media and about their Credibility**

*(Figures in %)*

| State Name | *Between Media and Politician who has more credibility* | | | | *Should there be restrictions on media publishing poll surveys* | | |
|---|---|---|---|---|---|---|---|
| | *Media* | *Politician* | *None* | *Both* | *Yes* | *No* | *DK* |
| Andhra Pradesh | 35 | 39 | 5 | 17 | 55 | 38 | 7 |
| Tamil Nadu | 19 | 13 | 13 | 47 | 20 | 72 | 8 |
| Karnataka | 58 | 16 | 1 | 8 | 16 | 70 | 13 |
| Kerala | 37 | 32 | 9 | 6 | 52 | 27 | 20 |
| West Bengal | 46 | 16 | 17 | 16 | 46 | 40 | 14 |
| Assam | 17 | 48 | 6 | 28 | 47 | 53 | - |
| Orissa | 60 | 12 | 5 | 10 | 3 | 77 | 21 |
| Bihar | 66 | 6 | 13 | 9 | 71 | 25 | 4 |
| Jharkhand | 11 | 41 | 2 | 46 | 54 | 46 | 1 |
| Uttar Pradesh | 63 | 21 | 3 | 10 | 15 | 78 | 7 |
| Madhya Pradesh | 55 | 15 | 5 | 24 | 16 | 80 | 3 |
| Chattisgarh | 50 | 22 | 12 | 14 | 23 | 68 | 9 |
| Haryana | 41 | 41 | 7 | 9 | 29 | 66 | 4 |
| Himachal Pradesh | 61 | 3 | 7 | 28 | 36 | 64 | 1 |
| Rajasthan | 48 | 17 | 14 | 18 | 39 | 51 | 10 |
| Delhi | 55 | 23 | 14 | 8 | 36 | 53 | 11 |
| Gujarat | 31 | 28 | 9 | 36 | 43 | 50 | 6 |
| Maharashtra | 30 | 17 | 18 | 13 | 33 | 63 | 5 |

*CMS Survey 2008*

enhance the quality of poll campaigns. As P.N.Vasanti wrote in *Mint (May 1, 2009)* in the wake of 2009 polls, surveys should not be "preemptive of citizen activism, provocative of our divides and not be dictated by conflict of interest of news media and the survey agency. The assertions in the coverage should be explanatory, not conclusive. The analyses should be objective and not one sided. And it should differentiate between sponsored content, views and news". But since pre-poll surveys have the potential to become part of party campaign, rather than be independent and / or objective exercises, the way such surveys are presented could vitiate the poll process.

**Readers' Interest in Poll Surveys in Media**

CMS had enquired more than once about views of readers and viewers on restraining news media covering poll surveys. The sample was large and covered most States. The respondents were adults and selected randomly as a part of a larger study in 2008 on corruption that a citizen encounters in availing basic public utilities / services. This enquiry about poll surveys was limited to readers or / and viewers of television. However, this study was meant to derive general insights on the subject, not to draw linkage. The enquiry was in the context of ongoing debate at that time about restrictions on news coverage of poll surveys, including exit polls. Also, although the respondents were adults of voting age, only about two-third were voters.

Readers were divided about publishing of poll surveys in newspapers. A majority of them do not favour any restrictions on publishing surveys. One-third however do think there is need for some restrictions on newspapers publishing poll surveys on the eve of elections as they try to influence voters in favor or against one or other political party or candidate – intentionally or unintentionally.

But, marginally more viewers of TV news channels were for restrictions than in the case of newspaper readers. However, even in the case of viewers, a majority are not for restrictions on the coverage of poll surveys. In Bihar, Andhrapradesh, Jharkhand, Assam and Kerala, more than 45 per cent were for restrictions. The reason why some 35 percent viewers are for restrictions on news channels is more for the way the poll surveys are highlighted. In fact, more interestingly, relatively a higher percent of viewers are for restrictions on sex, crime and such other contents of TV, than in the case of restrictions on the converge of poll surveys by news channels. This perhaps is because women's groups are vocal for restrictions on TV portrayal of women, whereas, in the case of coverage of poll surveys, there is no section of citizenry including academic bodies criticizing the hype of poll surveys. This is despite that surveys covered on channels had gone wrong more often than they were right – in the last one decade. Interestingly, in most States, a much higher percent of people consider news media as having higher credibility than politicians.

**Surveys Syndrome**

There was a classic case of election to Delhi Assembly in 1996 when Sushma Swaraj was BJP's candidate for Chief Ministership. She relied rather on surveys (carried out by an overenthusiastic new entrant – at the time into conducting poll surveys) all out for her strategy and surprisingly lost the poll. Ashok Gehlot in Rajasthan and Ajit Jogi in Chattisgarh lost in 1998. Both relied on one or other surveys (their first exposure to such surveys) and, further, one depended on Cable TV network and the other on news media more for support. In 2002, Mulayam Singh Yadav lost in Uttar Pradesh. He relied on surveys (by a loyalist) and glamour more. In 2004 Chandrababu Naidu in Andhra Pradesh and Amrendra Singh in Punjab too lost their polls. They depended even more on surveys and media publicity. Chandrababu Naidu's case was unparallel (as he had several rounds of surveys and by more agencies). In 2009 Rajasekhar Reddy scraped through in Andhra Pradesh after insisting victory in two-thirds seats all through the campaign (nearly half of Ministers in his cabinet lost the poll). No Chief Minister ever before in India got so many surveys (more than 20) conducted (in one year), pre-occupied so much with news media and spent so much on media advertising as Rajasekhar Reddy did in Andhra Pradesh in 2009 and his predecessor in 2004. However, Dr Reddy, a better communicator individually, personally reached out more people more than once in a year in the previous four and half years before the election than any other leader before.

One thing common in all these cases, apart from performance related factor of the parties in context, is their "media driven campaigns" and "surveys determined strategies". Dependence on these two interventions by an incumbent leader/ party signals certain disconnect with immediate concerns of voters, mood of larger public and the undercurrents. In this process, they forgot the fact that public opinion today is allusive and like an air balloon and all that it takes to bust the balloon is a hair pin. Each case of course was unique; The examples of Reddy in Andhra Pradesh in 2009 and Mayawati in 2006 offers two different models and signal a dilemma that political leaders are going through. Most political leaders do not seem to learn from goings on or do not remember even the recent past experience.

Poll surveys more particularly when sponsored or commissioned by or conducted on behalf of an incumbent Chief Minister, they suffer from inherent pit fall of bias either in the very design or in the field work or in the data analysis or in all the three ways. This was the case with surveys for Sushma Swaraj in 1998, for Chandrababu Naidu in 2004 and 2009 and for Chiranjeevi's PRP/ Rajasekhar Reddy in 2009. These surveys were assigned to those individuals/ agencies who are commercially driven or and do not have all the insights into psephological aspects (as more and more of them were from public relations or market research or from journalism) or from party ranks. Nor did they have critical understanding of the larger picture, or appropriate skills to capture the psych of voters or specific under currents over time. Adding to this is that most political leaders/candidates generally do not have the kind of discipline or temperament not to get trapped by such surveys. Very few of them know how to discern the findings but reprocess for insights. The anxiety was to show large sample (as if that makes a survey scientific!) and interest was on getting maximum patronage out of the survey assignment. The advertising campaign for the polls goes by a briefing from out of such poll surveys and vise versa. Such surveys end up being good enough only when the going is good even otherwise.

On the other hand Narendra Modi in Gujarat or Basu in West Bengal have never depended on surveys. So also Karunanidhi in the initial years, although he attributed his win to a CMS survey (1996), but sponsored by his opponent!. On the other hand, Ashok Gehlot losing out in 1994 in Rajasthan was a good example of not being able to deduce sense out of a pre-poll survey.

What started as an assessment of prospects or chances of winning an election, has become the very basis for electoral strategy including selection of candidates, issues to be taken up and advertising campaign. In this process, from one poll survey in 1996, they have become half a dozen surveys by 2004 and two dozen in 2009. This number of surveys is in addition to what individual leaders and potential candidates get. Taking some of these surveys too seriously and on face value, many of them had gone into complacency cycle or relied on a single track approach. The high point is that hardly anyone realizes the potential risk of getting into trap of such commissioned surveys – the same way as news TV channels got into in a TRP trap. Political parties / leaders should know the limits of surveys and save themselves from getting into a survey syndrome as elections approach, particularly the incumbent/ leaders.

Voters, when overwhelmed by news media's coverage of leaders/ parties against their own expectations and experience on ground, give scope for a boomerang particularly by incumbent parties/ leaders. Phenomenon of boomerang is more obvious recently as if there was certain "over doing" or "media fatigue" had set in on voters and that voters get repulsive of the candidates, claims and arguments. Most often the situation is somewhat like losing a tree for the wood!.

This, however, does not mean that surveys per se mislead although that is for sure when not designed and undertaken professionally and understood critically. Hence they should not drive or dictate a poll campaign, strategy or even candidates election, the way they are today. Each one calls a methodology different in some respect or other.

The problem is one of how surveys should be taken or used by political leaders and be sensitive about the limitations of surveys. They need to realize that surveys can only be for supplementary or complementary role in an electoral democracy.

# 5

# Exit Polls

Had there been no restriction on exit polls in 2009, there would have been more than a dozen exit polls in between the polling phases between April and May 2009 – against about 10 exit polls in 2004 and about 6 in 1999. With an increase in the number of news channels and consequent competition, the number of exit polls too multiplied between 1996 and 2009. The fact that there were six Lok Sabha elections in the last two decades (1991 – 2009) each with 3 to 5 phases of polling and exit polls conducted by two or more news media for each phase, the nation had witnessed more than 20 exit polls for Lok Sabha between 1991 and 2004 (1996, 1998, 1999 and 2004). And then there were Assembly elections during the period when exit polls were conducted and prominently covered by the news media. These exit polls must have been conducted on more than 50 occasions in all (Four Lok Sabha and more than 40 for State Assembly elections). During this period exit polls for Lok Sabha elections were carried out by more than six different agencies (like CSDS, Neilson, DRS, C-Voter, CMS, Cfore, GfK Mode)

Theoretically, an exit poll is conducted as a voter steps out of a polling booth after casting his or her vote. The voter is presented with a dummy ballot paper with names of candidates or/and symbols and asked to mark the choice he or she opted inside the booth. Exit polls have become part of poll process and coverage of polls by news media after 1991.

Exit polls are not the final verdict as they are not based on actual counting of votes polled. An exit poll is expected to be indicative of things to come on the counting day and its findings cater to the curiosity and anxiety of a large section of people. Because of unusually staggered poll schedules, exit polls have attracted more attention. They are expected to be more accurate than pre-poll surveys though their record has been no better. But there should not be so much variation from one exit poll to another in the same election. An Exit Poll is conducted, as in the case of pre-poll surveys, on the basis of systematic sampling of polling booths and constituencies.

## Relevance of Exit Polls

Relevance of an exit-poll in India is because of time gap between the polling day and the counting day which is more than a couple of days. Time schedule of 1999, 2004 and 2009 elections was rather unusual. The time gap between the first polling day and the last polling day itself was a month with three to five phases of election. That is how exit polls acquired their relevance. Exit polls by their very nature do not end the suspense. Rather they add and even prolong certain speculations about the poll outcome. Anxiety of voters and leaders would of course be there to know the outcome the same day of polling. The news media want to cater to such anxiety by taking to

**Number of Phases of Polling**

| *Year* | *Phases* | *Gap between polling dates* |
|---|---|---|
| **Lok Sabha** | | |
| 2009 | 5 | 16, 23, 30 April, 7, 13 May |
| 2004 | 6 | 20, 22, 26 April, 5,10, 31, May |
| 1999 | 7 | 5, 11, 18, 25, 28 September, 3, 4 October |
| **Assembly: Uttar Pradesh** | | |
| 2007 | 3 | 14, 18, 21 February |
| 2002 | 7 | 7, 13, 18, 23, 28 April, 3, 8 May |

exit polls. Even the parties and individual leaders / candidates get exit polls conducted for each phase for campaign use as well as part of strategy. But then given the kind of complexities and track record of exit polls in 1998, 1999 and 2004, they have caused more agony - to voters and political parties and the news media alike.

**Lok Sabha 1999:**
**Exit Polls and Actual Results**

| *News Media* | *BJP+ NDA* | *Congress+* | *Others* |
|---|---|---|---|
| DD | 287 | 174 | 77 |
| Star TV | 295-305 | 145-155 | 85-95 |
| Jain TV | 291 | 147 | 87 |
| LOK MAT | 242 | 227 | 69 |
| **Actual Result (October 5, 1999)** | **296** | **134** | **107** |

A general impression of exit polls during the last couple of national elections, is that they are not necessarily more reliable as they are expected to be and, in fact, the probability of their being right is no better than in the case pre-poll surveys. The variation between exit polls of same election and between exit poll and the actual result should not be so much as happened in the case of the four exit polls on four television channels in 1999 and five or six in 2004 not to talk of the ones in the case of the exit polls conducted on the eve of Assembly polls. Theoretically speaking, the variation between the findings of various surveys, particularly exit polls, should not be more than marginal. But that assumes that the surveys were conducted using similar procedures for selecting the respondents. A critical appraisal of whatever limited information was made available by the television channels about these various exit polls and their estimates, is not possible to validate.

**Exit Poll, not an Exact Poll!**

Strictly speaking an exit poll cannot be an exact poll for various reasons. Firstly, what an exit poll comes out with is also an estimation as in the case of a pre-poll survey perhaps with the possibility for better accuracy level. Secondly, the logistics of conducting an exit poll for a more reliable finding can never be uniform because of ground level realities around polling booths. Thirdly, representative character of the sample cannot be any better than in the case of pre-poll survey even though the sample size in exit poll is likely to be much larger. Apart from sampling related errors, problems to do with logistics on ground often vitiate the results of an exit poll. For example, once the person conducting the exit poll is noticed at the booth with or without a ballot box, party workers often try to influence the exercise by forcefully filling the dummy ballot box. Representative character of voters who respond to in an exit poll is less than in the case of a pre-poll survey, where the voter or the household is pre-selected on certain criteria. Even more important, it is not always possible to know how representative the respondent voters are in an exit poll, so that the same could be corrected before projecting the outcome.

What purpose does an exit poll on Lok Sabha serve? It has no value addition to voters as it has for middlemen involved in party politics and commercial dealings. An exit poll vitiates, if there is subsequent (re)polling in subsequent days. A pre-poll survey on the other hand, has some potential to help the parties as well as the voters; bring to the fore issues that concern voters, their preferences and help improve the relevance and quality of campaigns.

The concern about poll surveys today arises for different reasons. These include : Proliferation of poll surveys in the media, often without transparency about methodology used; use of such surveys by political parties as a part of their campaigns; and the way the media uses poll surveys in a conclusive way, giving "authenticity" impression for the survey findings. In a staggered poll schedule to the Lok Sabha or the Assembly, an exit poll, when showcased on news media before completion of all phases, is bound to vitiate the process in the subsequent phases of polling. If it does not, why in the first instance they are being conducted at considerable cost.

Presenting the findings of an exit poll in the midst of a poll process, could be misleading. Exit poll findings have often been presented as if they are the "final results". Even more, when exit poll is presented on Doordarshan channel, it has the potential of being viewed in every nook and corner of the country and some tend to view news on Doordarshan as having "official endorsement" and a few even think of such presentation as "result of the poll" just held during the day, particularly because leaders of parties were discussing it. The kind of discussion orchestrated in television studios based on an exit poll is "much a do about nothing" with full of hypothesis. These programmes based on exit poll add further suspense among all and confusion among some. By roping in political party representatives in the discussions, the programmes try to give the impression of "that was the way poll outcome has been". That was how exit poll based programmes have been presented on channels when, in fact the exit poll findings are not the final verdict of an election.

**How Reliable are Exit Polls?**

In February 1998, the estimates of (three) exit polls were mixed- one TV channel had gone wrong totally; the other one had gone wrong with key states although at the national level its findings were within acceptable level but only with respect to one or other party. (The variation in the case of some states was so much *that the very direction* of the exit poll estimate was just the opposite of the actual result. That is how the very relevance and methodology of *exit polls itself was questioned*, not only by those parties who were adversely shown in the programme, but by others too. Then of course is the very credibility of some of the research agencies which conducted these exit polls and their track record and transparency in their operations. There were atleast four exit polls in 1999 and the variation between them was so much that it dented the credibility of the channel, although it might have earned some revenue out of that presentation. Similar is the case with 2004 Lok Sabha poll. The last day of five phased 2009 Lok Sabha polls had 16 news channels presenting exit polls.

**Lok Sabha 2004: Exit Polls and Actual Results**

| *News Media* | *NDA* | *Cong+* | *Others* |
|---|---|---|---|
| Sahara Samay | 263-278 | 92-102 | 171-181 |
| Star News | 263-275 | 174-186 | 86-98 |
| Aaj Tak | 248 | 189 | 105 |
| Zee News | 249 | 117 | 176 |
| NDTV-IE | 230-250 | 190-205 | 100-130 |
| **Actual Result (May 25, 2004)** | **185** | **220** | **137** |

**Andhra Pradesh: Exit poll forecast Lok Sabha 2009**

| *Channel* | *Congress* | *TDP+* | *PRP* | *Others* |
|---|---|---|---|---|
| NDTV | 29 | 12 | - | 1 |
| Times Now | 15 | 22 | 4 | 1 |
| Star News | 23 | 15 | 3 | 1 |
| Headlines Today | 22 | 19 | - | 1 |
| **Actual Results** | **33** | **8** | **-** | **1** |

**Andhra Pradesh Assembly: Exit poll forecast 2009**

| *Channel* | *Congress* | *TDP+* | *PRP* | *Others* |
|---|---|---|---|---|
| NTV | 155-169 | 92-110 | 30-35 | 7-9 |
| Sakshi | 181 | 64 | 12 | -- |
| I News | 85-105 | 140-150 | 40-60 | 4-9 |
| **Actual Results** | **156** | **107** | **18** | **13** |

**Tamil Nadu: Exit poll forecast Lok Sabha 2009**

| *Channel* | *DMK+* | *AIADMK+* | *Others* |
|---|---|---|---|
| NDTV | 20 | 18 | 1 |
| India TV | 12 | 26 | 1 |
| Aaj Tak | 12 | 27 | 0 |
| CNN-IBN | 11 | 28 | 1 |
| Star News | 24 | 11 | 4 |
| **Actual Results** | **26** | **11** | **2** |

**DMK+** DMK/Congress
**AIADMK+** AIADMK/CPI/CPM

## Exit polls going wrong yet again!

To nobody's surprise, all exit polls of 2009 Lok Sabha poll, broadcast across the country on May 13 by 16 channels (!), were "off the mark" as was the case in the 2004. Regional language channels in most cases carried the exit poll outcome of one or more national channel. No wonder, speaking in a TV interview two days after the 2009 poll results were out, Dr. S Y Quraishi, Election Commissioner of India, said that "we believe that exit polls and opinion polls are manipulated. They do influence free and fair polls and every political party opposed it" (Karan Thaper show CNN/IBN, reported in Pioneer, 19 May 2009). (Dr. S Y Quraishi should know what he was talking as he has also been a researcher with published works to his credit). Both Times of India and the Hindustan Times too commented adversely about exit polls. Hindustan Times concluded that "election predictions is a most inexact science". It observed "some predictions were altogether wrong, a couple of them were closer although no where near but better than 2004. But most had indicated the direction and trend correctly although some argued that for such kind of general forecast, one does not need exit polls needing massive exercise and promotion. It is generally viewed by most in the media, politics and outside that exit polls have added to the suspense and confusion and served no purpose except allowing channels to mount debating programmes next couple of days until the results on the counting day started pouring in".

**2009 Lok Sabha Poll**
**News channels which carried exit polls on the last day of polling**

| | List of Channels |
|---|---|
| | **English** |
| 1 | NDTV 24x7 |
| 2 | CNN-IBN |
| 3 | Headlines Today |
| 4 | News X |
| 5 | Times Now |
| | **Hindi** |
| 6 | Star News |
| 7 | India TV |
| 8 | Live India |
| 9 | News 24 |
| 10 | NDTV India |
| 11 | IBN-7 |
| 12 | India News |
| 13 | Voice of India |
| 14 | Total TV |
| | **Business** |
| 15 | UTVi |
| 16 | Zee Business |

on 13 May 2009. Some carried it to two days

*Source : CMS Media Lab*

An editorial in Tribune (19 February 2009) "No to opinion polls" aptly brought out this dilemma. The editorial said "there is no denying that opinion polls tend to influence the voter in the smooth exercise of his/her franchise. If free and fair elections are sine qua non of a democratic form of government, opinion polls set to sometimes negate this concept because these have the potential of either influencing or confusing the voting behaviour. More important, experience in the past few decades suggests that the opinion polls, based on small sample surveys, instead of reflecting the popular opinion, have misled the voters by projecting an unreal picture despite the best of intentions… Inaccurate opinion and exit polls can hardly help the democratic process. Essentially, the debate on the issue is focused on two independent questions – how reliable are these polls?. And how right is it to allow them during the electoral process?. Unfortunately, the proponents of exit polls are yet to give cogent and credible answers to these questions". These two editorials in reputed national daily newspapers sum up the feelings of citizens.

Exit poll was covered by some channels over a period of three days. Although all the three national news channels did exit poll, CNN/IBN devoted its entire (The Verdict 2009) prime news for three days about and based on exit poll it conducted. Zee News, Aaj Tak, and Doordarshan, the other main line news channels did not conduct exit poll. In 2009, unusually, a larger number (6) of smaller players or new news channels conducted exit poll to present on the last day of the five phased poll.

Most exit polls on national channels were way behind, by a deviation of any where between 16 to 35 percent in the case of the UPA. Yet some channels claimed accuracy of its exit poll. In the case of some States, exit polls were off the mark by more than 50 percent (Tamil Nadu, West Bengal, Uttar Pradesh, Andhra Pradesh). In fact, a couple of new channels kept reminding its viewers "how accurate" the channel's exit poll was when in fact what they were right was only in indicating the direction. Theoretically speaking, the variation in the projections between exit polls of the same five phased

**News channels' coverage of Exit Polls for Lok Sabha polls, 2009**

| *Channel* | *Date* | *Exit Poll* | *Total News time* | *Total prime time (including ad)* |
|---|---|---|---|---|
| CNN-IBN | 13 – 15 May | 532 minutes | 532 minutes | 720 minutes |
| NDTV 24x7 | 13 – 14 May | 163 minutes | 323 minutes | 480 minutes |
| Star News | 13 May | 111 minutes | 154 minutes | 240 minutes |

*Prime time (7.00 p.m. – 11.00 p.m) Source : CMS Media Lab*

## Lok Sabha 2009:
## Exit Polls and Actual Results

| *News Media* | *NDA* | *UPA* | *Third front* | *Others* |
|---|---|---|---|---|
| CNN-IBN | 165-180 (135-150) | 185-205 (145-160) | 110-130 | 20-30 |
| Times Now | 183 | 198 | 112 | 50 |
| Headlines Today | 180 | 191 | 38 | 134 |
| India TV-C voter | 189(143) | 195 (152) | 113 | 14 |
| News X | 191 | 199 | 104 | 48 |
| Star News – Nielson | 198 (154) | 202 (157) | 97 | 12 |
| Zee Business | 208(157) | 182 (145) | 109 | 14 |
| UTVI | 195 | 183-195 | 105 -121 | |
| News 24 | 194 | 218 | 101 | |
| NDTV | 177 | 216 | 105 | 45 |
| Congress (own survey) | 168 | 205 | 164 | |
| BJP (own survey) | 220 | 170 | 153 | |
| Mumbai satta bazar | 190-200 | 160-180 | | |
| Rajasthan satta bazar | 125 | 145 | | |
| **Actual Results (16th May, 2009)** | **157 (116)** | **262 (206)** | **80** | **44** |

* Figures in bracket are for Congress party and BJP on their own

election, should be minimal. However, in 2009 it varied from 15 percent to 55 percent.

Exit poll based TV programmes were made popular by newscaster turned psephologist Prannoy Roy. The poll surveys that appeared earlier in the newspapers never received similar kind of public attention. That being the case, in 1999 once again more than one exit poll and by more than one research agency had become the highlight. Also because the exit poll in 1998, claiming over 1,00,000 sample size, on a TV channel had gone wrong. In fact, its projection was in the reverse direction. The other exit poll on Doordarshan had gone off the mark in the case of key states. Nevertheless, they acquired a large viewership on the election day also because of the kind of programme promotion and animated and heated discussion that TV channels had mounted based on the results of exit polls. In fact, glaring deviation of exit polls since 1999, inconsistencies between exit polls themselves and outright commercialization of these programmes on TV channels, had dented the very credibility of poll surveys to the extent of such programmes were described as "entertaining". But, on a more serious count, the contentious nature of exit polls on news media, had created sensitivity among larger public about such poll surveys. Accuracy of exit polls has never mattered much for the news media because they have continued to sponsor and feature exit polls as if such programmes are inevitable part of poll coverage. Even Doordarshan devoted one hour of its prime time for presenting an exit poll in 1999 against 30 minutes by other channels. This poll survey too was off the mark over all and even in the opposite direction in the case of more than a couple of key states. Although that presentation was commissioned;. Doordarshan made no effort to keep its stakes protected. On the contrary, it allowed deliberate effort as if Doordarshan did the exit poll and the discussion was by it.

Interestingly, at the height of the controversy on the credibility of exit polls, one controversial "psephologists", (whose forecast turned out to be in the opposite direction on the counting day) innocently tried to defend "psephology" as a "science". As an exercise, exit polls or even pre-poll surveys are enabled by several different disciplinary positions, sampling and probability theories from statistics being at the core. Psephology is concerned more with converting voting intentions into number of seats with plausible explanations. Given the kind of peculiarities of coalition politics, election contests and campaigning, and last minute variables, this conversion process is full of subjective assumptions since local political scene is never static or uniform across constituencies. The accuracy of results of an exit poll depends not only on the representative nature of the constituencies and booths sampled but the conditions under which the actual operation of an exit poll at polling booths was actually conducted. Of course, thanks to Election Commission, "booth capturing", (impersonation in voting) are things of the past. Of course, new ways of "rigging" are being discovered as, for example, cyclical voting by election agents or/and polling officers themselves). One channel (NTV) tried to defend the poll survey with the argument that the agency which conducted the exit poll ( A C Neilson) was "most authentic" and "internationally reputed" as if that is god enough for the accuracy aspect.

The other reason for exit poll not coming out with any better track record (between 1996-2009) is the competition between channels. For example, in the beginning (before 1996), an exit poll programme on a channel was at 8 or 9 pm on the polling day. With more channels taking to exit polls, this competition lead to telecast of exit poll at 7 pm (in 1998) and at 5 pm (1999-2004) that is as soon as the polling ends. To do an exit poll programme on a channel at 5 pm or even at 6 pm, the field work for the poll at polling booths should end a couple of hours before, that is at around 3 pm so that booth-wise data could be passed on to a central point for processing and conversion into seats and then be able to identify significant trends in the voting pattern. This means the exit poll has to miss the pattern of voting in the last two or more hours of polling. Had there been an exit poll on the day of polling in 2009 in Andhra Pradesh, for example, it would have missed the unusual and significant turnout particularly of women in the last one hour of the polling on April 23, 2009. In fact, in many booths the polling went on until 9 pm (the Election Commission allowed all voters in the queue to cast their vote beyond 5 pm). One can imagine what would have been the fate of that exit poll. There is also tendency of certain section of voters casting their vote in the last one hour (agricultural labourers on their return from field, housewife coming out of their homes when the temperature falls below 44 degree, etc). This "missing vote" in an exit poll could make it off the mark or even go in the reverse direction. Then there is practical difficulty of taking an individual sample as the tendency in many regions/ among certain communities is to go for voting in groups. And in such situations, sampling a particular voter as they start come out of the booth, is not easy or can not be consistent. This problem too effects the forecast.

A general impression of the exit polls (in 1996, 1998, 1999, 2004 and 2009) that has gained ground is that exit polls are not necessarily as reliable as they are expected to be. The need for reconsidering the kind of methodologies used for exit polls is too obvious. The problems to do with logistics at poll booths too require reconsideration. The distance from polling booth for standing with the dummy ballot box has been increased to 100 meters in 2009. Till 1996 and before, it was possible to reach out the voter as he/she comes out the booth.

The wide difference between the projections of various poll surveys in 1998, 1999, 2004 and 2009 and, more glaringly in the case of "exit polls" with actual results on counting day has raised doubts once again about the very reliability of poll surveys. It has led to believe that such surveys could at best be "guess works" and that "statistics are a bunch of lies". However, that media themselves were responsible for sponsoring pollsters of known and unknown origin or with doubtful qualification for undertaking such surveys, pre-polls and exit polls. In fact, the way the State owned Doordarshan itself has telecast exit polls, going off the mark, has made people believe that such poll surveys are not always without political motivation. Subsequently, in 1999, 2004 and 2009, such an impression of political motivations about some channels gained ground.

Although 2009 Lok Sabha polls had not seen exit polls on channels between April 16 and May 14, the rumour mill was active with findings of exit polls doing rounds in private conversations. However, this took place without claiming or attributing to any particular "exit poll" per se. These were newspaper columns of analysts and experts and news channel discussions. This is because of the gap between the first phase of polling and the counting day (May 16). [P.N.Vasanti, "Surveys and Exit polls in our mediated elections", Mint, May 1, 2009]

With as many pre-poll surveys as well as exit polls going off the mark or had gone wrong in the last 15 years, the Election Commission had revived the proposal to restrict publication or broadcasting of exit polls in between the polling phases. In fact, in most democracies, one or other kind of restriction is there on announcing the findings of pre-poll surveys and exit poll surveys before the completion of the polling all over. Because such surveys were prone to influence voters same way as felt by the Election Commissioner of India Dr S. Y. Quraishi. If they have no influence on voters and poll campaigns, as some argue, they would not have received the kind of attention they get particularly both from political parties and news media. But exit poll programmes on TV attracts advertisers hence there are stakes of channels, market researchers, public relation firms and of course, advertisers.

## Why Efforts to Restrain Poll Surveys?

The Election Commission tried first in 1996 to get exit polls and pre-poll survey restrained from publishing or telecast in between polling phases. However, it was only in 2008, that the Government took the initiative of bringing an ordinance to that effect. The Government is yet (2009 July) to get the amendment (to restrain surveys / exit poll) passed in the Parliament as put forward before the Supreme Court. What is interesting is that the Election Commission was supported in its move by all political parties. The Election Commission, the Government and the political parties are keen on restraining exit polls and poll surveys, but could not succeed until the Supreme Court reconsidered its own judgment in 2008.

By making Election Commission withdraw its directive in 1998 to restrain poll surveys and exit polls to certain timings, the Supreme Court in 1999 had gone more by the book than by the spirit of the Election Commission's guidelines. The Election Commission took the initiative in 2008 with an understanding that such a restraint helps free and fair election. The contention of the Election Commission was that exit polls and pre-poll surveys are a hindrance for free and fair conduct of elections. Because such surveys are not the same as the reports of journalists as surveys are presented in the news media as if they are "scientific" and hence reliable, objective and authentic about the poll outcome. Poll surveys when reported in the news media are assumed to have potential of influencing poll process in one way or other. The Election Commission had also pointed to the practice in this regard even in USA.

## Should Media Coverage of Poll Surveys be Restrained?

When Election Commission of India first mooted measures to restrain poll surveys in 1998 and again in 1999 it was scuttled by the Supreme Court on the filing of an appeal by N Ram of The Hindu. The Union Cabinet ventured after considerable bickerings to take the decision for an amendment to the Representation of Peoples Act (is yet to be passed by the Parliament). The government move however was not for a ban of pre-poll surveys and exit polls as reported in a section of news media. It wanted to restrain publication or broadcast of the findings of pre-poll surveys and exit polls in between different phases of polling days. By doing so the government acknowledged that news media influences voters. Channels should be happy about this acknowledgement of its power to influence. But news media do not want any such restrictions as they know that it amounts not only restraining their "freedom", their "political role" and but also effects advertising revenue. How come all political parties supported the idea to restrain publication of poll surveys?. Why the Government which is otherwise restrained in tinkering with "freedom of press", was driven to such a move?. Why did the Election Commission consider publication or broadcast of poll surveys as an interference in "free and fair" conduct of electoral process?. It took ten years for the Commission to succeed in these efforts to restrain poll surveys during the poll schedule. During this ten year period, the country witnessed three Lok Sabha polls and more than a half a dozen Assembly polls with staggered poll schedules and had seen proliferation of news media particularly news channels.

The news media in 2008 were even more powerful, particularly news channels, than in 2003 or 2004. Not only because the number of news channels proliferated but because some prominent news channels, belonging mostly to newspaper groups, formed into an Association (NBA). They resist any move to restrain poll coverage by any and views it as against their interests and as an infringement of "freedom of press". Even Editors Guild, which otherwise has declined in its stature, has rallied around against any "infringement on the freedom of the press". The Guild viewed that such a move "would severely restrict the citizen and voter's right to information". It does not agree "that opinion and exit polls are harmful to the electoral process". On the contrary, it stated that, " poll surveys generally help to understand the trends in public opinion" (Tribune 6 December 2008). This view, some felt is editors' echoing commercial and political interest of owners of media.

That is why in 2008 on the eve of polls for (Madhya Pradesh, Chattisgarh and Delhi) Assemblies, once again the Government came close to issuing an Ordinance. But, even after announcing the Government backed out again as if at the instance of NBA and the Guild. Instead, it initiated a Bill in the Parliament to amend the Representation of People's Act empowering the Election Commission to restrain opinion polls and exit polls. The Bill in 2008 was passed in the Rajya Sabha but could not come up to Lok Sabha before the elections to State Assemblies were announced in 2008. It was at this point, that the Supreme Court at the instance of a PIL by one D K Thakore, with a different Chief Justice heading the Bench, gave the Election Commission a free hand to ban exit polls- even pending a Bill in the Parliament. This was on the basis of argument of Additional Solicitor General, Amarendra Saran that the Court should allow the Election Commission to regulate the media. (The Election Commission had withdrawn much earlier when the Court observed that the Election Commission had no power to frame guidelines on exit polls pending a legislation. Agreeing with his argument, the Supreme Court lifted any ban on guidelines of Election Commission and asked it to even issue fresh guidelines for exit and "instant polls" telecast or published by the media. The Hindu which has been opposing any such guidelines and based on whose petition the Court earlier went along, was also a respondent in 2009 and also argued again on the same lines as before.

It places a particular party in an advantageous position and simultaneously rendered its opponent demoralized. "interfering with free and fair elections. It was an attack on democracy itself". It was based on this argument, the supreme court reconsidered its earlier views.

Banning poll surveys is, however, not the only course, other options should be tried. In fact, it is not feasible to implement a ban even otherwise (as 2009 Lok Sabha poll had shown) with globalization of the media as well as the emergence of newer media – such as the Internet and other non-conventional methods of passing on certain information. However, in the interest of free and fair elections, some guidelines, more by way of self-discipline are desirable.

Self-discipline is needed both for polling agencies and the news media. Self imposed discipline is far better. Both freedom of media as well as holding of free and fair polls are important. As the duration of Lok Sabha election 2009 was spread over five phases and one month, the desirability of restraining coverage of exit polls and poll surveys in media in between the polling phases was important.

**Is Election Commission's Restriction Futile?**

Election Commission's 2008 notification restraining poll surveys in between poll schedules contains conditions which are too elaborate and rigid. According to it, "no result of any opinion poll or exit poll conducted at any time would be published, publicized or disseminated..."from 48 hours before the first poll to until the polling on the last leg. Even "circulation by means of any pamphlet, poster, placard, handbill or any other document" is prohibited. The expression "election matter" in the notification has been defined as "any matter intended or calculated to influence or effect the result of an election". The Commission further specified that panel discussions, debates and interview with political personalities might be telecast, "provided they are not in the nature of an election campaign or promoting or prejudicing the prospects of any particular party or candidate".

However, exit polls have not ceased from being conducted in the country by political parties / leaders, powerful lobbies and advertising agencies (read market research agencies) as they are restricted only from being used in public communication channels. But, reference to such (private) exit polls in between the phases of 2009 poll was obvious in some news media although only one channel was given (oral) notice in Andhra Pradesh for telecasting an "exit poll like" programme on three consecutive days. But that happened more because the competing channels had complained to the local Election Commission. From the first phase and the fourth phase the number of news media that had followed one or other way of forecasting poll outcome has increased. A day before the fourth phase of voting on May 6, the Times of India front paged a table giving its state wise party win forecast of seats. Under headline "It seems a photo – finish as BJP plays catch up". The TOI claimed that the forecast was "based on the tracking of poll's progress by its political bureaus and its network of correspondents" to give "best estimates of the likely results" (TOI, 6 May). A similar news story with a table giving forecast was there in Dainik Bhaskar on 5$^{th}$ May 2009. After the third phase Saakshi Telugu daily banner headlined on the front page indicating that all surveys so far had pointed "UPA's majority" and went on recapitulating pre-poll surveys to put forward a new set of figures to that effect. Times of India had headlined on the front page "BSP may struggle to cross 30 seats in UP" and reports that "inputs from three phases of voting suggests". NDTV's 24x7 too did a replica of exit poll based animated discussion by stating that an exit poll will be presented on the last date of the polling (13 th May).

Examples for such specific effort are many more. After the first phase of poll on April 16, *Economic Times*, *The Tribune, Asian Age, Pioneer,* Hindi daily *Dainik Bhaskar* and a couple of news channels carried columns or news prominently with prediction of the outcome for individual phases of polling, referring or attributing to one or other "survey". The Economic Times of April 21, 2009, in its lead column on editorial page referred to the result of "exit polls" of first phase of election (on 16th April), more specifically in the context of Andhra Pradesh. Similarly, The Tribune of April 21, 2009 in its prominent feature in centre page "Delhi Darbar" had the headline "Congress ahead of BJP" and wrote "even though exit polls have been banned by the Supreme Court in the election to the 15 th Lok Sabha, there are enough predictions being made by the advertising agencies to their clients" and continues to write in the next para "one such exit poll predicts that out of 543 seats, the Congress will get 139 and the BJP 136, making it a neck to neck race... It gave the BSP 35 seats out of 80 in Uttar Pradesh and 21 to the Samajwadi Party". In the next para it wrote that "The exit poll predicts that the Congress will get seats from Rajasthan, Andhra Pradesh. The poll also predicted that the CPI(M) would get 30 seats from West Bengal…".

*Dainik Bhaskar* of 21st April 2009 published two days before the second phase of the polling "Saptahik poll meter" with heading "teesara morcha picheda" and had given the number of seats each Front was projected to get state wise in a chart and attributed it to staff reporters of Bhaskar / DNS. Pioneer of Sunday 26 April 2009, had a front page banner story, "Left could go down to 22 seats in Bengal". The news story with a byline goes "According to conservative estimates cutting across party lines, the Trinamool Congress – Congress alliance could notch up an impressive tally of 14 to 17 of the 42 seats in the State". "If the popular mood prevailing from North to South, Bengal is any indication, the opposition could end up winning anything between 18 and 20 seats".

Asian Age of 18th April 2009, two days after the first phase of the poll, prominently published a four column news on the front page, "BJP survey shows gain in UP and Bihar, loss in Orissa". The news goes on "The Saffron camp's internal survey, which reached the BJP headquarters on Friday evening, (the day of poll) has shown gains in Bihar, Uttar Pradesh and Assam…". In the next para it went on. 'The survey carried out by saffron spin doctors stated that the BJP was gaining…' it went on "the survey agreed that the Congress and the UPA allies, not doing well in States..." and gives the seats different parties are likely to get as per that "survey". Asian Age of 26th April 2009 went ahead and published Arun Nehru's column, as before at the beginning of poll campaign, with a chart for possible alliances and State wise seat projections and the likely outcome of the elections giving likely "swings". The same column was also carried on the editorial page of Pioneer of April 27.

Vaarta Telugu daily too, published prominently a news item on front page on April 17 sourcing it to its "analysts", the number of seats each party was going to get in each round of polling in Andhra Pradesh. NTV, Telugu news channel, had put out a 30 minutes programme on April 25th (after the second round poll in Andhra Pradesh was over) recapitulating what pre-poll surveys had forecast about Lok Sabha poll and AP State Assembly election and held a discussion around those surveys by different news media. Similarly, after the second phase of polling on April 23, NDTV had presented on the same day, a review of days polling with inputs of "GfK Mode" giving the impression that the polling agency did a poll on the polling day. Of course no where it mentioned "exit poll" or even "survey"; instead, it mentioned "inputs from field from Gfk Mode", a professional polling agency. All these predictions imply advantage to one or the other party. Maha TV, hardly a few months old Telugu news channel, went further soon after completion of polls in Andhra Pradesh and had detailed "field analysis" based programmme projecting the number of seats for each party district wise.

Times Now channel featured on May 10, 2009 (two days before the final round of polls) a one hour programme, "Number Game 2009" based on Times of India's projections published on May 6,2009. "Psephologists", but really all senior journalists, discussed at length seats various parties were likely to get and which combination of parties had chances to form the Govt. This progmme, like most others referred to above, may not amount to violation of Election Commission's directives, but if voters and cadres watch the discussion, it is bound to enlighten and also influence "fence sitters" both among voters and, more importantly, the ones likely to get elected!. Numbers are used to facilitate discussion, Goswami of Times Now claimed.

This was how news media gave "coverage" in between the five phased Lok Sabha poll of 2009. It is obvious that political parties and survey agencies themselves (at the behest of one or other interested sponsor) had conducted surveys and got them into news media informally. What intrigued most was high and unprecedented turnout of women on the last leg of the poll in Andhra Pradesh. News media cannot avoid analyzing such trends. However, instead of going only by the claims of party spokespersons or leaders, an analysis of what different parties had offered to women as part of their manifesto or electoral promises would have revealed more. Yet another way is to take to "case approach" of women voters in one community or of members of a self-help group.

Without exit polls being formally allowed, news media, party leaders and television anchors alike found it difficult to deliberate in between the phases. They cannot be expected to stop deliberations on the likely scenario based on voting on the polling day. Alternative models of analyzing a poll scene have to be found. What could be such alternative?. P N Vasanti of the CMS had suggested some ways of going about in her column in *Mint* midway of 2009 polls

(Mint 10 May 2009). Thanks to the Election Commission's restrictions, news channels and newspapers tried to fulfill the function they are expected during the month long five phased poll process without having the benefit of exit polls. They explored different programme formats as if they realised the limits of poll surveys. The urge for alternative models in covering the polls was being felt even otherwise.

The Election Commission's notification was too restrictive and even preventive. Strictly going by it, news media cannot play a role, any role, to further democracy and strengthen the electoral process. Instead, the Commission's guidelines should be indicative of elements that should be avoided in the interest of "free and fairness" objective of the poll process. The Election Commission should have formally or informally formed an ombudsman group for the limited period. Before the Election Commission's restrictions on poll surveys become a farce, it should do something so that the media plays its due role better than before. Over all, news media should be appreciated for not blatantly violating the notification by publication or presenting exit poll or pre-poll survey in between the phases.

**2009 Election without Exit Polls in between the Phases!**

2009 Lok Sabha and Assembly polls in Andhra Pradesh and Orissa had seen no exit polls covered in the news media. In 2004 Lok Sabha poll there were six polls and atleast three exit polls covered Andhra Pradesh Assembly polls. Exit polls come handy to news media particularly news channels, to mount lengthy discussions, rope in leaders of parties and make them argue out and even get into "cock fights" based on hypothetical outcomes of exit polls. They help conduct a debate on post poll prospects of parties in forming the next Government – all based on exit polls. This they could do until the day of counting. That is "shelf time" of exit polls could be any where from one month in the case of the first phase of Lok Sabha poll to 3 or 4 days in the case of final phase of polling. Studio based interactions

*(Contd.)*

*Contd. from previous page*

make a difference in the public discourse of parties, between leaders and political interlocutress (even start negotiating support, etc). Exit poll based programmes pep up the mood of cadres of the party shown in exit polls as winning while others get into blame games or look for explanations for the likely defeat.

2009 polls missed all that as exit polls were restrained from being published or covered in the public communication channels. News media missed exit polls to explain their viewers and generate hours of discourse based on their findings. News media were compelled to look for alternative ways of having such discourse.

Thanks to the Election Commission, in the absence of exit poll based programmes in the news media, political parties and cadres of all parties continued to claim victory and some also celebrated. Andhra Pradesh witnessed such celebrations since the final day of polling for Assembly and until the day of counting – about three weeks (April 23 to May 16 counting) – by the three major Parties (Congress, TDP and PRP). There were firecrackers and sweets distribution at the head quarters of the three political parties. They would have been deprived of this enjoyment with exit polls around in between poll phases.

But, on the other hand, one had seen definite change in the nature of discourse. With exit polls the discussions earlier were more on hypothetical assumptions. Absence of exit polls helped the discussions become open ended and were on contentious issues and lot more real and serious. These in fact have helped leaders of opposing parties share experiences, concerns and even helped bring some level playing and focus (on public thinking as to) post poll concerns. But at the same time absence of exit poll has increased anxiety and boosted undesirable elements. (by way of threats to likely winners).

In the absence of exit polls, betting (as to who wins or loses) picked up in many constituencies and pockets of the country. In one Assembly in Ongolu district of Andhra Pradesh, the money involved

*Contd. on next page*

*Contd. from previous page*

in betting was Rs.3 crores according to news media. (April 30, TV9). The amount as well as the extent or the number of bets across the country had multiplied. Telugu daily, Saakshi (May1) estimated that betting on poll outcome in Andhra Pradesh involved Rs.400 crores. Interestingly, one bet included exchange of signed MOU between rivals to resign from an elected local post in case of win or defeat in this election.

The Election Commission's notification on pre-poll and exit polls between polling phases is restrictive of the kind of role news media are expected to play during poll season. Secondly, given the kind of news media scenario in the country, it is unfair to expect news media to limit their role during Lok Sabha / Assembly elections. That is what the notification implies. It is unfair to the public even more not to expect news media to play a proactive role in covering the polls. In fact, the news media cannot be expected to keep off from discussing the emerging scenario, projecting seats expected by parties and allow political leaders make claims and explain their propositions. The Election Commission should explore other ways of going about the issue. So also the news media outlets, so that their own "excesses" do not effect the entire news media scene.

Perhaps because it was the first time that media operated without poll surveys they did not fully explore ways of going about with tackling the suspense until the counting day. Some tried with some success. Since the nation is not going to have a poll in one or two phases in the near future and counting same or even the immediate day after, they need to evolve alternative ways of capturing the same.

Restrictions by the Election Commission or not on media coverage, the 2009 poll provided an opportunity to the news media, particularly the news channels, to experiment with alternative ways and evolve new formats and methods of presenting most anxiously awaited period of electoral process, instead of relying on poll surveys. Post-poll

*Contd. on next page*

*Contd. from previous page*

surveys of the kind by CSDS, for example, provide far more insights. Should winning a poll only become all out concern of media to report about or should means be as much? Poll?. Cause and consequences should matter as much or far more. The onus should also be of political parties / leaders to restrain from giving to media with their internal exit polls.

# 6

# Elusiveness of Public Opinion and Illusion of Poll Surveys

## Elusive Opinions

Opinion surveys in the context of electoral politics are what is known as poll surveys or polls in short. Walter Lippmann and Herald Lasswell were the first to bring out the significance of public opinion in a democracy. The public opinion is a freeze point of view or a snapshot account of a moment of an on going process. Certain fuzziness of opinion or flux in opinion is bound to be there, more in a pluralistic country like India. This is based on surfing or surface scratching of top of mind phenomenon. If the phenomenon of opinion is elusive as it is, outcome of poll surveys can only be illusionary to that extent. Public opinion is a bubble and all it takes to burst is a needle. Most of what gets reflected as public opinion in the media is elusive. It gets crystallised in a response mode, not necessarily based on information level or considered view. The skills for such a response are neither uniform nor compatible in most instances and external stimulai, provocations or compulsions are too many, popping up until the last moment of actual vote casting.

Opinion surveys or channels of opinion are often vague, misleading or managed as a design in the context of a problem or situation. Not always opinions in fact are indicative or reflective of preference or behaviour. In the case of television, erratic bytes are presented in isolation as public opinion. It is more to do with obsession with opinion poll culture of media to interest their consumers day in and day out. In the case of poll surveys, the opinions are in the context of cues of grass root politics and campaign strategies of parties/candidates over a short period depending upon which election is in context. Quantification of such a phenomenon is what lends a form or a structure. Opinion surveys serve temporal quest of media, more as an offshoot of consumerism. However, surveys help generate public interest and even involvement. The passiveness of citizens in general and articulative skills of people determine the sensitivity of surveys. So is the researcher's methodology in capturing such a phenomenon. It is sensitivity of research methodology that determines the extent of illusion of poll surveys. The methodology need to be constantly conscious of that phenomenon and provide for minimisation of elusiveness in quantifying public opinion. This section deals with some of the methods involved in that process.

**Illusion of Poll Surveys**

There could be a dozen reasons for a pre-poll survey going off the mark. These might have to do with inadequate or inappropriate sampling, faulty or inconsistent field work, irrelevant analysis of field data and lack of understanding of political dynamics, processes or inconsequential responses of respondents or a combination of them.

After 2004 Lok Sabha polls news media and survey agencies claimed by way of advertisements, how right they were with forecast of their poll surveys, irrespective of whether and to what extent they were right. Even in 2009, some channels claimed on the day of counting, how right their pre-poll and exit polls were. Some went out of way to thank their psephologist. In the case of sample surveys conducted in the context of markets and social issues, one could get away without being assessed for the accuracy even in a couple of months time frame. Similarly, e-surveys, on public issues never get validated. But not so in the case of exit poll surveys as their accuracy will be known within a few days. But credibility of many stakeholders - news media, survey agency and also a psephologist in some cases, will be under scrutiny on the day of counting and thereafter. Hence it is useful to know how or when one could claim being right with the forecast of an election outcome. This could be truly assessed only at the end of counting of votes when full details including votes polled by each party/ candidate are known.

Reliability of projections of an election survey depends on external variables, on which a research agency may have little control. But the design and methodology related variables are important for reliability and credibility of its findings. These depend on two or more aspects. One is to do with the very design of the survey and the other is how field investigation is conducted. The pre-disposition of field investigators indicate the quality of such data. The CMS used to administer a survey - first among its own field investigators to ascertain their own political bias. Discipline in following the selection procedures of respondents is critical. And then how well the interview was carried out and also recorded so that someone else, some where else, could decode the responses and computerize the same. Another factor is how well consistency in asking questions from one respondent to another was maintained as answers depend on how a particular question was asked. Then of course supervisory methods followed – to check back with sampled respondents and also see how well responses were elicited and whether there was consistency in the response pattern of questions about voting preference. All these aspects matter. Every survey requires some training and supervision of field investigators in these respects.

For example, in 2008 Karnataka Assembly elections, Cfore, a relatively new agency (Swarn TV, New Indian Express and Asianet TV) was more accurate than the poll surveys conducted by experienced agencies with much larger samples like that of CSDS – CNN IBN. C fore used students of a local business school as investigators for the survey who apparently worked with more enthusiasm and less fatigue and political bias.

Another important aspect is how well a questionnaire or interview schedule is designed and whether it pre-tested and whether local language is a easily understandable in the same way by different section of voters. How a questionnaire is designed or how a question is asked about voting intentions or candidate preference could very well predetermine the response pattern.

For example, whether a question about preference for PM post was asked without suggestion of alternatives or was it open-ended and only spontaneous responses were recorded, and if options were given to choose from alternatives.

Another factor which sometime matters more for the quality aspects of field work, particularly of poll surveys, is mode of payment to investigators. In 40 years of survey research this author never allowed payment to field investigators on "per interview" basis. The obvious difference is tendency to do a higher number of interviews in a day even at the cost of quality in the field work. Most agencies pay investigators on per call basis. This often effects selection procedure of respondents and encourages round the corner interviews.

Poll surveys covered by newspapers and television channels in the context of Assembly and Lok Sabha elections are based on interface interviews. Telephone surveys are yet to become reliable and representative. When market research companies ventured into poll surveys, they initially relied on interviews in restaurants, bus stands and similar public places rather than specific households as per a sample design.

Some newspapers having a network of reporters at block level, as in the case of Eenadu, have trained their own staff to conduct rapid surveys including on political issues and election related. It was Ramoji Rao's idea that his reporters should have the skills and discipline for conducting systematic surveys. That is how way back in 1979, he got his correspondents trained by an experienced professional. That initiative enabled Eenadu to undertake several surveys on issues of concern and of contentious nature with fairly large and well spread sample. This enabled the newspaper to go beyond government claims and official press releases. Eenadu was able to do faster, with much higher sample size than what market research agencies would have done and at a much less cost. This practice of course has its pros and cons. The positive aspect is that reporters know better whom to interview specific to the subject of enquiry. The negative aspect of this practice is that newspaper or TV reporters are influenced by the 'angle' of that news media and respondents themselves may have inhibition in their response pattern when the interview is by a local media reporter. Neutrality dimension on the part of investigators may suffer. This practice, in any case is better than SMS-based and phone-in surveys that news media these days rely on. But when the survey is to find out voting intentions, in a pre-poll or exit poll, this familiarity factor of investigator need to be concerned about.

**Sampling – More is not Merrier**

A general impression among political parties / leaders as well as news media is the higher the sample size of a poll survey beyond what is statistically needed, the more reliable or authentic its findings are. Polling agencies, on the other hand, would like to show larger sample (than what is good enough for such surveys) as that would justify claiming higher fee for the survey.

That is, the bigger the sample, more likely the error in the forecast. That is the case when more respondents are of the same category rather than proportional representative of the variations in the characteristics of the population in the universe. This is more likely when the sample is spread geographically within a constituency or a State. Quite often, in most surveys female, poor, minority and voters in remote constituencies get underrepresented and more articulate sections get over sampled. Knowing about it and correcting it with appropriate weightage or to ensure coverage of such sections is important but that does not always happen. Then there is a need quite often of representation of certain sections of voters in a given electoral scene. It could be, for example, Jats or Gujjars in Rajasthan or Kapus in Andhra Pradesh in 2009, considering their significance in a particular electoral situation. It may be relevant to have a purposive sample of such section of voters as in the case of the first time voters, who carry certain weightage in the context of an election.

This author has been writing that the more is not always merrier as far as accuracy of a field survey is concerned. On the contrary, more the sample could mean more the margin of error or the extent of misleading of such a finding. What is critical about the size of a sample is how well it is spread across the constituency in context. More than a decade ago, in early 1990s, the CMS developed an SSS model as part of its poll survey methodology. The three S stand for size, spread and selection of the sample. The size of a sample for an Assembly in a pre-poll survey depends on at what point of poll schedule and whether it is for projecting seats or to bring out the trends. The CMS model has demonstrated more than a couple of times that with a sample of 200 voters for Lok Sabha constituency spread across two to four assembly segments could give as reliable findings as a survey with a sample size of double that in the normal situation, all other aspects being equal. For example, in a poll survey to know the general trend for Andhra Pradesh Assembly towards end of 2008, a sample of 80 – 100 voters was good enough for Assembly constituency including an additional sample for taking into account the Chiranjeevi factor. But closer to polls when more reliable seat/ vote share projection is required for the State, a sample of 100 – 125 voters per Assembly is good enough in 30 to 36 carefully selected constituencies. If, on the other hand, Assembly constituency specific projections are required, 350 to 300 voters are good enough even when the main contest is between three parties.

The basic frame of reference for selecting voters is the updated local voters list. Since voters lists are updated until a couple of weeks before the poll dates, the selection could be from the blocks/ wards or booth area households. Within a selected household the respondent should be 18 plus member. Out of them male, female and age groups will be selected as per the sample design.

Sometimes sub-sample or purposive sample is used to take into account peculiar poll realities on ground. This enables specific or more focused analysis of preferences of critical section of voters in the particular election. Psephological exercise could be more focused when such sensitivity is there in sampling.

## Questionnaire

Election eve surveys depend on primary data collection from voters on a systematic basis. Most agencies use personal interview methods. As and when telecommunication connectivity goes beyond 70 percent across all sections of voters, the interview could be done by a phone. In such interviews, it would not be possible to do the kind of detailed enquiry that is possible in personal interviews. In either case, a structured questionnaire is used. The structure and scope of a questionnaire in many ways determine the reliability of estimates of a poll outcome. This sequence and enquiry in questionnaire depend on agencies / investigators, their past experience, often on both. Knowing inconsistencies in response pattern is important.

A poll survey questionnaire tries to ascertain individual information about respondent (age, community, profession), past voting and present intentions, preferences of party, assessment or outlook about sitting and potential candidates and factors that are likely to determine or influence actual voting. The questionnaire of the CMS and the MDRA enquires into the elements discussed earlier i.e., psychological, sociological, political, demographic and local issues. The questionnaire is supposed to be in local language and pre-tested to see the flow, clarity and ensure consistency in responses and at the same time the interview should not be irritating and loaded. The questionnaire should enquire and help cross check responses on voting intentions, preferences and factors that go into that decision. One could argue that there could be an element of violation of privacy in such enquiry. Investigators need to be conscious of that. This depends upon rappot on credibility that investigators establish about their own neutrality vis-à-vis political parties / candidates or even caste / community – with each respondent. Respondent cooperation is critical in such enquiries. The reliability of poll surveys depend on the nature of cooperation of respondents.

Some of the questions will be open ended where responses are recorded verbatim, while some other seek yes/no response or choose from a scale of three or five. Some questions will enquire about specific names in case of PM or CM. In each case there are pros and cons. For example, if the names of potential ones are not indicated, the response could be too diffused but on the other hand when names are limited, the survey may miss potential local names. This enquiry could be at different levels so that both kinds of responses are captured.

Opinion polls covered in news media, including the ones in the context of elections, tend to view every contentious issue in terms of yes or no response. Whereas, in reality, most issues being complex, people do not view the issues in a polarised manner, as news media tend to look at. As such yes-no type polls can present a weird picture about what that particular section of people stand for in a misleading way. Most SMS polls in media, in particular, belong to this category. In the name of simplifying issues, yes-no based surveys in media create an illusion of polarised outlook and tend to divide people further. Poll surveys by marketing research agencies tend to optimise the time of field investigators and look for such simpler ways of analysis of responses.

Market research agencies tend to add rider questions unrelated to the election (to make field surveys cost viable) and make the questionnaire lengthy. The longer the interview, the less likely reliability of cooperation of respondent. Temptation to include too many questions, always haunts researchers everywhere. While the CSDS questionnaire is thorough, it becomes too long to sustain interest of respondents beyond 30 minutes in one sitting. CMS questionnaires are compact and shorter to be able to completes within 30 minutes.

Interview with rural women beyond 15 minutes tend to get converted into group interview.

How questions are framed?. A loaded question tries to make a voter respond in certain way and constrain the respondent to limit the response. Also important is how a question is asked by investigators. 'No answer' to a question does not always mean 'do not know'. The findings of a survey and the poll forecast may be misleading or unreliable because of bias or limitation in the questionnaire and the way it is administered. If the psephologist is not familiar with the scope of questionnaire and response pattern, but goes only by the findings, interpretation may end up constrained and forecast off the mark. This happens often in the studio discussions of poll surveys. The discussions assume that the survey in context was conducted without such limitations and cooperation of the respondents.

Field surveys during elections, when hectic campaigning is on, sometimes miss on taking into account the ongoing events while the field work is underway even when such developments may have significance to the poll outcome. If a poll survey was undertaken just before the terrorist attack on Mumbai in November 2008 for an election to be held there after as was the case of election to Rajasthan Assembly in December 2008, the findings of that survey need to be reinterpreted or redone among a small sample of voters. Similarly, if a manifesto released with populist proposal of a party, as in the case of TDP's cash transfer in 2009, while the field work was on, the questionnaire need to be revised or some questions added. If it is too late then a sub-sample of women voters, or as the case may be, need to be included.

**Sanctity of Surveys in Peoples Perceptions**

Why should any individual participate or respond to a set of questions that he or she is posed with by known or unknown person on phone or is person? Either he or she responds only when some benefit is perceived from such cooperation or it is viewed as a government agency requirement or sees it as part of an educational pursuit. The benefit or some other aspect of a survey (and the perceptions about it eventually) is what makes of opinions elusive. Participation in a survey could be viewed as a waste of time or as trying to intrude into privacy (as to voting intentions on behalf of someone clandestinely). In either case, participation and the extent of cooperation to respond to a set of questions get effected. Also, if it is felt that surveys on polls do not reflect opinions objectively, why they will cooperate? Sooner or later survey research and poll surveys will face this dilemma.

Then of course is the variation in response pattern from one set of respondents to another because of differences in the comprehension levels to the issues in questions and also articulation skills of different sections of respondents, particularly in the case of open-ended questions. These are issues beyond research methodology, survey design, referred in field work.

Sooner or later, polling agencies have to face the issues arising out of these aspects and provide for alternatives in the sampling and intervening. But the cooperation and willing participation in a survey still remains an issue for reliability of surveys. If a respondent had participated in surveys earlier and he or she never heard anything about the outcome of that, his or her pattern of response will not be the same.

This dimension of voter's motivation to participate in a poll survey and also the extent of cooperation to respond to all queries get effected if people think that surveys in media do not reflect their views or ever serve their interest. May be a day is not far when some incentive (cost or gift) is required to make people to respond to poll surveys (this practice of giving an incentive or gift has already started in some countries). Participants in focus group based surveys in India are already being paid incentive by market researchers, engaged in doing commercial research for a brand or a product.

### Analysis of Responses

When a field survey is undertaken in the context of an Assembly or Lok Sabha election with large sample, the questionnaire needs to be coded and responses entered into computer along with software to yield the tabulation of the data that the researcher or psephologist requires to come up with a summative analysis and forecast thereafter. In this process, the research agency tries to group responses to open-ended questions into broad categories. A cross tabulation of responses brings out the undercurrent more than a straight analysis. For example, knowing details about undecided voters or those who are likely to change their voting intention close to polling day, gives better insight for forecasting the outcome. With mega power computers' and sophisticated software, handling of large survey data and analysis has become easier, faster and more reliable. It facilitates desegregated analysis of responses. What used to take weeks two decades ago, is an overnight job today. If analysis of field data was done by someone other than those responsible for the field work or survey design, it needs to be stated in the survey report. Depending on the analytical tools used, the outcome could be different sometimes. With sophisticated IT tools and software models and data mining facilities, with it is possible to do specialised analysis for focussed insights from field surveys.

**Presentation of Survey Data**

There are several instances of what is covered or presented in news media as survey finding is misleading. Often, either the agency which conducted the survey or the sponsor of the survey makes out a press release with the highlight of the findings. In doing so, certain vital findings get missed. Irrespective of such a possibility, the news media at its end either headlines what it understood or what it wants to and even skips some findings from the text for whatever reason, including on account of its own political leanings. But more often, it is also because of lack of sensitivity at the news desk.

Most of the time what is highlighted in the news media is who is likely to win and what is the number of seats the key contending parties are likely to get – based on surveys conducted may be a couple of months before when polling dates are not even known.

When the percentage of "undecided" and "no response" or "could not answer" is likely to be high and cannot be ignored from being reported. Quite often this happens because the journalists are not aware or might not have gone through the survey findings fully as they are always in a hurry to be the first to report or bring out certain aspects first.

**Who are the Field Investigators?**

These days some newspapers publish pre-poll surveys claiming large samples. They claim that the survey was conducted by their own reporters. That may include stringers. If such field reporters are trained or are familiar with structured poll surveys, importance of sample of respondents and know how a structured questionnaire need to be administered, they could be used. But generally that is not. Also, the local standing of field reporters of said news media and its known political leanings do matter in an enquiry on voting preference. Because when a reporter goes to a voter with pre-identified familiarity, the response may not be reliable, since news media themselves are often known for their political preferences, response may not be natural. To which party, one had voted earlier and to whom intend to vote for now is something not every respondent would like to share, particularly with those who have been around and associated with a local news media known for its political leanings.

The question is who analyses the field data?. If the newspaper has designed the field survey, gets it conducted with its own field reporters and stringers and also analyse the data, the reliability of such survey cannot be the same as when it is undertaken by an "independent agency". There are hardly any examples where a newspaper has ever published a field survey on an Assembly or Lok Sabha election going against its known political position. One such example was in Andhra Pradesh. But that was more than two decades ago, Eenadu featured prominently on its front page during 1980 Lok Sabha elections a survey conducted by its own reporters which concluded that Mrs. Indira Gandhi was ahead and winning the election decisively.

Such field surveys by news media in the context of an election would have better credibility if they are undertaken in collaboration with or under supervision of an independent research agency.

Conflict of interest is something that needs to be taken into account if a poll survey findings are presented in news media. This includes aspects like who funded the survey, at whose instance it was conducted, who has actually conducted the field survey, etc. Stating these aspects is likely to enhance credibility of a survey. Publishing survey findings without indicating who has conducted it or who is responsible for the survey and when and how it was carried out, obviously create doubts on the very intentions of publishing the results of a poll survey.

Against the background of exit polls and pre-poll surveys going off the mark beyond margin of error, it is important that the issues raised in this section are taken note of. It is in the interest of everyone – the news media, political parties, voters and the very democratic culture – that pros and cons of field survey conducted during elections are understood. Transparent and credible surveys have potential to strengthen democratic traditions, institutions and the processes. They are an opportunity for news media to expand and even ensure their own credibility among its clientele.

**Responsibility and Accountability**

Girilal Jain of Times of India was one of the foremost editors to commission poll surveys in early 1980s. He insisted that the write up on the survey findings in the front page should go with the by-line of the person who was responsible for conducting it. His view was that credibility of that person should also be on test, not just of the newspaper. Jain waited for two days before publishing a pre-poll survey commissioned by Times of India as he wanted to make sure that the findings of the pre-poll survey for Haryana Assembly were based on reliable field work and were also written objectively, as that survey concluded significant majority for the then opposition party.

The actual result on the counting day was exactly what the newspaper commissioned survey came up with and what the paper headlined.

Today, although, poll surveys are published or broadcast giving the name of the poll agency, the name of the person(s) in that agency responsible for conducting the survey and projections, is seldom indicated. And, the identity of polling agency is not always known or clear, particularly because the agency uses different names each time and conducts for two opposing parties / candidates in the same election. CSDS surveys, presented by Yogendra Yadav leave no scope for such ambiguity.

A self appraisal of poll surveys on the evening of counting day by the same agency/ person which had conducted the surveys would add to the credibility of the agency as well as of the news media. But very rarely this is done.

The CMS and the MDRA, two well known survey agencies, are associated and use each other's resources for conducting research studies. Both these agencies always indicate the professional of the organization who is responsible for the particular survey. But these agencies never used the two names simultaneously in the same election or put out two different reports for same party or two opposing parties as some other agencies like AC Neilson or DRS do, to mention as an example.

On the other hand, in the case of certain organizations the identity is not clear. For example, AC Neilson – ORG – MARG publish without identifying any individual at all. The three are not different entities. Together, it is one corporate entity and yet surveys were published or broadcast using one or the other name separately or a combination of the three names of AC Neilson – ORG - MARG. In the last couple of years, surveys for political parties / candidates are conducted in the name of AC Neilson as if to enable sponsoring media claim that the survey was conducted by an "internationally reputed agency". And, even more curiously, the same organisation was getting surveys commissioned by opposing parties / candidates and even news media in the same election. Whether same field data is used for both the claimed surveys was anyone's guess.

**Transparency in Conducting Surveys:**

Transparency is missing in the news media coverage of poll surveys. Who should be considered responsible for coverage of surveys in the news media?. The news media often assumes that the methodology used for the survey is known to readers/ viewers and that by attributing to a "survey" it becomes objective in reporting. Consider for example CNN IBN-CSDS surveys together with a newspaper. In these surveys, while field work is attributed to one agency, the exercise of projection of seats/ votes is attributed to some one else and interpretation of the findings is done by a third person mostly of the channel. Even in the case of NDTV that is how it has been. Who should be considered responsible for the media coverage?. If such surveys remain as internal exercise, public need not be concerned about but if they are prominently covered in the news media, someone should be responsible?. Also, after the announcement of results, rarely news media compare the actual results with what had been projected. And yet news media tend to claim how right they were although they were in fact only partially right or better than the projections by another agency or news media, as if they know that these poll survey are illusionary and viewers will not even remember them next day or week.

**Conflict of Interest!**

There is a catch 22 situation here. Psephologists who conduct poll surveys are a new set of people whom politicians tend to pamper for obvious reasons. In this process, some move closer to the party in government and the ministers. There was a classic case of a state chief of a party on assuming ministry in the Union Cabinet, writes a letter to a public sector unit under his ministry to engage the research agency which did poll surveys for his party and presented the findings favourable to the party in the news media. Another example for the nexus between politician and pollster is of the State governments engaging the research agency which projected a win for the party through its surveys and ensured coverage in the news media. A more recent example is that a psephologist who did poll surveys for the incumbent chief minister, hires the psephologist as official "media advisor". Yet another example is where a State government assigns a research agency through State HIV/AIDS organization to conduct poll surveys directly under the nose of the chief minister. The survey came out well before the poll schedule with findings that the party in power is going to sweep the poll. A Central minister assigns a psephologist to do a survey in a State where he wished to go as chief minister and assigns a research project of the ministry, amounting to quid pro quo. An important point is that such linkage was known to the journalists in each of these examples and yet that never bothered them in covering the survey in their respective media – as if it was a jugalbandi between them. Obviously, all this has implications to the way poll surveys are covered by the news media and the journalists. Such a "conflict of interest" is a new phenomenon which is bound to erode the very credibility of surveys covered in the media. The onus about such nexus is more on the news media. For, they should be aware of the implications and make sure to indicate any such linkage while covering poll surveys. This of course does not mean that all psephologists and research agencies fall into such syndrome. Nevertheless, in the interest of free and fairness of elections and credibility of both pollster and the news media such links should be stated explicitly. News media should themselves verify credentials of pollsters before engaging them or publish their surveys. There were instances of news agencies releasing poll survey findings knowing well that no such survey was ever conducted. This author also knows that more than two daily newspapers publishing surveys on front page prominently without ever conducting any poll survey of any kind indicating "large sample size" as the base. There are also news channels with similar credentials, not all of them are small or new.

In 1996 the Press Council of India (PCI), a statutory body, came out with an appeal to media to reveal basic facts about surveys but with little compliance. In 1998, Election Commission, (EC), constitutionally responsible for conducting free and fair elections in India, restrained media coverage of pre-poll and exit poll once the campaign period ends, that is 48 hours prior to the actual polling day until polling of all phases all over the country is complete. In 1998, *Frontline*, a prestigious magazine of The Hindu Group, went ahead and published a poll survey to test the validity of Election Commission's notification as an interference in to press freedom. This case remained pending with Supreme Court until 1999 Lok Sabha poll when in view of five phased poll schedule stretched over a month, the Election Commission issued guidelines banning media from the use of pre-poll surveys and exit polls once after the poll campaign ends until the last phase of polling is over. This time the Times of India too went against Election Commission's ban with contention that the EC had no jurisdiction on the fundamental right of the press for freedom of expression. Jain TV appealed to the Supreme Court against the Election Commission's order and the Election Commission itself went to the Supreme Court for judicial sustenance of its guidelines. The Supreme Court verdict was that that Election Commission's guidelines banning publication or telecast of opinion or exit polls was without legal sanction and not binding. The judgment did not go into merits of the EC argument on the implications or impact aspect of media coverage of such surveys during the course of a poll schedule. The Election Commission suggested for a national debate on the implications. But is such a debate possible once news media takes a stand?. Post-poll surveys of the CMS and the CSDS conducted immediately after 1996 and 1998 Lok Sabha elections had indicated that poll surveys do influence voting intentions, marginally or significantly, depending upon the keenness of the contests and differently in different parts of the country. A CMS post-poll survey of 1998 had brought out that pre-poll and exit poll surveys, affect voters in three different ways (a) bandwagon, (b) boomerang and (c) complacency. And such effect would be more when the percent of "undecided voters" is more.

One school of thought in India is that opinion polls do influence voters, while another school thinks that notwithstanding research evidence, they do not influence the voters as people who read these polls are educated enough and politically savvy and that in any case voters have a right to know such findings. While banning publication of survey findings is not a solution, a certain code both for polling agencies and the news media which use or sponsor poll surveys is desirable, more in the long term interest of news media. This issue however was settled by Supreme Court itself in 2008 as discussed in another section of this book.

## Precaution Needed

Realizing that some poll surveys covered in media could be politically motivated, CMS in 1998 had cautioned readers by way of a small advertisement not to get swayed by opinion surveys (Pioneer, Hindustan). A code developed by Market Research Association of India for agencies in general is neither known to the political parties nor to the public and the news media. In any case most of those psephologists are not members of the Market Research Association and each election sees a couple of names and even agencies never heard before. Vinod Mehta, editor of *Outlook* magazine felt that exit polls are a travesty and they mislead specially during elections when the latter are staggered. Referring to exit polls as fabricated, eminent journalist, Khushwant Singh, said. "It is the responsibility of media to see that their credibility does not suffer" (September 22, 1999 - Observer). "Poll surveys unethical" headlined The Hindu in October, 1999. Realising such a possibility, this author had called way back in 1987 for safeguards to prevent distortion of public opinion polls in media. He suggested that news media should invariably refer to aspects like (a) sample size, (b) selection procedures, (c) margin of error in the estimates, (d) at whose instance the survey was conducted, (e) identify the agency which conducted the survey and who did the psephological exercise and (f) percentage of undecided voters, etc. Yogendra Yadav invariably refers to these aspects in his presentations and also to the shortcomings and limitations and imponderables that may have effect on the analysis of the poll survey.

**Need for guidelines:** Some motive- driven pre-poll surveys, like the one by an advertising agency in Andhra Pradesh in 1995 (which Congress party's Chief Minister got it done and covered in the media prominently. The party lost the election overwhelmingly), have led to controversies and affected the very relevance of such surveys. In 2004 the TDP used surveys, including exit poll in Andhra Pradesh in such a way that the survey agency and the psephologist loses credibility – atleast for some time. The *exit poll* on the eve of the Maharashtra Assembly poll in 1995 is yet another example of eroding the very credibility of poll-eve surveys. There are other examples too for Lok Sabha polls since 1998 when news media themselves had succumbed to plants or bias of surveys. The onus of avoiding such instances of motive-driven surveys, however isolated they may be, should be on the media. Hence the need for guidelines or a code for the media, particularly since not all editors in all news media can be expected to be discriminatory enough, nor do they have the background to judge research methodologies, also, because more and more news media are becoming politically inclined. According to a recent CMS analysis, nearly one-third of news media in the country in 2009 have direct or indirect links with one or other political entity.

Writing in India Today's Media Monitor (July / August 1987) and A&M magazine (July 1989) more than 20 years ago, this author called for a guideline for pollsters, as well as for news media, so that sanctity of surveys are not tampered with by black sheep as they are found in any profession. This is what Dr. Jayaprakash Narayan of Lok Satta party warned about after accusing the media at the end of the polling for Andhra Pradesh Assembly on 23rd April 2009 (Sakshi and Eenadu).

## New Trend in 2009

Arun Nehru, a former Minister in the Union Home Ministry, writes a newspaper column where he forecasts State wise seats each party is likely to get and keep revising the forecast in subsequent columns week after week. His column appears prominently in a couple of newspapers, hence it gets into circulation of political networks. He also appears sometimes on TV discussions on electoral outcome. He never describes his methodology of forecasting the figures. Apparently he does so by virtue of insights gained from what he did during his days in the Home Ministry more than two decades ago and using his personal contacts in various parts of the country. He presents a chart with State wise figures as if to give quantitative touch. In doing so, he might be taking into account what poll surveys by others have come up with. And, in fact, some surveys may even be taking into account what Arun Nehru had forecast. The "domino effect" of Arun Nehru's column in 2009 is described elsewhere. There are also a few other columnists, mostly journalists, who also venture into such "general forecasts" of seats and trends without explaining any basis for the figures given. More often, than not, they are not based on any field sample survey. Such general forecasts use their own personal understanding or of a few experts. 2009 polls had seen more news media taking to such forecast of seats. In fact, Election Commission curbs on surveys had given push to such initiatives by news media. But the point is that all such ways imply certain erosion in the very standing of sample surveys on polls in media.

# 7

# Polling Agencies, Psephologists and Analysts

A pollster is one who conducts a field sample survey in the context of an up coming election. His findings are used to forecast the outcome of an election. A psephologist is the one who on the basis of field survey data / past voting pattern, projects the outcome of an election in terms of seats taking into account various elements including the ones outside the purview of a survey and explains the linkages and trends there in. A political analyst is the one who sums up a situation by not only a field survey /past voting trends but also weighs the characteristics of leaders and parties in a given context. A psephologist can also be a pollster and political analyst. Not all political analysts are pollsters or psephologists. An analyst is most likely to avail output of a pollster and a psephologist. A pollster too can be a psephologist and analyst although one may or may not be wearing all the hats in a given case. For example, Yogendra Yadav functions as a pollster and political analyst at CNN/IBN. Some years ago, he was a psephologist and an analyst. Rajeeva Karandikar provides psephological support to Yogendra Yadav. Dorab Sopariwala is a market researcher whom Prannoy Roy introduces as a psephologist. He no longer conducts surveys. But he serves well as Roy's sounding board on TV shows because of their initial association on TV. News media describes differently those engaged in poll surveys, in projecting seats that parties are likely to get in an election, and those engaged in moderating or commenting on the goings on in a poll scene.

Dr. N Bhaskara Rao started first as a pollster being a specialist in survey research. He later took up to the other two roles. Dr. Prannoy Roy was a psephologist to start with. He later expertised in political analysis with the help of graphics. In fact, he made election analysis popular. Roy himself has never conducted poll surveys. He relied always on an external polling agency. Both Yadav and Rao are also from political science academics. Roy was from economics and finance.

Most of the agencies like A C Neilson or GfK Mode or IMRB are premier market research agencies with experienced investigators in the field. Their specialisation in psephology or political analysis has never been indicated or showcased as in the case of field surveys. The individuals associated with these agencies involved in poll surveys have not been indicated perhaps because they relied on external sources or links.

It is better that distinctions between agencies and people being quoted or attributed with poll surveys are identified and known. Because every time there is an election, news media comes up with new names without even indicating the identities of professionals involved even when it is their first ever survey projected in the media. For survey to acquire credibility, identities are important. This is also a first step for transparency. It is also important to know the people in such pursuit. Forecasting anywhere has potential to attract frauds, conmen and fly by night operations. Even in fundamental sciences one finds such instances. Psephology is no exception. News media should make identities explicit.

**News Media taking to Surveys**

The credit for carrying poll surveys first in India by a daily news media goes to The Hindustan Times. But that was 1960s and in a limited way. It was India Today (late 1970s) which took to surveys more seriously and as a professional exercise in the context of national elections. It was Aroon Purie's initiative, along with his editors Chhotu Karadia and S Venkat Narayan.

Ramoji Rao and Girilal Jain were editors of leading daily newspapers to go for poll surveys at the very outset in late 1970s. M J Akbar and Vinod Mehta too used surveys in 1990s in their publications. Rajdeep Sardesai had taken to surveys from the very outset at CNN/ IBN. Ramoji Rao of Eenadu deserves praise for his foresight. He was one of the foremost editors of regional media to realise the potential of rapid field surveys, including poll surveys (1979). That was when he requested this author to acquaint Eenadu journalists with technicalities of conducting field surveys. In fact, despite opposing Indira Gandhi all out, Eenadu published a front page banner story on how Indira Gandhi outweighs all other political contenders, based on field survey conducted by Eenadu's own field reporters on the eve of the crucial 1980 Lok Sabha poll which brought her back to power. Since then Eenadu has been using its own reporters to conduct field surveys on a range of public issues, government claims and implementation of public schemes.

Times of India's Dileep Padgaonkar too deserves credit for taking to surveys to bring out opinion of people on contentious socio-economic and political issues as early as in mid 1970s. This author conducted them and also wrote the analysis for the newspaper with by-line. Letter, these surveys used to appear as a special feature under his name and that of S Venkat Narayan, a senior editor. Narayan used to edit initial draft for publication. It was confidence in doing field surveys on substantial issues that made Jain to go for poll surveys too. Later, it was Gautam Adhikari who took initiative and convinced Ashok Jain of Times of India to commission CMS and MDRA for Lok Sabha poll surveys (1998).

The Hindu newspaper too had gone for poll surveys but very selectively. Initially, in early 1980s, it carried surveys conducted by this author and then after 1999 mostly by Yogendra Yadav of CSDS. The credit of analyzing the methodologies of poll surveys threadbare, once after actual results were out goes to The Hindu and its sister publication, Frontline. Of course, The Hindu never sponsored exit polls. Its Editor N Ram opposed (1998) the Supreme Court restrictions in publishing or broadcasting exit polls. It was based on his PIL the apex court held Election Commission's initiative to restrain poll surveys and exit polls as void. But it goes to the credit of Ram that once restrictions were imposed on covering exit polls in between polling phases, his newspaper set an example by not violating and yet fully covering the process.

Times of India is another daily newspaper which took to poll surveys much earlier during the last phase of its renowned editor Girilal Jain and associate editor Dileep Padgaonkar. But the emphasis during his period was on issues and process aspects. After a gap of some years, TOI took up again and this time Ashok Jain himself was in the picture and together with Adhikari talked to the author about the modalities and reliability of poll surveys. CMS – TOI poll survey made a mark. Adhikari and his special correspondent S Balakrishna focused more on poll outcome and projection of the seats. The Times of India shifted to DRS and continued with it for more than a couple of elections. TOI – DRS surveys were covered extensively in its sister publications like the Economic Times and Nav Bharat Times.

Times of India's half a page stories during 2009 poll campaign, one week before the polling day, quoting IMRB survey in Madhya Pradesh was of different type. This Times story did not even bother to mention who had sponsored this survey, when it was done and what was the sample. The saving grace was that they did not give the projection of seats and votes for the Assembly or Lok Sabha elections. Three such stories based on IMRB survey were published within a fortnight. Nevertheless, Times-IMRB model 2009 is a more desirable one with potential to help the poll process positively. Mint–

MDRA – 2009 too chalked out a new path by using surveys to bring out the issues and analyse the undercurrents and not be preoccupied with poll outcome in terms of seats and voters. The Hindustan Times also refrained from psephological exercise after 2004. In fact, The Hindustan Times model has been one of using surveys for performance appraisal. The Hindu and the Indian Express (Delhi) followed the best course of poll coverage - they avoided forecast based reporting and avoided peddling poll surveys.

Indian Express went for poll surveys in a small way only once when Prabhu Chawla was its Editor for a brief period (1995 – 96). The CMS did two rounds of surveys for Indian Express, Delhi. Later, it also featured poll-eve surveys in collaboration with a channel.

With the coming of satellite television, people remember the pioneering efforts of Dr. Prannoy Roy. In fact it was his first poll programme on television which brought poll surveys to limelight. It is interesting that it was the "two gentlemen" from academics (Dr Ashok Lahiri and Dr Prannoy Roy) doing economic analysis for India Today who ventured into poll forecasting based on field surveys conducted by MARG (merged later with ORG and AC Nielson). Dr Lahiri and Roy were academicians from Delhi School of Economics and not from market research background. While one had sound background in statistics and econometrics, the other was impressive with presentation style. And there was no competition on television, Doordarshan being the only channel at that time.

**Polling Agencies**

Field surveys in the context of elections are being conducted with one frequency or the other, by some two dozen organisations or individuals in all. Some of these are one-man operations. Of these, a dozen are active at national /state level and have done surveys for more than one Lok Sabha/State election. These include independent research institutes, private limited companies, individuals with their own outfit, floating individuals(operating individually), academicians and journalists. While something or the other is known about some of these agencies, nothing or not much is known about others. There is no transparency about professional background of many of them.

Most agencies that conduct poll surveys are based in Mumbai and New Delhi. While, Mumbai based are mostly market research organizations, New Delhi- ones are individuals or survey research outfits. Most of the others, outside these two cities, are from either University departments or from journalism. There is no evidence of any institution building efforts even by those who have been conducting poll surveys for some years now.

**Some Poll Survey Agencies**

1. Centre for the Study of Developing Societies (CSDS)
2. Centre for Media Studies (CMS)
3. Development and Research Services (DRS)
4. Research and Development Initiatives (RDI)
5. Insights Research Group
6. Centre for Voting Opinion and Trends in Election Research **(C-Voter)**
7. GfK-MODE
8. Midstream Marketing Research (MMR)
9. TNS Global
10. Marketing and Development Research Associates (MDRA)
11. Centre for Forecasting and Research (C-Fore)
12. Nielsen (AC Nielsen-ORG-Marg)
13. IMRB International
14. Synovate India Pvt. Ltd.
15. Todays Chanakya
16. Hansa Research Group
17. Quality Research Services (P)
18. Indian Council of Medical Research (ICMR)
19. Taleem

*This is not an exhaustive list. These were the agencies figured in the media in the last decade Some regional ones are not mentioned. Nor match is known about some of these.*

**IIPO:** The Indian Institute of Public Opinion (IIPO), launched in 1956 deserves special mention for its pioneering initiatives under its founder, Eric P.W. da' Costa, an economic journalist, for pre-poll public opinion surveys. He was influenced by George Gallup. In fact, the IIPO was an Indian associate of global Gallup. Although, the IIPO was concerned with political and economic issues, it was the first agency outside academics to use survey methodology for pre-poll surveys but limited to four metro cities. The IIPO used small samples (500-1500) for its pre-poll surveys to project votes of political parties in the fray. The IIPO also introduced the concept of omnibus surveys on socio-economic topics. Since 1980s, it has ceased to be a serious agency with Eric P.W. da Costa's retirement to Bangalore. He died in 2003.

**CSDS:** Centre for Study of Developing Societies (CSDS) founded by eminent political scientists Dr. Rajni Kothari, Dr. Bashiruddin Ahmed, Dr.Ramashray Roy and Dr. D.L. Seth, is a pioneering organisation started in early 1960s, with specialisation in election studies. Supported by some US universities, initially its main emphasis was trend analysis, theory building and studying the process of the working of a democracy. Besides depending on secondary data, the CSDS has also adopted survey research methodology since early 1990s. In fact, since 1995 with media emerging as sponsors of poll surveys, the CSDS has ventured into pre-poll surveys as well as exit polls and post-poll studies with more visibility. Yogendra Yadav at the CSDS deserve particular mention in this regard although he came into picture after 1990. While Prannoy Roy get recognition, more because of television and graphics, Yadav gave professional standing to pre-poll eve surveys with his lucid Hindi and English explanations both on TV channels and through his writings in daily newspapers.

Centre for Media Studies (CMS) was founded by Dr. N Bhaskara Rao in 1989 as an independent not-for—profit outfit. It revised poll survey methodology to capture fast changing political and media scene in the country. Its surveys were sponsored by various media as well as taken up on its own. Some of its poll surveys were add- ons or riders of its larger ongoing studies as in the case of more recent 'note for vote' which it did nationwide along with its survey on corruption and the citizen. There are half a dozen active pollsters / psephologists in the market now who branched out from the CMS. Over the years the CMS has emerged as an independent research institution with the motto that research is not an end in itself rather it should help equality in the country. Its priorities are not sponsor-driven. Social psychologist P N Vasanti, heads CMS (1997).

Madras University (Loyala College) department of political science has been conducting pre-poll surveys for the State Assembly and Lok Sabha constituencies. Narayan Tutorial Colleges and ICFAI, are two other examples where students are used for conducting poll surveys locally.

In Hyderabad, a journalist who is otherwise known as a critic of the State Government was roped in 2008 to conduct poll surveys. The money was paid from State AIDS Control Council as a research assignment. In some other States too that was the modus operandi, whether it is Rajasthan, Uttar Pradesh or Madhya Pradesh. The difference is in the source of funding for the poll survey. Most of these surveys however, do not get featured in news media. They are however used by a chief minister or some other political leader to bolster the confidence level of cadres and to quantify claims being made otherwise in the news media.

There are also "other" category of those who conduct or sponsor surveys without having any infrastructure or data base on previous elections. Some of them belong to an industry or such other interest (lobby) group or a PR agency. They take initiative and get poll surveys organised through students, or employees, and even by funding professional agencies in support of one or more political leaders. The number of poll surveys in this category has been on increase since 1998. In 2009, their number was more than the ones formally conducted or covered by news media.

Cement companies, mining companies, civil contractors and even corporates like Satyam Computers sponsored or funded surveys (at the instance of one or the other politician). This is happening all over the country in the context of Lok Sabha and Assembly elections. For example, C.C. Reddy of Vishu Cements, a close confident of Dr. Y S Rajasekhar Reddy, organised surveys and "got them covered" in the news media on the eve of 2004 elections to the State Assembly. The other agency is MARCH, a small in-house market research outfit (2004-06) of ICFAI (which was waiting at that time for State Government's approval of its expansion plans). Assam chief minister too got surveys done through a cement company. Then there are public relations concerns who get surveys undertaken for individual leaders or parties these are given only as examples.

There are many leaders who commission surveys individually for their constituency and for their friends and even for the entire State. L Rajgopal, MP (2004-09) of Vijayawada had commissioned more than a couple of rounds of pre-poll surveys for the State in 2004 and 2009 and many exit polls and surveys for his own Lok Sabba constituency. He also commissioned and paid from his own source for surveys in Uttar Pradesh, Gujarat, etc in Assembly elections held since 2004. Kamal Nath is another leader who sponsors surveys frequently. Industrialist Tyagarajan of Chennai is another example, although not a candidate, who sponsors surveys as a means of advising political leaders and chief ministerial contenders.

Chandrasekhar group of industries in Karnataka, or Advani group in Gujarat are only a few examples. More than a couple of industry groups in Mumbai sponsor surveys for one or other parties / leaders. Advertising agencies and public relation firms are others who mediate poll surveys. Some news media houses who sponsor surveys also share the findings with political leaders before hand.

While something or other is known about the CSDS and the CMS, as not-for-profit professional institutes, not much is known about A C Neilson, IMRB, GFK MODE or Synovate. Their origin or corporate identity is not known. For example, A C Neilson is described as "international", "most authentic" etc. Their various business interests are not known. Nor it is known that they are owned and controlled by foreign corporates. It is important to know the vested interest aspect about these agencies. For example, it is not known what is their main source of sustenance and what other related activities they are engaged in. Many others including the CMS, sustain on research projects they get from government departments, States and Centre, foreign organizations and Indian corporates. Poll surveys get connectivity to these agencies or individuals for expanding business interests. Media coverage of surveys help them to get patronage, directly or indirectly, from governments and corporates.

It is difficult however to attribute political motives to most of these agencies or individuals undertaking poll surveys. Three or four kinds of bias/ conflict of interest in the outcome of poll surveys and the way they are presented in the news media is possible. Even in the normal course, "sponsor bias" is expected in any survey research where the outcome or findings are likely to be "favourable" (not against) to serve the interests of the sponsor or those who commissioned the survey. A second bias could be that of the news media involved in presenting the survey findings. A third bias could be arising out of "vested interest" aspect, where support is expected once in power when the very methodology (that is sample, questionnaire, analysis, etc) itself may be tailored to yield certain outcome.

The surveys sponsored by news media are expected and supposed to be objective and independent – without source bias. But news media too often have their own "angle" in a given election, which is not always obvious to know. But with more and more news media already known for their political proximity, their coverage of poll surveys is in tune with such leaning, known and unknown. A recent exercise of the CMS had indicated that one-third of channels and even a higher percent of newspapers have links with one or other political party or leader, directly or indirectly. For example, news channels and newspapers in three Southern States (Kerala,

Tamil Nadu and Andhra Pradesh), with a total of half of readers or viewers have ownership links with one or other political party/leader. Similar picture in this regard in other States too is emerging. With such conflict of interest ridden media scene, the methodology of surveys and the way they are covered in the media too could go through change – so that credibility aspect is relooked into. Saakshi Telugu daily and Saakshi News channel, setting new standards in this regard in Andhra Pradesh, are not an exception or is it happening for the first time. This, however, does not mean that all field surveys are biased.

Who owns these polling agencies? Not much is known about many of them. All are not corporates. For example, that AC Neilson is a fully owned foreign global conglomerate. It is not known to most well informed people of India, even those who frequently engage it for poll surveys. The CMS is known as a not-for-profit registered body. The MDRA is registered under the Companies Act. The DRS is a registered company and its chief G.V.L. Narasimha Rao, is its face and it is always indicated. Taleem is a Zee TV's research body. It is well not known in the market. Similarly that the ICMR is a totally owned division of the IIPM is not known. In the case of the NYCD, its corporate character is not indicated nor any name of a professional involved is indicated. Other than the name of director, nothing else is known about C-Voter or Cfore. But surveys conducted by them are quite often published in news media.

When a survey is attributed to a news agency, its identity should be given. It is the responsibility of news media which refers to such poll survey findings. Poll surveys conducted by the CSDS are credited or attributed to Yogendra Yadav and, even the names of team members are indicated. But in the case of AC Neilson, ORG-MARG, IMRB, GfK-MODE, etc. the names of professionals associated with the survey are not known as they never indicated. In fact, whether these agencies have any expert psephologist on their staff also is not known. And yet, they are engaged by competing news media as well as competing parties and even competing candidates, without even knowing what is pertinent to know. A C Neilson is an example. Ranjit Chib has been on "contract basis" with Neilson –ORG- Marg to secure assignments from political parties / news media and coordinate the surveys.

Yet another confusion exists about A.C. Neilson – ORG – MARG. Legally the three names together are one corporate entity. The field investigators used for surveys are the same. But often, either only A C Neilson name is mentioned while some other times, A.C.Neilson – MARG or A C Neilson- ORG is used for public identity. The name of concerned individual(s) in these outfits responsible for the servey is not indicated; For example, the professional whom L Rajgopal (Member of Parliament from Vijayawada) engaged in one election is no longer there in AC Neilson. He still engages the agency, more because of its name. There are other industrialist – MPs, who commission poll surveys because of "flexibility" or "confidentiality" aspect.

It was this author's initiative at ORG (1972 – 89) to expand the very scope of that organisation as country's first large market research (MR) outfit and take to poll surveys that lead to the MR firms taking to poll surveys as a serious portfolio. It was a decade later that MARG came into picture as a splinter group of IMRB. India Today's Aroon Purie roped in Titoo Aluwalia of MARG into poll surveys for which Dr Prannoy Roy did the analysis and forecast. It was Roy's first attempt and break through. This author was supposed to have done that survey (1979) from ORG but had to go to ADB on a prior committed assignment. This association between MARG, India Today and Roy continued in the next decade.

The MDRA is another market research organization, founded by Dr. N Bhaskara Rao, which has been engaged in poll surveys for over a decade. Its poll surveyes were identified with Naveen Surapaneni (1998 – 2007). Its professionals, individually made mark with their analysis on television discussion programmes and its poll surveys for news media too were identified with professional of the organisation. The MDRA takes up poll surveys selectively and has been keeping away from the poll season race since 2004. In a front page story Asian Age (February 16, 2002) described how Dr. Rao's research organizations were monopoling poll surveys in the country. As if taking cue from this report Dr. Bhaskara Rao had shifted to teaching and advising on survey research and media research methodologies. The other reason for Dr. Rao to keep away was that he had become a critic of the hurry with which poll surveys were being conducted and, even more, the way the survey findings were being (mis) used by news media.

Dr. Rajeev Karandhikar, Vice President of Granes Software Inventing Limited, did the projection by conversion of votes into seats for CNN/IBN in 2004 and 2009 Lok Sabha as he had been teaming up with Yogendra Yadav for the previous decade. Karandhikar was earlier on the faculty on India's premier Indian Statistical Institute from where he developed this software for projecting seats based on pre-poll surveys and exit Polls as well as on counting day for TV channels.

The independent identity of ORG and MARG was fully availed by A.C. Neilson taking credit for the surveys. In 2004 and 2009 Lok Sabha polls, Neilson monopolised almost half of poll eve surveys conducted for news media as well as political parties and individual candidates / leaders across the country.

IMRB, GfK Mode and Synovate are other market research organizations. They also do not showcase any professional background in election studies. All these agencies are also foreign owned and controlled. A C Neilson and IMRB has unique advantage of having field investigators with experience of conducting year round and countrywide field research of all kind. IMRB is a leader in market research business in India as is A C Neilson – ORG-MARG. It is a division of British Market Research Bureau (BMRB). It entered the field of election eve surveys late in 1990s. It has "added surveys" on polls riding over its other field surveys. They got published prominently in Times of India. It seems IMRB had deliberately avoided doing psephological exercise for news media. It has been taking monitoring surveys including for Doordarshan using a new name as its division. For example, counting day operations for Doordarshan with several lacks of rupees, was undertaken by IMRB in 2009 in the name of BIRD. It also did the same project for Zee News in 2009 using different name because of exclusive condition of Doordarshan.

**Psephologists**

Over two decades ago only one "psephologist" was known in the news media. That was Prannoy Roy. Today more than a dozen are in circulation in the news media. News channels discover them in the first instance. Broadly, there are three types of people who are engaged in conducting poll surveys, psephology and analysis or punditry.

There are a few who are journalists or anchors turned analysts of poll surveys. News channels often introduce an analyst as "psephologist" in the panel in an election eve studio discussion. There are, of course, expectations from psephologist to explains patterns and forecast poll outcomes. Mahesh Rangarajan, Vinod Dua, Gautam Adhikari, Paranjoy Guha Thakurta, etc, are introduced as psephologists. They have been analysing outcome of poll surveys conducted by one or other polling agency. Senior editors like N Ram, M J Akbar, Vinod Mehta, Chandan Mitra, Alok Mehta, Shekhar Gupta, Dileep Padgaonkar, Neeraja Chouwdhary, etc, are among those who appear in most New Delhi based studio discussions on polls and are introduced as experts to do political analysis.

Regionally, there are more than a couple of such analysts in most States described by channels as psephologists every time there is a programme on polls. Some of them with no background – they are neither working journalists, pollsters nor psephologists. Neverthless they are drafted to comment on and discuss poll scenario.

**Dr. Prannoy Roy:** Dr Prannoy Roy is an economist turned psephologist turned broadcaster – media baron today. He never conducted field surveys. He always relied on a survey agency. For long, it was MARG, then for sometime CSDS and after 2006 other agencies. He used a third party, a market research veteran (Dorab Sopariwala) to validate the survey procedures and findings and be his sounding board on survey based poll discussions. He relied on Dorab unmindful of his insights into political dynamics of the country. Dr. Roy made a mark and has become a role model for many anchors, broadcasters and also psephologists and a guide to aspiring politicians. His merit initially was simple analysis, good graphics and impressive delivery. Although he confines to English, he reaches nationally. To reach Hindi viewers, he went in initially for a equally well known co-anchor Vinod Dua, a veteran in broadcasting having entered the field through Yuvavani of All India Radio in 1970s. Dua too never conducted or involved in field surveys, nor had the background of psephology. But he made a mark anchoring survey-based programmes on NDTV channel. He had even evolved and innovated interactive field programmes with different section of voters and in a personalised style.

**Political scientist - Yogendra Yadav:** Yogendera Yadav of CSDS is a political science scholar from grassroots India. He has the best of advantage to do poll surveys professionally and also analyse the findings lucidly. Although he entered the field only in 1990s, he has the advantage of the CSDS which has been an independent institute with right kind of resources for electoral studies as no one else in India. No other institute or individual has the kind of special advantage that Yogendra Yadav enjoys. To add to all this, he has the discipline of not falling into lures that competitive politics and competitive media often offers. His methodological rigour in field work stands out and at the same time transparent as no one else. He is also the only one who does not go "over board" with survey findings and psephological exercise and rightly reminds the limitation that one need to be aware of.

**Proactive psephologist: G.V.L. Narasimha Rao,** agriculture graduate, rural researcher, was trained under Dr. N Bhaskara Rao for nearly a decade and came into limelight through CMS. G V L made a mark on the national scene for surveys for Doordarshan and

Times of India late 1990s. Having started his own outfit, DRS, GVL mastered too quickly tact of catering to more than one news media and more than one politician simultaneously and court potential politicians and tag on to them. In this process he has come to be identified with one political party and ended becoming an embedded psephologist. He is hard working, enterprising and has better writing skills than anchoring. While he could be credited for rapid poll surveys, with considerable smartness in presenting the findings, some of his exit polls were in the "opposite direction" of actual results. A high point for his blatant ways of using surveys was the press conference (arranged by the party in government for which he did poll surveys) insisting how accurate his exit poll was when in fact the result was too much off the mark. Such hasty steps had dampened his otherwise impressive potential to innovate in the market place. He made a mark in recycling field survey data. GVLN's understanding of grassroot dynamics is better than many other psephologists in business today. So also his analytical skills. His over jealousness "to beat everyone" and over enthusiasm to present his findings as if "that is how it is" when in fact the poll process is yet to be over, deprived him from better recognition that he deserved otherwise. He is now a member of BJP's national executive and sounding board for the BJP leaders. He was even made as an advisor to the chief minister of MP in recognition of his support through poll surveys in the media.

**Yeshwant Deshmukh :** Yeshwant Deshmukh, data operator (with a news agency) turned psephologist, is a new star in opinion survey business in India. He operates as a loner using C-Voter name. He has been conducting polls for some news media in print and broadcasting for more than a decade. His analysis in studio discussions on polls are impressive and appreciated. Of late, he has got into surveys for media on other subjects besides election eve polls. His strength is his quick learning spirit and good data base for past elections. He is no longer associated with any political party, but his (unknown) international links (since 2004) are his latest strength. He has mastered to do poll surveys anytime anywhere.

He has better grasp of poll dynamics than most other one person polling agencies.

**Ranjit Chib :** Ranjit Chib is a pioneer in market research (MR). He started MRAS in mid 1980s and sold it to a foreign MR outfit and become a freelancer. A Delhi based socialite, his strength is business procurement and getting surveys organised. He also operates as a front of Neilson – ORG Marg and secures for them poll survey business. A good task master with uncanny knack of gaining confidence of opposing political parties.

**Dr. Vinod Aggrawal:** Anthropologist with impressive credentials. He was a senior social researcher at ISRO for over two decades. He heads Zee TV's outfit, Taleem, based in Ahmedabad and more recently moved in to education field. He dabbled into poll surveys at the instance of Zee TV. His pioneering background, has not lead to any new approach to poll surveys as could be expected from a social anthropologist as a counter to market research driven models.

**Dr. Devender Kumar:** Devender Kumar is another pollster who had made dent on poll surveys and even changed the scope of these surveys. A Ph.D. from JNU, Debu, as he is known, had his initial training in the CMS and was inducted into psephology by Dr. N Bhaskara Rao, the same way as GVLN was. He also worked at DRS, before launching his own Research & Development Initiative (RDI). His strength as pollster includes tracking campaign trends, monitoring election campaigns and rival strategies. He apparently does more assignments for political parties than for news media. His caste analysis model for Hindi belt states and his model for tracking poll prospects with timely feedback to political parties /leaders has sustained RDI in the past decade. He has taken to research projects involving large scale surveys.

**Premchand Palety:** As an engineering graduate with business school education, he has become a prolific surveyor for news media in no time, since (2003). His surveys on newly launched regional news TV channels (TV9 and Swarna) earned him entry into psephology more recently. He started his research and survey experience from MDRA (2001). Cfore's (Centre for Forecasting and Research) "rating of sitting legislators" of Delhi Assembly (2008) for the Hindustan Times had upscaled its potential. More importantly, he had demonstrated that by using "fresh-field investigators" one could do better in cases like forecast for Assembly poll. Cfore's ranking of B-Schools of the country has given it the advantage of roping in B-School graduates for field investigation of poll surveys. Starting with Outlook magazine, he has been doing surveys for The Hindustan Times for a couple of years not only on elections but on other subjects of immediate interests.

**Naveen Surapaneni:** Naveen Surapaneni, an engineer with MBA, turned into a psephologist having got initiated into by Dr. N Bhaskara Rao. As Director of MDRA (Marketing and Development Research Associates), he did several rounds of poll surveys. But he made his dent in the news channels circuit with his chaste Hindi and cool and insightful analysis of poll trends better than his seniors in the field. The names described here are only as an indication. Many others could not be given here for want of information. Their could be neither comprehensive or without a mistake or omessions.

**Embedded psephologist of political parties**: A blatant example of how poll surveys have become part of party campaigns figured in 2004. A survey flashed on the front page of a leading daily in Andhra Pradesh two days before the first phase of the Assembly poll. The other one was an exit poll in between the two- phased poll to Andhra Pradesh Assembly in 2004. Both indicated a sweep for the TDP. Both the surveys were not only off the mark but were in reverse direction, including the exit poll (April 20, 2004). The high point was that the psephologist concerned with the two surveys addressed a press conference organised by the government PR department to defend blatantly pro TDP survey and justified the findings which was prominently covered in most local media. Political parties, irrespective of in power or out, have been going all out to rope in enthusiastic survey agencies and pollsters for such an all out cooperation, formally and informally. Such "embedded psephologists" now work over time in support of political parties and leaders who provide them inputs about evolving election scenario. Towards the close of last poll phases of 2009 Lok Sabha poll, both Congress and BJP released to media their own internal pre-poll and exit poll survey reports. Why?. With counting three days away. If agencies and pollsters do not realize that such linkage eventually effect the very credibility of poll surveys, not just of one, but all in a matter of time, surveys are bound to lose their relevance and utility. Where as political parties and leaders, on the other, would like to have embedded pollsters / psephologists. This would be neither in the interest of news media nor political parties.

To formalise such an arrangement with news media, agencies or pollsters use dummy names. Why?. The well established ones do not want take the risk of tarnishing reputation by having direct linkage with political parties/ leaders but at the same they do not want to lose the business opportunity and also patronage in the government. They use names like Centre for Political Research and Analysis, Chanakya, Globe, Bird, Insight, etc without indicating the linkage with parent organization. News media despite knowing the linkage tend to avoid reference.

A new move after 2004 Lok Sabha polls has come into being News Broadcasters Association. It commissioned A C Neilson to do field research for poll surveys of its member channels, including counting day monitoring of results. If this experiment succeeds and if this outfit sustain itself next couple of years, it could also take to the idea of "common field work" for poll surveys.

Among political leaders who could be given credit for encouraging surveys in public domain initially include Rajiv Gandhi, L K Advani, N Chandrababu Naidu and, more recently, Dr. Y S Rajasekhar Reddy as chief minister. He had taken more interest in poll surveys more than his predecessor Chief Minister. Reddy did not take surveys seriously in the earlier years. But as 2009 polls approached, the uncertainty made him to go for poll surveys. In fact, this author could recall that Reddy would have come to power five years earlier in 1998 had he believed that field surveys can provide insights into voter behaviour and help strategize poll campaigns. It was as if with vengeance that he commissioned or relied on more than two dozen surveys in the last one year (2008 – 2009) of his first tenure as Chief Minister.

Poll surveys conducted for the BJP provide relatively more inputs to the party's outlook and poll strategy than the ones conducted for Congress party. This is because the BJP is more proactive in the very process of commissioning surveys. It interacts with the survey agency before and after the polls. By providing patronage to the survey agency with government assignments on an ongoing basis once in power in the State or Centre, the BJP nurtures certain relationships with research agencies and "psephologists. Where as Congress party leadership has neither the kind of active temperament to get most out of poll surveys nor it trusts the agency to the extent needed to design an insightful survey. Also, in Congress party leaders do not share survey findings with each other to get most out of them. Until Rahul Gandhi came into picture there was certain self righteousness view of Congress leaders as if they already knew everything. But Ahmed Patel is the master strategist of Congress party with grasp of grassroot dynamics state wise. Jairam Ramesh is another one with big picture view and good analytical understanding of electoral situations. Vishwajit Singh is a long standing resource in Congress party with a mine of poll data and tools for presentation. With one or two others joining time to time they configure, commission and track election surveys in that party.

In BJP late Pramod Mahajan was initiating poll surveys for long, later it was Venkaiah Naidu, Arun Jaitely, Sushma Swaraj and more recently the party President L K Advani himself was doing orchestrating surveys of all kind. These observations are made with some understanding of this author on how different political parties or leaders availed or commissioned poll surveys, including exit poll.

Over all, BJP leaders benefitted organisationally far more from poll surveys than Congress party. BJP's pro-activeness has even helped shape the very scope of poll surveys.

**Use and Misuse of Poll Surveys**

A recent example of how channels "help" parties / leaders, intentionally or unintentionally, was Star News channel's pre-poll survey in November 2008. AC Neilson did a survey first for the CM of Delhi directly (paid by an industrialist) in October 2008 based on which Star channel presented "Star-Neilson poll survey at 8 pm. in an half an hour discussion programme showing that Congress party was way ahead in Delhi Assembly poll in terms of seats and votes. Going further, in an unusual way, Star News channel presented another Neilson survey on 26 November, at primetime 8 p.m. showing that Congress party had further improved its position since its first survey on November 1st. The survey shown on November 26 was conducted as per the news stories between November 15 and 20th. Why the channel had to wait for 6 days to present the findings of a survey in Delhi?. There was no precedent where a news channel presented two pre-poll surveys conducted by the same agency within a fortnight in the context of an election for the same State Assembly.

The programme presented on November 26 was after BJP leaders peaked their aggressive campaign in Delhi and almost on the last day of the campaign for the November 29 polling. There were more such examples where news media blatantly went about as if using surveys in support of a party. NTV channel in Telugu is an extreme example. The channel got three surveys by A C Neilson and prominently featured them on the channel each round for a couple of days starting five months before the poll schedule was announced. That the channel was trying to announce its support to the chief minister was obvious. In fact, incumbent parties in power both at the Centre and in the States have been spending government money to get many poll surveys conducted by many agencies and also "manage" to get them covered prominently by newspapers and TV channels. These surveys are mentioned only as a examples to indicate the trend. A C Neilson was the agency in both the States and also in the case of Lok Sabha poll. No wonder why most newspapers which published the first round of survey of Star – Neilson did not bother to cover this second round of the survey. The Hindu in a brief summing of that second survey was careful instead of repeating a PTI story as it is. Whether it was a "press release" sent to PTI by the party or by Star News or by A C Neilson could not be verified.

## Recycling or Reuse of Surveys?

With poll surveys becoming a commercial and quid pro activity, it is perhaps natural for polling agencies to become greedy. The greed is for quick money as well as for patronage from the winners in the electoral race once in power. This quest becomes easy when political leaders or potential candidate too become anxious to hear positive things from poll surveys. Poll surveys have become the medium for such ego trips. This requires getting surveys conducted frequently and as many once the poll schedule is known with many aspiring candidates seeking surveys. Polling agencies started to cater and cope with such a demand by reprocessing old survey data or/ and reuse the previous survey irrespective of who had conducted it. There are instances of recycling data of earlier surveys and reuse data of a latest survey to cater to an altogether different client. There are also instances of polling agencies reusing data of another competing candidate / party showing same or a different name for the polling agency. Then fudging poll data to fit into the news media's policy or suit a leaders' requirement is another way of "manipulation" of surveys. To avoid any contradiction in findings some survey agencies "moderate" field data.

News media should be sensitive to such possibilities and practices. News media should be able to discern survey findings received while poll campaign is on. A majority of pollsters and psephologists are one man operations. There is no effort to institutionalise the activity to do with elections or voting behaviour or integrate with larger phenomenon of life styles and development.

# 8

# Slogans to Schemes to Surveys

**Populist Schemes**

The extent to which political parties went about luring voters in 2008 and 2009 Assembly elections was as if the sky was the limit and that they could get away with any promise. It was a rat race between political parties. These initiatives of parties / government do make a difference to the poll campaign and tend to contribute to accuracy level of poll surveys. Earlier in 2006 in Tamil Nadu, the incumbent offered "free color television" sets to voters as a part of its manifesto. Many parties have come to believe that inducement had helped the DMK to come back to power in Tamil Nadu. In 1955 mid-term poll to Andhra Pradesh Assembly, Communist Party had offered "two bullock and 5 acres" to landless (zamindari system was still around) families. That did not help. In 1967, it was MGR in Tamil Nadu who introduced mid-day meal scheme for school children and Rs. 2 per kg rice for below poverty line households. In 1983 NTR of the TDP in Andhra Pradesh made such an offer and romped home. Chhattisgarh and Madhya Pradesh in 2008 had witnessed virtual competition in offering "free bees" to voters on the eve of going to Assembly polls and to a certain section of voters. In 2008 and 2009, all parties were in competition in making such populist offers to lure voters. The TDP chief Chandrababu Naidu in Andhra Pradesh was described by his opponents as *"all free Babu"*.

Elections were fought in between years on emotional appeals which meant taking to slogans, like "*garibi hatavo...*" or "aam admi" "pride of Andhras..." "*mahengipadi Congress*" to woo voters.

**The Incumbency Advantage?**

The parties in power start worrying about the next election much before and take up populist schemes to woo voters. With the spread and proliferation of news media and their constant pre-occupation with politics, parties/leaders take to "image" building as a priority. That is how electoral campaigns have moved focus from slogans to populistic schemes again and use poll surveys. Going for surveys indicate the public standing of parties / leaders or schemes force such measures. In this process, "getting into media", has become a preoccupation of parties and leaders. That is how political leaders once in power go all out "to coopt news media" in such a way that they give positive coverage to the leadership and their governments. That is how "PR" apparatus of governments are becoming fat with more and more funds. For example, against a budget of Rs.150 crores of the TDP Government's PR Department, over Rs. 500 crores was spent by Congress Government in Andhra Pradesh in the last years of its stint.

In 2008, Andhra Pradesh presented yet another extreme case of populistic schemes and "publicity-surveys". Though elections were more than 6 months away, the party in government had managed news media for "carpet advertising" as a way of eliciting the support of news media and persuasive propaganda. In this process "surveys" have become means to echo public support in the news media and influence voters for a bandwagon effect. With increased competitiveness in contests, political parties have been taking to populistic inducements in successive election. It is no longer limited to incumbent party but by all contenders. If one party offers rice at Rs. 3/- per kg on the eve of a poll, the other party promises same at Rs. 2 per kg and yet another one offers giving higher quantity of rice per family per month even at Rs.1/-. And, if there is a fourth party it could offer rice even free. The DMK victory in 2002 Assembly election was credited partly to the party offering "color television" to voters. Timing of such temptations also could be a factor. For example, on the last leg of the campaign in Chhattisgarh Assembly election 2008, the incumbent party BJP announced wheat at Rs.1/- per kg when it released its manifesto four days before the polling day. Although the success of this party to retain power cannot be attributed to this lure alone, any change in voting preference because of such inducements could not be taken into account in pre poll surveys. These and other such efforts could effect accuracy of poll surveys.

The incumbent governments whether at the State level or at the Centre have been going full blast in publicising achievements of their government in the context of forthcoming elections and starting much before the Election Commission announces the schedule for the election. What the Government of Andhra Pradesh did in the three months prior to January 2009 announcement of poll schedule for the Assembly election was perhaps an unprecedented example. It gives an idea of emerging scenario in other States and the country. The party in government went about as if "saturated advertisement" ensures the return of the party in power and unconcerned with lessons from its own predecessors in the State. There are three classic cases. Indira Gandhi government's "decade of achievement" campaign in 1977, Vajpayee's Governments "India Shinning" campaign in 2004 and Chandrababu Naidu Government's "Vision 2020" campaign in the 2004 Assembly elections. In all these three cases the incumbent governments lost the election as if boomerang of over doing was so obvious.

## Blurred Differences between the Government and the Party

Over the years the distinction between the government of the day and the party in power has been on decline. That is even more so and glaringly when it comes to advertising and publicity by the government of the day in the interest of the party and such a way to give it advantage at the polls. This trend is as if political parties and leaders do not learn lessons or get any insights from the past. There is no evidence that saturated level of advertising and publicity by the government for helping the party and leader in the preceding months to an election will always help the return of the party to power. In fact, recent trends project a different picture. The party in government goes all out in using funds and machinery to reach out and lure voters with all out publicity around schemes specially designed for such effort. And, it starts several months before the Election Commission's embargo.

The government machinery is used to project the party and the incumbent chief minister. In this process, surveys are unleashed at Government's cost as another way of "endorsing" or projecting popularity of the party in power in the news media.

Since the coalition era at the Centre and in some States in the last decade, this phenomenon of government taking to all out publicity blitz for giving the party an advantage has increased as if there are no restraints. The "media wars", where the party in power uses its powers to muscle news media, directly and indirectly, and even starts its own outfits. Surveys of all kinds have become part of that process and more often a source for stirring and steering political scenario towards an electoral advantage of the ruling party.

In this respect the poll scene in Andhra Pradesh, both in 2004 and 2009, is a case in extreme. The parties in power were all out, in using the government machinery and resources for projecting one individual – the chief minister of the day. All public meetings and visits to districts by the CM were organised to help the party. The advertisement campaign, sponsored and surrogate, was unprecedented at saturation level in the mass media of all kinds and at the cost of the government. And, in 2009 it was mostly camouflaged or surreptitious. Programmes of TV channels were sponsored by the government but giving the impression that they were part of the routine schedule. "Mr CM", a stage managed interview based by select journalists on

TV-9 was an example. For six months before the election the programme enabled the CM to say whatever and how he wanted to say – with selected journalists asking questions in a pre-designed way. A studio was set up for this programme at the CM's residence. The journalists who participated were briefed about questions. Realising that news channels in the State are proliferating and TV-9 is no longer the prime mover, the government initiated author programme– "AP Weekly Report" – which the PR department of the State government distributes to channels with prior arrangement to position the programme as an "important reviews of events" of the week – but in fact featuring Chief Minister interacting or wooing a particular section of voters about "achievements of his government" as well as failures of the previous government. 'Mr. C M' continued during the campaign till the end of the polls. Closer to the election, in January 2009, the government even revoked a licensing condition of cinema theatres to screen "Government documentary" (with achievements of the CM) as a mandatory. All this was not for the first time. In several other States also this was going on. It is blatant now. An estimate of what the government of Andhra Pradesh spent on such and other publicity (directly and indirectly) in the one year preceding the Assembly - Lok Sabha election of 2009 was about Rs. 800 crores (against 200 – 250 crores earlier during 2004). The government had to revise budgetary allocations to DIPR thrice in 2008 – 2009. This does not include what each department / programmes like Jala Yagnam, Rajiv Griha, Rajiv Health..., etc spent on advertisements. Interestingly, some of these schemes targetting at one or the other section of people, were designed so imaginatively as if a consumer brand is being promoted in a market place. As if to counter "fake surveys" by some newspapers, the State government came up with "surrogate news stories" in the form of "banner news" on the front pages of all Telugu newspapers showing the "hand of CM" initially without mentioning anywhere that it was a "paid advertisement" and later mentioning in small letters in an inside page that it was provided by DPRO.

**Eenadu** **February 9, 2009**

The government commissioned several rounds of surveys for "poll inputs" for the party in power from out of government funds whether it is of HIV – AIDS society or of some other government agency. All this was arranged before the formal announcement of Poll Schedule by the Election Commission.

The chief minister himself tried to justify in "orchestrated TV discussions" that all was meant to communicate about the schemes of the government to all sections in the State. This has been a standard model of successive governments.

In India, increasingly the State governments and even the Centre have been using government resources to use media. The Election Commission writ comes into effect only from the date it announces a schedule for the election. Since this schedule is fairly well laid out, the party in power does its best in inducing, influencing and luring voters by anything well before that schedule is announced. Also, there is no instance of the Election Commission or any other body taking proactive initiatives in the case of news media's ways of hyping one or other party's interests. Poll surveys conducted in such an atmosphere in States are bound to get biased either way and going off the mark in their forecasts.

**Margin of Wins and Transferability of Votes**

The relevance and role of poll surveys vary depending upon keenness of contests and likely margin of victory or defeat. Fate of projections of seats based on poll surveys depend on several external factors. One such aspect is margin of victories between key contending parties and the competitiveness in the contests, both in the case of Lok Sabha and Assembly elections. Quest for "marginal vote" drives parties and politicians to divisive politics and polarise voters and win at any cost. The number of elections for Assembly and Lok Sabha that voters had experienced in a State in the previous 10 years, for example, also determines the competitiveness.

The number of contestants in Assembly / Lok Sabha elections in India has been on increase with rise of regional and local parties in most parts of the country. Even electoral postures or strategies of parties / candidates changing from one election to another. More complex of late is the kind of coalition politics that parties and leaders are engaged in. The composition of coalition of parties too is changing from one election to another. Individual leaders who carry with them certain communities / groups of voters for what ever reason, in some pockets of the country/State, make pre-election projection of seats further complicated and sample surveys less reliable. The dynamics of such vote banks close to a poll date could make survey projections go *heywire*...

**Narrow Margin of Victory – Lok Sabha Seats**

| *No. of Votes* | *1991* | *1996* | *1998* | *1999* | *2004* | *2009* |
|---|---|---|---|---|---|---|
| < 2000 | 15 | 12 | 13 | 8 | 11 | 9 |
| < 4000 | 24 | 21 | 21 | 25 | 21 | 13 |
| < 6000 | 33 | 32 | 33 | 37 | 28 | 9 |
| < 10000 | 47 | 51 | 64 | 56 | 46 | 23 |
| > 10000 | 487 | 492 | 479 | 487 | 493 | 489 |

*Source* : Election Commission.

About one-third of the districts of India, for example, are assessed as "under insurgency" where not only uncertainty in the normal course of civilian life but also factors like violence and intimidation dampen poll campaign and scope for normal voting. Poll outcome in such constituencies eventually depends on the intensity of such activities rather than any other reason as reflected in pre-poll surveys.

## Voter Turnout

Voter turnout is another factor which influences the fate of parties or candidates to some extent or other and what induces the turnout or otherwise is a link for the outcome of a poll. That is why political parties too take up campaigns to enroll voters and mobilise them on the voting day. Voter turnout is higher in rural and among poorer section of voters. It will be interesting to note here that voter turnout has been lower in pockets where presence of news media is higher. Although more research is required to analyse the relationship between exposure to news media and their priorities and voting behaviour, it could be observed that heavy users of news media are less likely to go out and vote on the polling day – as if they are contended with drawing room participation in front of the television. The way, channels cover the campaign and give the prospects of parties based on surveys is demotivating voters on the polling day. This factor too could eventually formetive Vitiate production of a Poll Surveys.

Coalition of parties formally or otherwise in an election too could decide the prospects of individual candidates. In the last decade or so in particular, there has been a cris crossing of political parties and political leaders from one election to another to somehow get elected or get a majority in the Assembly and Lok Sabha elections. In Andhra Pradesh, for example, in 2004 election to Assembly and Lok Sabha Congress party, the CPI, the CPI(M) and the TRS contested together against the TDP. In 2009 the CPI, the CPI(M) and the TRS were aligned with the TDP against Congress. Similar examples were there in Tamil Nadu, Uttar Pradesh and, Bihar. And, similarly, the stand of parties on certain lingering and contentious issues change from one election to another. The TRS which stood for the separation of Telengana aligned in 2009 with TDP and CPM which were against separation in the previous election. Similarly in Tamil Nadu the stand of the DMK and the AIADMK towards the LTTE and Tamil Elam in Sri Lanka was different from one election to another in the last decade. So also the INLD of Ajit Singh in Uttar Pradesh or the PMK of Ramodos in Tamil Nadu. The basic assumption in such situations is that voters too would vote accordingly. This assumes that 3+2 become 5. Whereas in fact, it could be only 4 or it could even be 6.

**Lok Sabha Election - Increase in Voter Turnout in Key Urban Clusters: 1998 - 2009**

| *State* | *Urban City* | *LS 1998* | *LS 1999* | *LS 2004* | *LS 2009* |
|---|---|---|---|---|---|
| Delhi | Delhi | 51.3 | 43.5 | 47.1 | 51.8 |
| Gujarat | Surat | 47.1 | 32.3 | 37.7 | 49.0 |
| Maharashtra | Thana | 33.0 | 33.7 | 40.5 | 41.7 |
| Punjab | Ludhiana | 53.2 | 45.8 | 55.8 | 64.6 |
| TN | Chennai | 47.8 | 45.8 | 47.6 | 62.4 |

*Source* : Election Commission.

**Alliance/Coalition: How different from election to election**

| | *1996* | *1998* | *1999* | *2004* | *2009* |
|---|---|---|---|---|---|
| **Andhra Pradesh** | | | | | |
| CPI/CPM | Left Front | United Front | No Alliance | Left Front | Left Front |
| TRS | | | | UPA | NDA |
| TDP | NDA | No Alliance | NDA | NDA | Left Front |
| **Uttar Pradesh** | | | | | |
| BSP | No Alliance | Jan Morcha | No Alliance | No Alliance | Left Front |
| RLD | | | NDA | SP | NDA |
| Kalayan Singh | | | No Alliance | No Alliance | Fourth Front |
| **Tamil Nadu** | | | | | |
| DMK | No Allinace | United Front | NDA | UPA | UPA |
| AIDMK | | NDA | UPA | NDA | Left Front |
| PMK | No Allinace | NDA | NDA | UPA | Left Front |
| MDMK | | NDA | NDA | UPA | Left Front |
| **West Bengal** | | | | | |
| AITC | | NDA | NDA | NDA | UPA |

**Lok Sabha Election - Decline in Voter Turnout in Key Urban Clusters where news media proliferated : 1998 - 2009**

| *State* | *Urban City* | *LS 1998* | *LS 1999* | *LS 2004* | *LS 2009* |
|---|---|---|---|---|---|
| Bihar | Patna | 44.7 | 55.2 | 51.8 | 33.6 |
| Maharashtra | Pune | 59.6 | 52.2 | 47.8 | 40.7 |
| Karnataka | Bangalore | 57.7 | 55.2 | 51.8 | 45.3 |
| UP | Kanpur | 49.1 | 44.8 | 43.4 | 36.9 |
| Maharashtra | Nagpur | 56.0 | 53.5 | 48.6 | 43.4 |
| UP | Meerut | 60.4 | 59.6 | 52.4 | 48.2 |
| AP | Hyderabad | 73.1 | 69.2 | 55.7 | 52.5 |
| UP | Agra | 53.8 | 51.4 | 44.9 | 42.0 |
| MP | Bhopal | 58.9 | 61.9 | 46.5 | 45.0 |
| MP | Indore | 60.1 | 56.5 | 50.9 | 50.8 |
| UP | Varanasi | 47.2 | 45.0 | 42.6 | 42.6 |
| UP | Lucknow | 49.8 | 48.6 | 35.3 | 35.3 |
| Haryana | Faridabad | 65.7 | 56.8 | 54.6 | 56.7 |
| Maharashtra | Nasik | 51.6 | 57.9 | 43.1 | 45.4 |
| Gujarat | Ahmedabad | 50.4 | 40.0 | 39.7 | 45.3 |
| Gujarat | Baroda | 57.9 | 41.5 | 39.4 | 49.0 |
| WB | Kolkata | 71.8 | 67.1 | 66.8 | 65.6 |
| Maharashtra | Mumbai | 50.3 | 44.9 | 47.2 | 41.4 |

*Source* : Election Commission.

In such situations, the parties are expected to come to terms promptly in the distribution or allocation of seats among the parties that have come together in an understanding and later campaign together. But in reality that is possible only when at booth level the leaders/ workers of the parties concerned work in tandem. At macro level, sometimes such arrangement is more psychological move and a strategy and less of arithmetic. Sometimes an individual leader joining one or the other major party is assumed to change the arithmetics. For example, if Kalyan Singh (former chief minister of Uttar Pradesh( BJP)) aligns with the SP as he did in 2009, it is assumed that nearly 3.5 percent voters of Lodh community that he belongs to will go with him and vote for the SP. But the question here is what percent of Lodh voters in fact had voted accordingly when the candidate is a non- Lodh. Such being the nature of coalition in electoral politics, poll surveys and psephological exercise could get into trouble if they are not sensitive to such grassroot realties.

## Number of Candidates in Contest

Poll survey forecasts have better chance of being closer when the contest is direct between two candidates in subsequent polls. Division of votes on account of number of candidates in a contest in a state or constituency could affect survey forecasts depending when the forecast was made after or before the names of contestants were known. The number of candidates in each election has been varying. The fluctuation in the number of candidates is so much that conversion of votes into seats becomes that much difficult. This is also because

**Lok Sabha election : Contestants Candidates**

| *Year* | *1998* | *1999* | *2004* | *2009* |
|---|---|---|---|---|
| Andhra Pradesh | 390 | 285 | 279 | 569 |
| Tamil Nadu | 296 | 362 | 571 | 823 |
| Uttar Pradesh | 1037 | 1208 | 1138 | 1368 |

*Source* : Election Commission.

**Assembly Election : Contestants Candidates**

| *Year* | *1991-94* | *1996-99* | *2001-04* | *2006-09* |
|---|---|---|---|---|
| Andhra Pradesh | 3219 | 2104 | 1896 | 3655 |
| Tamil Nadu | 2834 | 5017 | 1019 | 2586 |
| Uttar Pradesh | 9726 | 4429 | 5533 | 6086 |

of increased dissent in parties and aspiration of certain newer section of people in each election. In 1998 Lok Sabha poll, 390 contested for 42 seats in Andhra Pradesh against 569 in 2009. In Tamil Nadu 823 contested in 2009 for 38 seats against 296 in 1998; and 1368 in Uttar Pradesh in 2009 against 1037 in 1998.

The tendency of sample survey is to over or under represent candidates of certain local or small communities and newer candidate/ party depending upon the spread and selection procedure of respondents in the survey design and also in its execution in the field.

**Keen Contests: Some example - Number of Seats Won/Lost with Margin of Less than 2%**

**Lok Sabha Election**

| | *LS 1991* | *LS 1996* | *LS 1998* | *LS 1999* | *LS 2004* | *LS 2009* |
|---|---|---|---|---|---|---|
| Margin <2 % | 45 | 55 | 78 | 79 | 59 | 73 |
| Total Poll | 534 | 543 | 543 | 543 | 539 | 543 |

**Uttar Pradesh – Assembly Election**

| | *VS 1991* | *VS 1993* | *VS 1996* | *VS 2002* | *VS 2007* |
|---|---|---|---|---|---|
| Margin <2 % | 57 | 60 | 71 | 83 | 70 |
| Total Poll | 419 | 425 | 424 | 403 | 403 |

Recent studies on voting brings out that the percentage of loyal voters who vote consistently to same party election after election has been on decline. This means increase in the percentage of floating and undecided voters who tend to decide about their voting close to or on the polling day going by the inducements and motivation offered by contesting candidates/ parties and their campaigns. Going by election studies that this author has been conducting over three decades, it could be observed that today no political party enjoys one-third of electorate as loyal voters. And the percent of floating voters amenable for wooing by parties / candidate has been on increase and could be as high as one-third of electorate in some pockets. That being the case capturing the opinions and intentions of such floating votes in a poll survey becomes crucial.

These developments in the competitive politics, fragmentation of parties, populist appeals, pursuasive strategies, decline in party loyalties influence poll outcome to some extent or other. Hence the very relevance and reliability of poll surveys and sensitivities of methodologies used in the conversion of votes into seats also affected. Poll surveys are cause and effect of these various developments in the context of electoral politics. Surveys are used to strategise interventions, to come up with populist schemes and to pursue divisive politics or otherwise.

**Tracking Model**

In recent years the political climate in the country has become so volatile that it is now a "boiling pot". As such, it is not merely "voting intentions" which matter but "floating character", "migration trend" from one party to another and "perceptions" of voters about likely poll outcome also has become pertinent. Particularly because the percentage of "loyal voters" of political parties has declined over the years. To understand and analyse voting behaviour and also project the likely outcome of an election in qualitative terms, a more dynamic and transparent methodology is needed than the ones in vogue. If pre-poll surveys fail in indicating the direction and the outcome of a poll, they do not deserve the kind of public attention and media coverage they now get. For that, one round of survey is no not enough to capture the mood and the likely outcome of an election. More than one round of survey is likely to help fine-tune the exercise of capturing evolving perceptions, changing opinions, preferences and intentions and hence the projection of poll outcome in terms of seats. It has been brought out during the last decade that two or three surveys with small but well dispersed representative samples on the eve of a national poll are far more reliable and relevant if they are done at different times before and after the process has started for an election to the Assembly or Lok Sabha.

"Tracking poll survey" is an ongoing exercise to unravel changing electoral fortunes of candidates / parties once the electoral process is on with poll campaigns. This approach is far better way of forecasting than based on a one time survey. The CMS was the one in 1996 which advocated tracking surveys with a distinct research methodology. In 1998, for example, the CMS did three rounds of surveys to come up with more accurate prediction. A tracking survey is held at every key point in an electoral process. It could be 2 or 3 time points. The first survey could be even before the poll process had started. Usually this round of survey serves as a "benchmark" for the following rounds of surveys to check where candidate/party stands and what could be the factors and reasons for the poll outcome. The next round could be once after the poll schedule is indicated by the Election Commission. The next round of survey could be once after the candidate selection process is over and after the manifesto of the parties are released and at the height of the campaigns before the polling day. This tracking approach helps parties/candidates to take correctives. Among news media, India Today was the first one to take to such tracking surveys annually to find out changes in perceptions and voting intentions between two poll periods and also come up with prospects of parties and forecast of seats. Some political parties have narrowed the scope of tracking surveys to "feedback" about opposition party/candidate or about certain community leaders to assess their support (Gujjar leader or Kapu community).

A "CMS Tracking Model" was found far more appropriate to capture an emerging political scenario. The CMS tried this successfully in the 1998 poll also. The CMS undertook four polls in all, with a sample size ranging between 2800 and 8500 with field work of four days each. The day it was obvious that the country was heading for polls, first round of the CMS survey was conducted in two days using a small sample (2800 voters) and the findings were brought out as fast, within a day, and were published in the news media. Looking back we can now say that this tracking model has brought out the trend and direction at the national level as well as in the case of Tamil Nadu, Madhya Pradesh, Maharashtra and Andhra Pradesh fairly well and as good as the ones with large sample and 10 weeks before the actual election. It was based on such a survey that in 1997 the CMS had brought out at the very outset of that poll that the country was heading for a "hung" Parliament on 6$^{th}$ December,1997 (PTI) as it did in the case of the 1996 Lok Sabha polls. Secondly, a CMS pre-poll survey was conducted as soon as a formal announcement of election schedule was known with a bigger sample than the first round of survey (8400 voters). It was completed within 4 days (7$^{th}$ – 10$^{th}$ January) and it brought out the changes, momentum, the direction and, more importantly, "the undercurrents" of Lok Sabha poll. A third and final round of the CMS pre-poll survey was conducted mid way of the campaign within four days (28$^{th}$ – 30$^{th}$ Jan). Each CMS pre-poll survey helped fine-tune the trends in perceptions, apprehensions, aspirations and preferences of voters.

### "Note for Votes"

2008 polls to State Assemblies perhaps will go down as a watershed year in India's electoral history. For, it was this year that Karnataka went to polls for its Assembly when key contending political parties set new benchmark in money spent and cash distributed to voters. In both the respects the records were broken. According to the CMS tracking study the number of Assembly constituencies where more than 15 crore rupees were spent by candidates was more than a dozen and nearly half of the voters in the State were paid cash by candidates for their vote. The Election Commission itself confiscated over Rs.45 crores of cash in transit by different means, including by way of ambulances meant for emergency medical services. There is no precise way to know how much a voter was paid. But it was reported that in over a two dozen constituencies, minimum amount paid to a voter was Rs. 500/-. But in the 2009 Assembly polls in Andhra Pradesh, as per reports in most newspapers, voters were paid anywhere from Rs.200 to 1500 and in 40 Assembly constituencies Rs.20 crores was spent by each candidate. The Telugu newspapers gave specific names and description of the modus operandi of money disbursed to votes. All such lures in last couple of days of polling obviously will tell upon the accuracy levels of pre-poll surveys.

Liquor is another item distributed not only to cadres and opinion makers but also to voters, a day before the polling day as if it is a traditional "free" festive offer. The liquor sales in the constituency/ State going to polls goes up anywhere from 15 to 30 percent depending on the competitive scene. Even nation's capital Delhi had witnessed 17 percent increase in liquor sale in the week of polling in November 2008. Rs. 36 crore worth of liquor was sold in that week in Delhi. This was despite liquor sale was prohibited two days before the polling day.

This trend of increasing percent of voters being paid cash for vote in the last 24 hours of polling and liquor is distributed and such other inducements would upset forecasts of poll surveys in one way or the other.

The outcome of an election may sometime depend on what interest "polling staff" manning booths take on the polling day. They are normally employees of the State governments. For reasons, other than the preferences of voters, but if discontented with the party in government could go about helping some voters who are too old, handicapped, etc to vote in favour or against a candidate/ party. The TDP's loss in some Assembly constituencies in 2004 was attributed partly to such pro-activeness of "government employees" manning

**Those who had taken money or was given money for casting vote by Social Group (in the last 10 years)**

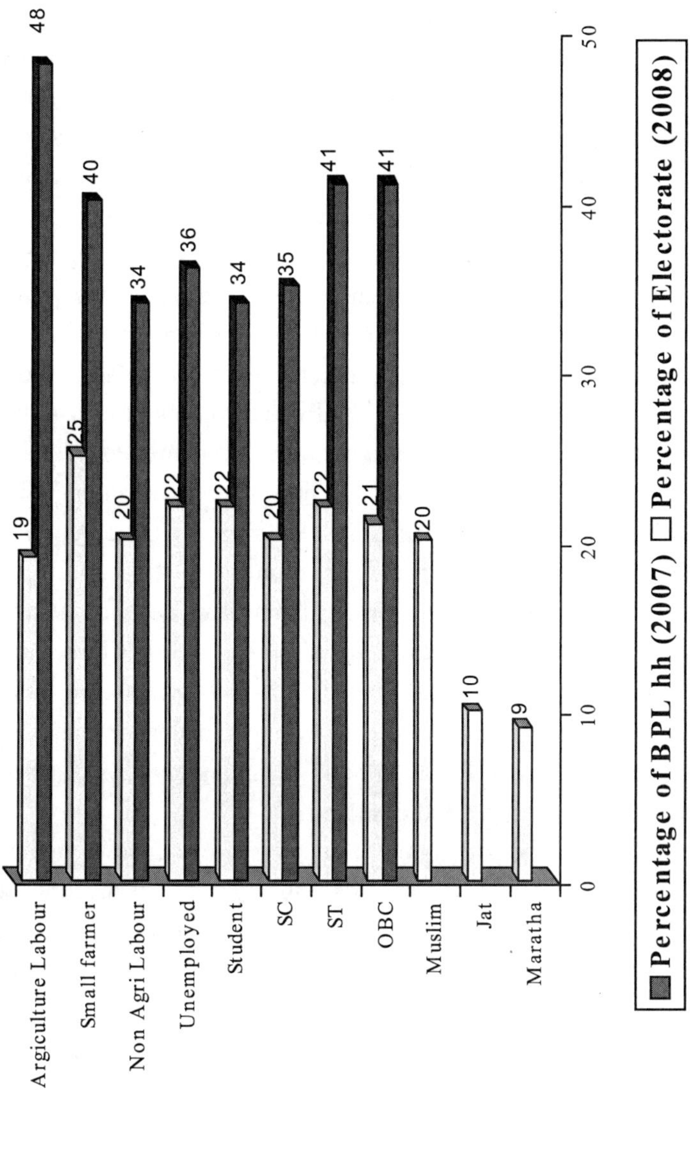


*Source* : *CMS Survey 2008*

polling booths as they were unhappy with the government's resolve to curtail employment in the government (presumably at the instance of the World Bank). There where other such examples elsewhere earlier.

**Winnability surveys**

In 1999 and 2004 more than a couple of times this author was approached on behalf of a national party to conduct field surveys to identify candidates for Lok Sabha election. This author argued that it was the leaders of political parties who should identify candidates and that the survey methodology, the way it was in vogue, does not yield such an outcome and on the contrary, could be misleading (as is evident in Andhra Pradesh Assembly in 2009 where half the Ministers and candidates lost despite using surveys). Surveys should not be a substitute for the political organisation to identify candidates to contest in the polls. As this author personally know cases of how rich and resourceful aspirants have used surveys to get nominated – showing survey reports as evidence for "popularity" or "winnability". There are even more polling agencies or individuals (researchers and journalists) in 2009 who could be commissioned for giving such (survey) reports. Now most parties themselves depend on surveys for selecting candidates and whether sitting ones should be continued or not. Polls in 2008 and 2009 for Lok Sabha and Assemblies have brought out how surveys were used to screen and select candidates, instead of using them for ascertaining winning chances of selected ones and for projecting poll outcome.

A shift in the paradigm of poll eve surveys in news media has come to fore in 2004 and 2009 Lok Sabha polls. This meant change in the concerns priorities of poll surveys. A couple of decades ago elections meant rekindling rank and file of party. Today "winning" in an election at any cost is all that matters. In this process, the emphasis of poll eve surveys has shifted from **needs orientation** (1970) of people to **pursuasion priority** (1998) to **winnability concerns** (2009). That is how selection of a winning candidate has become the concern of poll eve surveys. (than forecasting the outcome of an election or the issues and factors that matter at the polls). This outlook of parties and leaders has been obvious since 1998 elections to Lok Sabha and Assembly. But since 2004, this trend was even more obvious not only with national parties but also regional parties. In 2009 Lok Sabha polls, major contending parties got field surveys conducted for shortlisting candidates and help the process of selecting candidates. In fact, the BJP inducted into its executive council a psephologist who had been conducting poll surveys and exit polls for the party in the past decades and got them covered in the news media. So that surveys and analysis have become an ongoing affair in the party.

It was Davendra Kumar of the RDI and G V L Narasimha Rao of the DRS who had started using field surveys since 1998 – 1999 to identify "winnability candidates" as a confidential service to the party. The BJP relied on surveys in deciding about the sitting candidates and for selecting candidates in all elections to State Assemblies since 2004. Since 2004 Congress too engaged survey agencies for this purpose. The SP, the TDP, Akali Dal, and other regional parties too got surveys conducted for selecting their respective candidates for the 2004 and 2009 election to Lok Sabha. Three parties (Congress, the TDP and Praja Rajyam Party) in Andhra Pradesh got surveys in 2009 for selecting candidates for Assembly seats. This shift to rely on surveys for selecting candidates had come during 2008 elections to some State Assemblies (Madhya Pradesh, Rajasthan, Delhi and Chattisgarh). On the eve of 2009 Lok Sabha polls, field surveys were conducted for selecting candidates at three different levels – at the national level surveys were commissioned by national parties and state units of parties for assessing the prospects of candidate and alternates. Even individual aspirants/contenders got surveys conducted to assess winnability and submit the same to their "high command" as part of bio-data to promote their own candidature. They got surveys conducted to assess their prospects and used the survey report to convince the state and central leadership of their chances to win. Thirdly, individual leaders (like Kamal Nath) got surveys on their own to assess chances of candidates of their "group". In this process, survey agencies increased their business opportunities as the number of surveys needed had multiplied. The sample size of voters required per individual constituency for such survey is much higher than for projection of the seats. And sample size could be even larger depending upon the aspiring candidate's and peculiarities of certain constituencies.

Curious part is that the same agency was used by competing parties to conduct the surveys. AC Neilson – ORG – MARG has been the most commissioned agency not only by political parties and candidates but also by the news media despite its track record was no better than other agencies and that it has no public face to add to credibility of its surveys as in the case of Yogendra Yadav for the CSDS, G V L Narasimha Rao for the DRS or Yeshwant Deshmukh for C-Voter. It has however managed to project its "foreign" connection and volume capacity that it has to conduct surveys fast and anywhere in the country.

**CMS Model for Candidate Selection**

Based on experience in more than a couple of elections, the CMS had come up with an approach to the selection of candidate using field research. Such a way that the process consolidates the party organisation. A three or four stage approach is better to identify potential candidate than a one point field survey as party leaders tend to think. This is possible only if a party starts the process 4 to 6 months before the nomination dates. The party should recognise that involvement of party organisation in the candidate selection process is critical for sustaining the cadres. As such the first stage in any such exercise should be shortlisting the potential names by the district unit of the party. Based on these names a focus group discussion with local opinion makers should be conducted by an independent agency which should find out the unique features expected of the candidature to win the seat. It is after such an exercise and with the names that stand out from the focus group, the selection exercise could be taken forward. A quantitative survey in the field among voters should be organized thereafter to examine winnability of the shortlisted names. The names that emerge from such a field survey should then be considered by the selection committee of the party at the State or Centre level for final selection. In this process, bottom up approach i.e., desirability and winnability aspects should be considered.

In Andhra Pradesh, both Congress party and the TDP had conducted field surveys more than a couple of times during six months prior to 2009 poll to the Assembly. But that was more to perpetuate group politics and eliminate rather than to be an inclusive exercise and a need based assessment exercise.

Closer to nominations day of candidate, in April 2009, the number of suicide attempts in Andhra Pradesh in front of party offices, resignations and protests against party was unprecedented and reported prominently in the media. These incidents were indicative that there was something wrong in the way parties went about selecting candidates. Party offices were burnt down in more than a couple of places by supporters of those who were not selected or considered. In more than a dozen constituencies in the case of each party, workers dozed kerosene in an attempt to suicide. These selections were attributed (by the leaders of the party) to surveys conducted on the basis of "winnability criterion". If that was the case how such large scale dissentions can be there? Surveys were used by the major contesting parties as an excuse for nominating their own people. In fact, President of the party and the Chief Minister kept attributing to "surveys" and talking about as if it is a "mantra". Never before such resentment about selection of candidates was publicly demonstrated in either of the parties (Congress and the TDP). To what extent "surveys" were responsible for the internal dissentions and destabilisation of party organisation is something that need to be studied over time.

Chandrababu Naidu was an active user of poll surveys as chief minister and also as President of the TDP after losing at the poll. His loss of power in 2004 could be partly attributed to his over zealous approach of going by poll surveys. He never looked into motives of survey agency as with the findings and got swayed by the claims of the agency than about the appropriateness of the methodology. On the other, the SAD leaders in Punjab went in 2007 by poll surveys and won the Punjab Assembly poll. They conducted series of poll surveys by more than one agency and participated in the process closely after drawing the strengths from the two surveys. They engaged a more reliable agency for this methodology and took the researchers into confidence all through the campaign for prompt corrective inputs, including by way of sub-sample and small sample surveys. In fact, earlier, such an approach was availed by Ahmed Patel of Congress to win Delhi State from the BJP in 1998. It was Ahmed Patel's initiative that helped the party to win in majority of constituencies. This "winning model" basically consist of a combination of research methods, - starting with focussed group discussions with opinion makers, pre-poll sample surveys among voters at least twice, tracking certain constituencies or/and certain section of voters and monitoring of news media coverage for assessing competitive strategies and prompt correctives until the end of campaign period, 48 hours before the polling day.

The focus of surveys conducted for news media and political parties differ in their scope, methodology, analysis and structure of reports than when they are conducted for political parties particularly for selecting candidates. Quite often political parties informally get access to poll surveys conducted for news media and vice-versa. This author knows instances when editor of a news media quietly informs his close confident in one or other party / leader before the survey appears in the media. There are occasions when the publication is delayed or deferred or got the survey redone to moderate the findings. A recent (2004) example involves Zee News when it deferred the poll survey when it was about to telecast. Editor of a prominent weekly withheld a survey as its finding about a by-election showed the leader of an important party was losing the election in 2001. The editor in this case was right as it would have been an embarrassment, had he published that survey. For, the leader eventually made it. The point is surveys make sense, but can't be taken as a gospel's truth.

In 2009, in Andhra Pradesh the party in power used "surveys" to replace those sitting MLAs who were personally against the chief minister or / and to get nomination for those whom the Chief Minister preferred. Dr Rajasekhar Reddy had openly and repeatedly declared that the selection of candidates was on the basis of surveys. So also did Chandrababu Naidu. In all, Congress was reported to have got more than 30 poll surveys conducted during 2008 – nine against eight by the TDP and five surveys by the PRP of Chiranjeevi. Only a few of them in each case were by a private research agency and the others were by party cadres, students or faculty of a tutorial/ college (Prajatantra, May 15,2009).

Surveys are used to short circuit democratic processes and decentralised politics. Both Congress and BJP and some important regional parties like the TDP, Akali Dal, the NCP, the SP, etc have used surveys for nominating candidates. In this order, aspiring candidates tend to look for survey agencies for a favourable report. Both in Congress party and the BJP, there were more than a dozen such instances in 2009. In Rajasthan Assembly elections in 2008 there was a newspaper report alleging that a survey agency (or its investigators) took money from aspiring candidates. Interestingly, this was alleged by none other than G V L Narasimha Rao himself in his column in Mint. He was a well informed insider of the BJP and the one who has been carrying poll surveys for the party for some years. But such a phenomenon was not limited to that particular election or that State or even to that Party. In 2008 and 2009 elections, both for Lok Sabha and Assembly, surveys were used formally as a means for nomination of candidates. Unlike the earlier years, when aspiring candidates used to camp in Delhi for days to approach the party high command, in 2009 they were searching for contacts to approach survey agencies doing surveys for their respective parties.

Survey agencies which have become somewhat dedicated to parties as in the case of the DRS for the BJP and the RDI for the SP, have become the focal points for candidate selection. AC Neilson – ORG – MARG has become a sought after agency for such survey reports not only for Congress party but also for individual aspirants of that party. The wide spread revolt in the rank and file of the parties suffered was against the outcome of survey based approach of going about selecting candidates. It was as if more the claim of survey as the basis for candidate selection, the higher the possibility of revolt and more the number of rebel candidates.

Yet another snowballing issue is increased demand for provision in the ballot for option of "not any of these" or "none of the above". This movement could perhaps be attributed to increasing practice of preferring candidates by "surveys". Obviously those leaders / aspiring candidates who are in constant touch with a constituency, not just once in five years but engaged all through with the people and their problems, do not require a sample survey. Also, with increased dissidence or "groupism" in parties, the leaders take to surveys as a new way of "controlling" the party and managing "conflicts" and divides within the party. This increasing practice of using surveys to prefer "winnable candidates", as in 2008 and 2009, has dented the very objectivity of surveys. They are being viewed as a "confidential instrument" of leaders rather than as transparent way. And news media had taken in some cases to summative coverage of surveys leaked by political parties or individual leaders / candidates. Only positive aspect of this development is that news media are now back to basics and shifting their attention to basic issues in the election. Channels have shifted from studio based animated programmes based on surveys to real world field based live discourses. Surveys like the ones being relied by political parties do not help encourage decentralised politics nor sustains active cadres of parties.

Once it is known locally that surveys are the means for selecting candidates, resourceful individuals would devise methods of getting "recalled" in field surveys. So that they emerge as "preferred candidates". The tendency in field surveys is that voters recall more of those who had won or lost in the previous election or made extra effort for that. The methodology of surveys have to be different and it has to be a two or three days exercise. In this model, sample survey is only one input. Ideally in a democratic set up the selection process of candidates should start with the constituency, block or district unit of that party. The process is far more important for deepening democratic base. The prerogative of shortlisting should be more with the rank and file of the party from bottom up. The system of primaries as in US elections is a better way of selecting candidates. It is more democratic and more transparent way of going about identifying desirable and winnable ones. Lok Satta party in Andhra Pradesh demonstrated first time in Indian elections in 2009 in a couple of Assembly constituencies by conducting "primaries", a way of selecting candidates to contest for the Assembly. It is time that political parties explore adopting primaries more formally rather than depending on commercial surveys.

There were reports in news media before the 2009 Lok Sabha polls that some parties had even hired a private "detective agency" to "know more" about potential candidates so that adverse information about a "popular candidate" would not become a liability. Detectives were hired by parties not only to know more about their own potential candidates but also about the likely candidates of the opposing party.

Mrs Indira Gandhi's model (1970 – 80) of finalising candidates was relatively more democratic than selection through commercial surveys. She used to deliberately leak the name of a potential candidate and wait for any adverse feedback. This approach served her well for two Lok Sabha elections. But once her method was known, politicians knew how, or through whom, to counter or neutralise hurdles. In this model there are better checks and validation possibility than through a detective agency or a survey. But this method can be used only in the case of a select few contentious constituencies.

## Partywise share in poll advertising: 2004 - 2009

| | | | |
|---|---|---|---|
| ***On Radio*** | | | |
| | Jan-May | 2004 | 2009 |
| **Rank** | **Party** | **Share %** | **Share %** |
| 1 | Bharatiya Janata Party | - | 48 |
| 2 | Congress | - | 30 |
| 3 | Bahujan Samaj Party | - | 3 |
| 4 | Shiv Sena | - | 2 |
| **On Television** | | | |
| **Jan – May** | | **2004** | **2009** |
| 1 | Congress | 17 | 40 |
| 2 | Bharatiya Janata Party | 40 | 24 |
| 3 | BJP-Shiromani Akali Dal | 5 | 7 |
| 4 | Telugu Desam | 8 | 6 |
| 5 | Praja Rajyam | - | 5 |
| 6 | Sazhi Virasat Trust | 5 | - |
| **On Print** | | | |
| **Jan – May** | | **2004** | **2009** |
| 1 | Congress | 30 | 37 |
| 2 | Bharatiya Janata Party | 27 | 13 |
| 3 | Telugu Desam | 6 | 11 |
| 4 | Praja Rajyam | - | 6 |
| 5 | AIADMK | 6 | - |
| 6 | Samajwadi Party | 6 | 5 |

**Political Advertising**

Political advertising in 2009, particularly on TV, was as never before (Rs. 700 crore was the estimation), both in terms of advertisements and number of parties/ candidates (137 to 176) who went for advertising (Mint, May 16, 2009). The party in power is generally believed to outscore its rival parties in advertising.

There is no evidence that advertising campaign of political parties through mass media will sway voters either way. They are being viewed as necessary in the case of contending parties. But not viewed as determental. There is no research back up however to indicate that advertising in commercial formats helps but to what extent. The negative media advertising by Congress in 1982 was supposed to have helped Congress party at the Lok Sabha election.

**Back to Basics**

With too many surveys and of all kind in the market and in news media, and with political parties get inundated with survey reports of aspiring candidates, the credibility of surveys itself has declined to the extent that political parties tend to think in terms of "back to basics". And this is as if based on a realisation of limitation of surveys. That is, instead of depending on surveys, they rather would like to go back to traditional way of reporting elections and electoral politics. That is good in a way. So that surveys get back to their original stature. In fact, only then grass root politics get activated and get their due share of attention. Poll surveys in media without transparency and with pre-emptive role and way of reported in media are counter productive for a dynamic and inclusive democracy and for a free and fair electoral practice. Congress party in 2008, as the BJP did in 2004, had ample scope to realise this – but may be it was too late by then. The party commissioned so many surveys and so did its leaders, even more. Most of the applications that Congress party received for nomination were accompanied with one or other kind of field survey, preferably by a "foreign agency" so that it could be taken seriously ! The way news media went about with covering

2009 campaign, a shift from poll surveys could be expected in 2014 – from surveys to schemes and performance.

**Note for vote – phenomena of dampening democracy**
**The case of 2009 Lok Sabha Polls**

Has "note for vote" become a phenomena today to reckon with in poll campaigns or is it only an isolated practice in a few places? With Lok Sabha itself witnessing shocking note for vote in 2008, the incident repeated by news media several times and over several days, has this become a poll practice? How else we explain that in the last fortnight of March 2009 there were more than a dozen instances from around the country that we saw news channels showing cash in large volumes being transported or distributed by political leaders in the context of Lok Sabha poll. News channels, however vigilant they are, would not be expected to capture every such instance every where.

National channels have hyped incidents, involving Mulayam Singh Yadav in Uttar Pradesh and Member of Parliament Govinda in Mumbai, disbursing Rs.500 notes to a group of people and now a senior BJP leader Jaswant Singh doing so in Rajasthan. News channels in Andhra Pradesh in the last one week had shown instances, as part of their news bulletins, bundles of notes amounting lacs of rupees in the context of on going poll process. These reports were from Khammam, Karnool, Warangal, Karimnagar, Visakhapatnam, Adilabad, West Godavari, Srikakulam and Cuddapa districts. In each case, note bundles, the name of the party or the politician accused was mentioned. At all these places the cash involved was in several lacs and without proper explanation of the source. Except seizing the money, caught and arrest of a driver, or a security of a Minister involved, there were no follow up reports.

In fact, in 2008 local news channels in Tamil Nadu, Karnataka and Chattisgarh, had shown how a local Minister or senior politician distributed cash in a by-election. Without news channels' exposures of these incidents, nation would not have realized that the magnitude

*Contd. on next page*

*Contd. from previous page*

of note for vote phenomena is no longer isolated or limited to mine owners as in Karnataka. In Karnataka, ambulances were caught with crores of cash meant for distribution to voters. Even helicopter was used for carrying notes in one such instance. Note for vote is no longer a hush-hush affair or limited to a few.

Earlier, note for vote is what candidates used to be busy with after the campaign had come to an end officially. Now four weeks before the poll date instances are being witnessed all over. Cash in electoral process is used in three distinct poll phases: to leaders of party to get nominated; to cadres and competitors on the eve of filing nomination; and to voters on the eve of the polling. A candidate of TRS (for Secunderabad) had openly said to news channels that he had paid Rs.10 crores for getting the nomination as a candidate for Lok Sabha. Taking that statement *suo-moto*, the State Election Commission had issued notice to both the candidate and the leader of the party to whom he said gave the money. An aspirant from Andhra Pradesh was caught in Delhi airport with more than a couple of crores of rupees presumably meant for getting nomination of a party.

That voters are distributed money on the eve of voting is well known. But there is no empirical study nationally or state wise. Realizing this, CMS had undertaken such a study at three different points in the last couple of years. First in 2007, as part of its study on corruption involving BPL families, CMS enquired about the percent of voters who had ever received cash for vote. This study covered 23,000 BPL households across 29 States. Realizing that this phenomena was not limited to poor, in 2008 CMS did another round of enquiry among 18,000 voters from 19 States. Third, CMS did an exploratory study in December 2008 in eight intensely fought by-elections to Karnataka Assembly to find out how candidates of different parties gave money. Put together, these CMS surveys brought out mind-boggling

*Contd. on next page*

*Contd. from previous page*

phenomena of a high percent of voters are being paid cash to lure their vote.

Going by this study it appears that while in Uttar Pradesh and Bihar the muscle power is more at work, in Karnataka, Andhra Pradesh and Tamil Nadu money power is unleashed more during elections. Interestingly, it is in these southern States that political parties had more poll surveys conducted and it is in these states that more number of 24 hour news channels have been devoting considerable time for poll campaigns, including note for vote and such other lures in kind.

The CMS study brought out that note for vote phenomena has spread across all sections of voters irrespective of age group, income levels, educational levels and urban and rural. The only variable which seems has telling influence is dominance of cadre based parties and the party in power. Where parties are relatively better cadre based and party loyalties are higher, as in the case of Left party ruled States, the percent of voters involved in note for vote is lower than in other states. A much higher percent of voters in Karnataka, Tamil Nadu and Andhra Pradesh had acknowledged receiving cash as inducement for vote "in the last ten years" (that is one or two polls for Assembly/Lok Sabha) than in Bihar or Uttar Pradesh. The amount involved in these states in the North was much less than in the three Southern states. This 2009 Assembly election in Andhra Pradesh will go down as most expensive poll ever in India as nearly half of voters in all are expected to be distributed with Rs. 500 or more per vote.

CMS is now planning to study <u>influence</u> and <u>effect</u> of note for vote phenomena. The two are different. Influence is how voters are influenced as to their voting. Preliminary enquiry indicates three types of influence. First, voters vote for the candidate on behalf of whom they were given money. Second, although they received money, they voted as per their own plan otherwise irrespective of whether they received from only one candidate or from more. Third, abstain from voting because money was given to restrain some otherwise loyal

*Contd. on next page*

*Contd. from previous page*

voters of a particular party/candidate. Although there was evidence for all three types of influence, which CMS is yet to quantify. This is because note for vote works differently from constituency to constituency and one election to another.

**Regarding Effects**

This author considers note for vote as "mother of all corruptions" because it is here during elections that the vicious cycle starts. Voter is not realizing that for every 10 rupees that a citizen gets from a candidate as a lure for vote once in five years, he or she end up paying five to ten times more annually as bribe to avail basic services that a citizen is entitled from one or other Government service. Thus, this note for vote has direct effect on the kind of governance that we end up having. In this process, neither the winner nor defeated candidate, who have lured voters with money, can be expected to take the kind of interest of a responsible peoples' representative.

Interestingly, there is no evidence impact of note for vote on voter turnout as one could expect. Perhaps because cash is distributed not on demand from voters but by candidates due to local competition of contests. Also, because more and more candidates are new or strangers or far away from the constituency, or from those who made riches rather fast, or those who had opportunity of having unaccounted money. No other factors explains this phenomena of "competitive politics". The effect of cash for vote include depriving truly peoples' representatives of any chance of getting elected or having level playing opportunity.

This enquiry together with reports of news channels indicates that election favour has inflated poll expenditure in the country by five times or since 2004. That is what was Rs. 10 note earlier has now become Rs 100 and so on, in 2009 Lok Sabha polls.

Concerned about note for vote phenomena the Election Commission has taken initiatives recently. It has been appointing

*Contd. on next page*

*Contd. from previous page*

"expenditure observers" to track and validate expenditure on various kind of campaign activities. Second, it has made it obligatory for candidates to file expenditure statements couple of times during the campaign period. The provision that candidates must file their expenditure statement within specified weeks after the election has been there for long. But there is no evidence that has made any difference. The Election Commission for the first time in 2009 has disqualified some candidates from filing nomination of those who had not filed their expenditure statement after the earlier election. Election Commission confiscated more than Rs 40 crores in cash while being transported for distribution at the height of Karnataka Assembly poll in 2008. Beyond that what they did was not known as a deterrent except roping in Income Tax Department to keep track of expenditure by candidates. Even police has been alert now. But, more than all their initiatives, it is news media's vigilance that has been exposing the practice of note for vote. But then communication experts could say that the more such news reports on channels depicting bundles of cash being distributed, the more is the spread of the phenomena, inflating the amount involved and increasing voter expectations.

The best bet to discourage note for vote phenomena is voters themselves, by refusing to accept the lure. For this they need to understand the linkage between note for vote and bribe that citizen end up paying to get what he or she is entitled otherwise from one or other Government department and responsiveness of elected representatives. Second, civil society groups should mount their efforts against various lures of voters locally. Third, the Election Commission should come up with more stringent deterrent measures. Only then the poll process can be truly free and fair. The accuracy level of projection of Poll Surveys obviously will depend on such last minute lures.

***(from The Hindu, 6 April 2009 by Dr N Bhaskara Rao)***

# 9

# Is there a Rethink about Poll Surveys?

Coverage of 2009 Polls by news media signals a rethink about poll surveys on their part. The rethink is a result of the way surveys were availed of by news media in the recent years, the way they were being conducted by polling agencies and presented in the media. Reliability of their findings and the way political parties had pushed them for media coverage is yet another factor for the rethink. The realisation on the part of the news media is that surveys did not help in bolstering their credibility, nor expanded their reach. They only facilitated prolonged studio discourse. Surveys no longer enjoy the kind of positioning they had in the earlier years, before their proliferation and the competition among news media. The costs of the surveys had also increased. The cost of a survey for Lok Sabha had gone up from around Rs. 5 lacs in 1991 to Rs. 25 lacs in 2004 and Rs. 40 – 45 lacks in 2009, making them no longer cost efficient although they still offer political clout.

The rethink in 2009 was obvious. The rethink in news media about poll surveys is evident from the following trends in their coverage of 2009 Lok Sabha polls. First, the number of national pre-poll surveys in the media in the context of 2009 Lok Sabha poll was much less than in 2004. There were less than five in 2009 against a dozen or more in 2004 – despite the number of news channels in this period had proliferated. But in the case of exit polls, the number increased in 2009 as more new news channels took to them. Secondly, news media which featured / commissioned pre-poll surveys in the earlier Lok Sabha election have not gone for any such field survey in 2009. The examples include Times of India, Hindustan Times, Outlook, Zee News and Sahara Samay, etc. Thirdly, many news media that had not gone for surveys midway of poll schedule had taken to some other way of forecasting or projecting the outcome of the election. They experimented with other ways as in the case of Times of India, Hindustan Times, Nai Duniya, Dainik Bhaskar, NDTV, Times Now, etc.

Fourthly, those media that had gone for a pre-poll surveys as before tried to use the survey findings in 2009 differently than the way they did in the earlier years – in terms of scope and structure of presentation of the survey findings. Fifthly, unlike before, news media that had gone for pre-poll surveys in 2009 did not confine to only surveys. Instead, they also had gone for other type of programme as if surveys no longer are enough to reflect the mood of voters or the polls scene. NDTV's Editor's Choice and Big Fight are some examples.

Sixthly, there were no example of media houses coming together to jointly commission pre-poll surveys as in 2004 when CNN/IBN, HT and a regional daily together commissioned and featured survey of the CSDS. In 2009 too CNN/IBN tried with HT, but the latter did not go for the arrangement, nor it had its own surveys. Dainik Bhaskar did so only in the case of exit poll. Swarna TV in Karnataka joined with Asianet and New Indian Express in Karnataka. Times of India's projections, based on its own assessment, were also featured prominently but only on their own Times Now TV channel.

Seventhly, the Election Commission's curb on publication or broadcast of exit poll or such other surveys, after the closer of campaign time for the first phase was over on the evening of April

14th till the end of the last polling day on May 13, 2009, had helped the channels and also newspapers to come up with "other ways" of catching up with the expectations of viewers / readers. This had provided an opportunity to try out other ways of catering to the needs or expectation of people in between the polling phases. Most of the news channels and even some newspapers did dwell upon the trends in between without referring to any particular exit poll or field survey.

Eighthly, news media no longer pretend to be "independent" of political rivalries. In 2009 there were more news media which belong to one or the other political party / leader or relative or affiliate. Nearly one-third of news media falls in this category as to their origin / affiliation. That being the case, it suited them to chalk out their own path or methodology of projecting poll outcome instead of having to go by or veering around the findings of a pre-poll survey by an outside agency. A couple of examples are presented here to indicate the rethink of news media about surveys and their efforts to experiment with alternate ways of covering poll campaign. The trend in the country is that regional media, both in the case of newspapers and news channels, follow the programming pattern of one or other prominent ones at the national level like NDTV, CNN/IBN, or Times of India or Hindustan Times. That was how not many regional news media apparently had taken to poll surveys in 2009 and, instead, gone for programmes similar to those of national news media.

**Poll Surveys, their Use by Media**

During 1991 - 1996 poll eve surveys were more of curiosity interest and were driven by main line news media. Four developments during 1996 – 2004, with four Lok Sabha polls in between, changed the role and significance of media coverage of poll surveys. First, exit polls were being sought after by the media, irrespective of being right or wrong aspect of such surveys and the coverage based on them. Secondly, proliferation of news media in the last decade, particularly news channels, and increased competition between them for one-up-manship. Thirdly, with "coalition" becoming way of power politics in the country, suspense and curiosity factor has increased, not only at the centre but also in some States. Fourthly, with political parties using surveys for selecting candidates, they are not as much interested in making surveys available to news media, or make them available only selectively. In fact, this was what the BJP strategist Arun Jaitely pointed on a TV panel discussion (8 May, CNN/IBN). He said his party had learned to depend more on regional news media's assessment compiled with their own surveys conducted by internal psephologists. That perhaps why GVL Narasimha Rao who has been conducting commercial poll surveys for news media and parties from outside has now become embedded one and in 2009 the BJP used only his survey in the news media. These four trends together reflect the change in the very course and standing of poll surveys vis-à-vis news media. It was during 1996 – 2004, the poll surveys proliferated as if no concern for the implications of the way they were conducted or covered in news media and as if no restrain which could avoid intervention of the Election Commission. It is during this period that news media went all out in featuring and playing up poll surveys. News media were proactive with poll surveys as if they were part of election campaigns to the extent that surveys become "instruments" to influence the poll process. In that process parties / candidates have started viewing poll surveys as means to sway voters. Also, it was during this period that too many survey agencies and pollsters entered the field, many with no background to undertake structured sample surveys and psephological exercise. Many poll surveys had gone off the mark and even as many exit polls to the extent of spreading several doubts and apprehensions about poll surveys in news media.

The decline in credibility of poll surveys culminated, not necessarily for that reason but for likely impact on free and fairness of polls, with Election Commission's restrictions on the eve of 2009 poll on the media coverage of poll surveys and exit polls in between the poll schedule. That is how although 2009 Lok Sabha poll process started in November 2008, when it was obvious that Lok Sabha poll will be held as per schedule, only 2 or 3 pre-poll surveys had come up in the news media until formal announcement of the notification of the poll schedule by the Election Commission on March 23,2009. It was clear by then that 2009 Lok Sabha poll perhaps would not see so many poll surveys as the previous four Lok Sabha elections had witnessed. How come? First, there seems some rethink on the part of news media about extra-ordinary relevance of pre-poll surveys in the coverage of polls, (particularly for byte based presentation). Also, there is realisation that factors different from State to State and they can not be presented in one go based on one field survey based programe like earlier and that they need not gear up for exit polls as they cannot be covered. Secondly, political parties are now getting surveys conducted more for candidate selection than for forecasting of seats as "change" and anti-incumbency as a factor. Against this background, news media explored new ways of covering polls for interesting readers / viewers rather than relying on field surveys which are time taking and even expensive.

At the national level there were only two field surveys by the news media, one by the CNN-IBN with the CSDS (February 2009) and the other by Star News with A C Neilson. Both surveys projected state wise seats for Lok Sabha. Both the surveys did not indicate shifts in voting pattern or percentage of votes, parties were likely to poll. The findings of this pre-poll survey were presented over a week with daily 30 minutes studio based discussion with 2 or 3 senior journalists. The CNN-IBN did not succeed to rope in Hindustan Times as a sponsor of the survey as it had done more than once in the previous election. Beyond marginal difference in the presentation format in studio, there was no other change in the way the CNN IBN presented the findings of the pre-poll or in the analysis of the survey findings. The findings were stretched over seven days of prime time programme (with discussion on 2 or 3 States each day). The studio-based discussion (no audience) with principal researcher of the survey, Yogender Yadav, on the first day of presentation to briefly refer about the survey methodology (when, how, size of sample, etc).

Elections to six State Assemblies in November 2008 had seen only two pre-poll surveys in the news media including one in a news magazine (The Week) and the other in a news channel (Star News). The latter used one exit poll for Delhi on November 29. The earlier Assembly elections for four States in 2007 witnessed five or six pre-poll surveys and more than four exit polls. This decline in the number of field surveys was perhaps because of government's decision against exit poll surveys and proposal to restrain pre-poll surveys between polling schedules. It could also be because of certain restraint of news media themselves as about two dozen poll surveys including exit polls on the eve of 2004 election, had gone off the mark causing ridicule of news media's reliance on such surveys for covering elections. But there were also efforts in November 2008 by psephologists to present in news media forecasts for electoral outcome in the grab of journalistic analysis. *Mint* (November 24, 2008) carried a front page three column story by its pollster columnist; "Surveys and Public Mood" as the basis for such forecast.

**Reuters Snapshot Survey**

2009 Lok Sabha poll witnessed a couple of new models of covering poll instead of surveys. Realising that there was a vacuum in poll coverage in the absence of pre-poll surveys and exit polls, Reuters News Agency in India had experimented with a "survey" of opinions of select panel of "experts" in an earlier poll. This survey was limited to forecasting the outcome of the Lok Sabha election in terms of seats the key contending parties and alliances were likely to get and the prospects of PM candidates. Reuters poll conducted over telephone involved a panel of 14 experts, each from a distinct field (economics, polling, media, research, markets, academics, etc). It was conducted every Monday (starting March 16,2009) and the findings released to the news media. This approach, Reuters apparently felt, was good enough to cater to news media's concerns and cater to the curiosity of interested groups like investors, industrialists, etc at home and abroad who were its key subscribers.

**THE TRIBUNE, Wednesday, March 18**

# Reuters poll gives thumbs up to Cong coalition

**NEW DELHI, MARCH 17**

An alliance led by the ruling left-of-centre Congress Party is most likely to win the next general election but it could need communist support to build a majority, a Reuters poll of 14 leading analysts has predicted. The main battle of the April/May election will be between the Congress-led coalition, known as the United Progressive Alliance (UPA), and the National Democratic Alliance (NDA) led by the BJP.

A group of smaller political parties, including the communists, have formally launched a "Third Front" in a bid to provide an alternative to the two main national coalitions. On average, analysts said there was a 32 per cent chance a Congress-led alliance would win, but would need communist party support to stay in power. They said there was a 27 percent possibility the Congress would win without leftist support. The leftist parties withdrew their support last year for the government over a civilian nuclear deal with the United States, but some analysts say they could rejoin in order to stop the BJP from forming government.

Those polled said, on average, there was a 23 percent chance of an NDA victory and only an 18 percent possibility of a Third Front government. Reuters surveyed 14 analysts from a variety of backgrounds, including universities, pollsters and banks, on Monday and Tuesday. The poll aims to give readers a snapshot of how some of the leading India analysts are thinking. The following are the results of their replies.

**1. How many seats do you think the Congress and the BJP will win?**

Congress 144, median 143; BJP average 130, median 130

**2. Assign percentages to the following scenarios:**

a) A UPA-led government with communist support

Average 32 pc, median 30 pc

b) A UPA-led government without communist support

Average 27 pc, median 28 pc

c) An NDA-led government

Average 23 pc, median 25 pc

d) A Third Front-led coalition

Average 18 pc, median 10 pc

**3) Who will be the next Prime Minister of India?**

Dr Manmohan Singh: 12 choices; Foreign Minister Pranab Mukherjee: 1; UP CM Mayawati: 1; LK Advani (BJP leader): 0

**Those polled** were: Amulya Ganguli, independent analyst; Mahesh Rangarajan, independent analyst; Phani Sekhar, fund manager, Angel Broking; TK. Bhaumik, chief economist, JK organisation; Alastair Newton, political analyst, Nomura Securities; Rupa Rege Nitsure, chief economist, Bank of Baroda, MUMBAI: Pran Chopra, Independent political commentator; DH Pai Panandikar, The RPG Foundation; Dr N Bhaskara Rao, Centre for Media Studies; Professor Sudha Pai, Jawahar Lal Nehru University; Seema Desai, Eurasia Group, Vinod Mehta, Editor-in Chief, Outlook Magazine, V. Anantha Nageswaran, chief investment officer, Asia Pacific, Julius Baer; Yashwant Deshmukh, head of C-Voter polling agency. — Reuters

This poll was released by Reuters over four Mondays. While four questions were common, it added one new question every round. One was about likely economic policies of the new Government. It was this Reuters model which was taken up by few other news media using similar approach, including The Times of India, The Hindustan Times, etc.

The Times of India (March 6, and May 6, 2009) published its survey twice on the front page with a chart giving forecast of steatewise of Lok Sabha seats that parties are likely to get. The forecast, it claimed, was based on an assessment by its own staff reporters on the "prospects" of parities. This newspaper apparently realised that this way it can do a better job than what Arun Nehru was forecasting week after week based on his own individual "assessment and update" of poll prospects. The Times of India concluded that prediction of Indian elections has long been a "mug's game" and since that pollester's predictions are "more often than not have been wrong", why not to use the "brains of its own bureaus" to come up with an estimate of the poll outcome.

**The Times of India**

The anxiety and focus of The Times of India was more with the outcome by projecting seats that various parties were likely to get in the form of a chart. There by they added to the speculation and pushed rumour mill with potential to influence the mood of voters and enthuse cadres of parties in one way or the way sample surveys indicated. Such reporting by prominent news dailies, in turn, influences poll surveys and even exit polls. How else one could explain so many exit polls failing to capture an unfolding story and such an almost uniform undercurrent as in 2009 Lok Sabha polls.

The issue here is not one of accuracy of estimates. But the way they were presented by the leaders of news media. Also, this was more a show of punditry and one-upmanship (as against one man's estimates in Asian Age/ Pioneer) which has become a talked about exercise fueling rumour mills, sustaining satta market and often

• Times of India March 6, 2009

# TOI's estimate: UPA ahead, but only just

TNN

Trying to predict the outcome of Indian elections has long been recognised as a mug's game. That has, however, never prevented anybody — and certainly not the media — from playing the game. So here we go, setting the ball rolling.

Rather than hide behind some pollster's projections (which more often than not have been wrong), we decided to stick our neck out. We picked the brains of the bureaus across India as well as the national bureau. We argued and differed on some estimates. Finally, here's what we came up with. The UPA is likely to win 201 seats, the NDA 195, the Third Front 82 and Others 65.

That means that while Congress and BJP almost exactly repeat their 2004 performance, neither has a clear shot at forming the government — 272 being the majority mark. Mayawati's BSP, which in our projection should win about 56 seats, could well end up holding a lot of the aces.

There are, of course, a host of caveats. Some of these apply across the board, some specific to states. The most obvious is that a week is a long time in politics and we are presenting our assessment a good six weeks before the first of the states votes. Any dramatic event between now and the polls could radically alter the situation.

That is not all. Not all alliances are yet in place and how they shape up could hold the key to the outcome. The delimitation exercise, which has changed many constituencies beyond recognition, could upset old calculations. Finally, the parties are yet to come out with their full candidates lists. These are, and we repeat, our best estimates based on [illegible] of our reporters and the ability of their sources to read the tea leaves right. If that was all it took to get the results right, we wouldn't need the world's biggest exercise in democracy would we? We reserve the right to revise our estimates in the weeks ahead.

► SP-BSP fight in UP, P 14

## STATE-BY-STATE SCENARIO

| State | Cong | Allies | BJP | Allies | Left | Others | Total |
|---|---|---|---|---|---|---|---|
| Uttar Pradesh | 10 | 0 | 8 | 3 | 0 | 59 | 80 |
| Maharashtra | 10 | 14 | 20 | 14 | 0 | 0 | 48 |
| Andhra Pradesh | 21 | 0 | 0 | 0 | 2 | 19 | 42 |
| West Bengal | 8 | 8 | 0 | 0 | 26 | 0 | 42 |
| Bihar | 4 | 12 | 10 | 14 | 0 | 0 | 40 |
| Tamil Nadu | 5 | 11 | 0 | 0 | 2 | 21 | 39 |
| Madhya Pradesh | 8 | 0 | 20 | 0 | 0 | 1 | 29 |
| Karnataka | 6 | 0 | 18 | 0 | 0 | 2 | 28 |
| Gujarat | 6 | 0 | 20 | 0 | 0 | 0 | 26 |
| Rajasthan | 13 | 0 | 12 | 0 | 0 | 0 | 25 |
| Orissa | 4 | 0 | 3 | 14 | 0 | 0 | 21 |
| Kerala | 12 | 2 | 0 | 0 | 6 | 0 | 20 |
| Assam | 6 | 0 | 4 | 2 | 0 | 2 | 14 |
| Jharkhand | 3 | 2 | 9 | 0 | 0 | 0 | 14 |
| Punjab | 5 | 0 | 3 | 4 | 0 | 1 | 13 |
| Chhattisgarh | 3 | 0 | 8 | 0 | 0 | 0 | 11 |
| Haryana | 4 | 0 | 2 | 4 | 0 | 0 | 10 |
| Delhi | 5 | 0 | 2 | 0 | 0 | 0 | 7 |
| J&K | 2 | 3 | 1 | 0 | 0 | 0 | 6 |
| Uttarakhand | 1 | 0 | 4 | 0 | 0 | 0 | 5 |
| Himachal | 1 | 0 | 3 | 0 | 0 | 0 | 4 |
| Arunachal | 0 | 0 | 2 | 0 | 0 | 0 | 2 |
| Goa | 1 | 0 | 1 | 0 | 0 | 0 | 2 |
| Manipur | 1 | 0 | 0 | 0 | 0 | 1 | 2 |
| Meghalaya | 1 | 1 | 0 | 0 | 0 | 0 | 2 |
| Tripura | 0 | 0 | 0 | 0 | 2 | 0 | 2 |
| Mizoram | 1 | 0 | 0 | 0 | 0 | 0 | 1 |
| Nagaland | 0 | 0 | 0 | 1 | 0 | 0 | 1 |
| Sikkim | 0 | 0 | 0 | 0 | 0 | 1 | 1 |
| Andaman & Nicobar | 1 | 0 | 0 | 0 | 0 | 0 | 1 |
| Chandigarh | 1 | 0 | 0 | 0 | 0 | 0 | 1 |
| Dadra & Nagar Haveli | 1 | 0 | 0 | 0 | 0 | 0 | 1 |
| Daman & Diu | 0 | 1 | 0 | 0 | 0 | 0 | 1 |
| Lakshadweep | 0 | 0 | 0 | 1 | 0 | 0 | 1 |
| Puducherry | 0 | 1 | 0 | 0 | 0 | 0 | 1 |
| Total | 146 | 55 | 128 | 67 | 40 | 107 | 543 |

| UPA | NDA | Third Front | Others |
|---|---|---|---|
| 201 | 195 | 82 | 65 |

**LEAD INDIA**

• TOI handpicks 28 MPs who made an impact in Parliament in the last 5 yrs

PAGE 2

**DANCE OF DEMOCRACY**

• [illegible], P 17
• [illegible], P 17
• [illegible], P 11
• [illegible], P 11
• Poll dancing kicks off in Andhra Pradesh, P 17

**Pawar cloud over BJP-Sena alliance**

BJP and Shiv Sena ties hit another bump on Thursday with Maharashtra BJP chief Nitin Gadkari taking exception to Sena MP Sanjay Raut "supporting" NCP chief Sharad Pawar for prime minister. P 12

Dainik Bhaskar        An ril 5. 2009

## साप्ताहिक पोल मीटर

# भाजपा खेमे को मामूली बढ़त

**कांग्रेस : 174 - भाजपा : 188 अन्य : 181**

भास्कर/सीएनएक्स के साप्ताहिक द्वारा किए गए ताजा आकलन से पता चलता है कि भाजपा खेमे को कांग्रेस खेमे से मामूली बढ़त मिल गई है। हालांकि अंतिम चुनाव परिणाम किसी के भी पक्ष में आ सकते हैं।

| राज्य/यूटी | सियासी स्थिति | अनुमानित परिणाम - दल | | | कुल सीटें |
|---|---|---|---|---|---|
| | | कांग्रेस व सहयोगी दल | भाजपा व सहयोगी दल | अन्य | |
| आंध्रप्रदेश | टीआरएस, टीडीपी व लेफ्ट के बीच सीट बंटवारे के विवाद से कांग्रेस को हो सकता है फायदा | 18 | - | 24 | 42 |
| असम | अंदरूनी लड़ाई के बावजूद बीजेपी-एजीपी मजबूत | 4 | 9 | 1 | 14 |
| बिहार | सीट बंटवारा समझौता न होने से यूपीए को नुकसान | 4 | 26 | 10 | 40 |
| छत्तीसगढ़ | भाजपा का पलड़ा भारी, कांग्रेस को थोड़ा लाभ संभव | 2 | 9 | - | 11 |
| गुजरात | कांग्रेस के पास मोदी का जवाब नहीं | 8 | 18 | - | 26 |
| हरियाणा | बसपा, कांग्रेस के वोट काट सकती है, इससे भाजपा-इनेलो गठबंधन को फायदा | 7 | 2 | 1 | 10 |
| हिमाचल | विधानसभा चुनाव में जीत से भाजपा बराबर सीट पर | 1 | 3 | - | 4 |
| जम्मू और कश्मीर | विधानसभा चुनाव के नतीजों का प्रभाव लोकसभा चुनाव पर भी पड़ेगा | 4 | - | 2 | 6 |
| झारखंड | सीट बंटवारा समझौता न होने से यूपीए को नुकसान | 2 | 8 | 4 | 14 |
| कर्नाटक | भाजपा के मुकाबले कांग्रेस [illegible] | 6 | 19 | 3 | 28 |
| केरल | लेफ्ट में अंदरूनी लड़ाई से कांग्रेस को फायदा मिलेगा | 14 | - | 6 | 20 |
| मध्यप्रदेश | मुख्यमंत्री शिवराज की लोकप्रियता से भाजपा को मिल सकता है फायदा | 5 | 24 | - | 29 |
| महाराष्ट्र | भाजपा-शिवसेना गठबंधन से कांग्रेस-एनसीपी को खतरा | 22 | 26 | - | 48 |
| उड़ीसा | भाजपा-बीजेडी अलगाव से कांग्रेस को मिल सकता है फायदा | 7 | 2 | 12 | 21 |
| पंजाब, चंडीगढ़ | टाइटलर मामले में सिखों की नाराजगी से कांग्रेस को नुकसान | 8 | 6 | - | 14 |
| राजस्थान | विधानसभा चुनाव में कांग्रेस के लिए [illegible] | 14 | 10 | 1 | 25 |
| तमिलनाडु, पुडुचेरी | जयललिता की वापसी होगी, पीएमके के पाला बदलने से द्रमुक-कांग्रेस को नुकसान | 9 | - | 31 | 40 |
| उत्तरप्रदेश | अधिकतर सीटें सपा और बसपा के बीच बंटेंगी | 13 | 15 | 52 | 80 |
| उत्तराखंड | [illegible] भाजपा के पक्ष में रहेंगे आंकड़े | 2 | 3 | - | 5 |
| प. बंगाल | कांग्रेस-तृणमूल [illegible], लेकिन पूर्ण [illegible] नहीं | 15 | - | 27 | 42 |
| त्रिपुरा | किसी बदलाव की संभावना नहीं | - | - | 2 | 2 |
| [illegible] | किसी बदलाव की संभावना नहीं | 2 | 1 | 1 | 4 |
| दिल्ली | टाइटलर मामले से 'मजबूत' कांग्रेस को नुकसान संभव | 5 | 2 | - | 7 |
| गोवा | कांग्रेस सरकार लोकप्रिय नहीं, लेकिन बदलाव की संभावना नहीं | 1 | 1 | - | 2 |
| अरुणाचल, मणिपुर, मेघालय, मिजोरम, नागालैंड, सिक्किम | किसी बदलाव की संभावना नहीं | 4 | 2 | 3 | 9 |
| | कुल | 174 | 188 | 181 | 543 |
| | पिछले हफ्ते के आंकड़े | 188 | 183 | 172 | 543 |

catching up with individual equations. The Times of India published a second "survey" with chart based on the assessment of its own staff reporters/ from across the country. The Times of India propelled other daily newspapers as well as channels to take similar exercise of projecting poll outcome from their own experts / bureaus in the absence or as an alternative to sample surveys.

Some news media in 2009 had produced "surveys" overnight from within. Two newspapers in Telugu, one old and other relatively new, published front page banner story based on a "claimed survey". (A senior editor at that time of the daily told this author personally – how the editor–proprietor of the paper dictated the survey story on phone). Both newspapers claimed that their staff reporters in the districts interviewed voters. Perhaps it was not a coincidence that both dailies carried such survey based story on the same day but with opposite projections!. What message readers get?

**Star News – Neilson Survey**

Star News – Neilson's *Kaun Benega Pradhan Mantri* ("Who will become the PM") was covered on Sunday March 23,2009. This was second channel, after CNN/IBN to come out with a nationwide poll survey. Claiming a sample of about 50,000, the survey did not indicate any other facts about the field survey as to the States it covered, etc. The channel hyped the findings of its "Neilson Survey" next 24 hours and its highlights were released to news media who covered it in the next day's daily newspapers all over. One or two journalists were asked to comment while the results of each State were presented by Star News channel. Unlike earlier, there was no discussion on poll forecasts, in the studio or outside, about the survey findings with political party leaders. Nor there was any one from the survey agency to explain about the survey itself or its limitations in the forecast of seats, or other aspects like delimitation of constituencies, etc.

But the anchor presented the survey findings as if *"saaf ho chuke"* (it is already clear) and *"saaf hota hi"* (it is evident) without any reminder that the findings were only estimates based on a sample survey several weeks before the voting. Nor it gave any hint about "undecided voters". Nor was there any effort to bring out issues that matter or concerned the voters in that election to Lok Sabha. Within 24 hours of the telecast of this "Neilson Survey" by Star News, the BJP had commented that the field survey was conducted for Congress party and that it was meant to be a "PR for Congress party" as the programme tried to show that the UPA was ahead of the NDA in the race (press briefings of BJP, April 2008). Also interesting was that the same agency (A C Neilson) did field surveys for Congress party nationally and for the same party in the States and for some other channels (as in the case of NTV in Telugu. This survey was attributed to "Neilson" when in fact it was the same "Neilson – ORG – MARG" which did the survey. This is to enable some leaders like the CM of Andhra Pradesh to claim that "even international agencies" had come up with "conclusive" findings that Congress and UPA was ahead and coming back to power'.

Along with 2009 Lok Sabha elections, AP and Orissa also had Assembly elections. Andhra Pradesh witnessed intense triangular contests. With the number of Telugu news channels getting doubled from 3 in March 2004 to 8 in April 2009, there was keen competition among channels in covering the election. TV9 Telugu channel which had conducted field surveys in the 2004 election in the State, tried with three and a half hours long discussion based programme on 2009 elections at a stretch (10 am to 1.30) without using any pre-poll field survey. But it had indoor programme (not studio) with 10 to 12 representatives of political parties (with more than one leader from each major party). The Chief Editor, Ravi Prakash, experimented with a new format "to generate election heat" (or controversy?) as he did with a sample survey at the time of previous Assembly election in 2004.

A one year old Telugu channel NTV, on the other hand, experimented prominently through advertising in newspapers and channels about its commissioned pre-poll survey by "AC Neilson –

ORG – MARG" ("who is the best Chief Minister"). The findings of the first round of the survey were presented in a studio based discourse with invited leaders of political parties over a week with daily 30 minutes programme. The motivation for the survey was to position itself along with more popularly viewed news channels in the State and position itself as a potential political force – in support of the party in power in the State – that was how the survey by the NTV was generally perceived in the State. In fact, it was even accused by the opposition TDP as reported in newspapers.

**NTV Model**

Not withstanding motives about the NTV channel sponsoring and featuring the pre-poll survey and claims of the survey agency about the sample size and accuracy of its projections, this channel's experiment with the second round of the field survey by the same survey agency in March 2009 deserve notice. In fact, it signals a departure in the way media used surveys in 2009. For, it was an effort to use pre-poll surveys for making a qualitative difference in the poll scene. NTV's "Big Fight – whose success it is going to be" was advertised extensively in all media all over the State. This Big Fight programme was shown twice daily. It was a departure for several good reasons. First, it made an all out effort to base the discussion on specific major local issues that concerned the voters. Secondly, it was not merely studio based or a closed door type programme with "same old" political leaders and journalists. One programme of 60 minutes duration was held at a district head quarter town (6 – 7 pm) each day and it was truly a open house in a large auditorium where two anchors moderated 10 to 15 local leaders representing parties and public too took part in the discourse. It was a three way discussion. First, the political representatives made a position statement on specific issue and on which the opposition party representative responded and the independent representative or the anchor puts supplementary questions amidst acrimony. Some times a special interest group in the audience, like a tribal activist from among large audience of open house in Khammam (on 13 March 2009) made his/her position on the issue. Thus the discourse went much beyond right – wrong aspect of estimates by A C Neilson – ORG – Marg as was the case earlier in most channels which had commissioned a pre-poll survey.

Over all, this attempt of the NTV was a departure from the earlier limited use of pre-poll surveys. The NTV model brings out how pre-poll surveys could help qualitatively by way of enhancing the scope of political discourse, inclusively and taking locally relevant basic issues. This was an example for deepening democratic process instead of damping the process by merely hyping the findings of

**TV Coverage of Polls:**
**In Search of a New Model!**
**The Case of NTV**

Since 2004 Lok Sabha poll, CMS Media Lab has been tracking and analyzing trends in the news media coverage including electoral politics. Based on its field research on the impact of news media contents in the context of various social development efforts in the country, CMS had come up with idea of "pre-emptive journalism" – where instead of involving and activating citizens or voters, news media tend to make them passive with its presentation structure and content thrust. And, in that process, even dampens civic response. On the eve of Lok Sabha and Assembly elections until now most channels have been by and large following same structure and format of animated discussions and debate involving poll surveys, more in a restrictive way and more to generate heat and personalized controversy. In 2009 some of the channels however have been exploring new ways of covering polls.

Against this background, one year old Hyderabad based Telugu news channel, NTV had evolved a modified model – may not by design but on initiative of smart young reporters of the channel (Ramachander

*Contd. on next page*

surveys to the extent of pre-empting interests of voters and motivating them to vote.

**Mint Model**

Mint is relatively new daily of Hindustan Times group in collaboration with Wall Street Journal. No sooner after its launch, Mint made a difference in several ways of its coverage of politics, economics and other issues – more depth, quantitative and illustrated as much and involved as many outside columnists.

Mint carried a field survey by MDRA (one research agency which has conducted poll surveys for news media for nearly two

*Contd. from previous page*

Rao and Miss. Rehnna). Apparently it tried to compete with established ones and be different from the more popular channels.

As a new entrant into crowded news channel market, NTV too tried poll surveys to get into news and catch up with political leaders. **But as if realized too soon that such surveys on their own will neither add to credibility nor to the reach of the channel, it had gone beyond survey centered animated** studio discussions. After two rounds of expensive pre-poll surveys on electoral politics in the previous one year, NTV took to "Big Fight" in the context of Assembly elections.

NTV's poll coverage was in **three** different phases and in each phase it had different structure and format and timings. Initially it started with **one hour** ("who the winner is") studio presentation of survey results for **five** days. Later, from March first week the channel took to **one hour** live programme at each head quarter district for 23 continues days as Big Fight. This is open house with representatives of all local parties and largely attended by local public. The discussion between representatives of parties was specific to local issues. They argued out at length on contentious aspects of the issues. All through,

*Contd. on next page*

decades) in the context of 2009 Lok Sabha elections with distinction for two reasons. First, it presented only charts and graphs for the survey findings along with basic facts about methodology and a brief introduction about the agency which did the survey. The interpretation is left for the readers in a neutral way instead of concluding with "pre-emptive" statements. No "conclusions" were presented. No effort to showcase "punditry" as is the case with channels. Secondly, the six part series did not include any projection of outcome, neither in terms of seats or percentage of votes, with election more than a month away. The emphasis was to flag factors and issues. The concern was more about *process*, than with *outcome*. No where in

*Contd. from previous page*

the discussions were serious, no trivialization or any attempt to mix up or dilute the debate with entertainment angle. And without getting into physical clashes at any point despite heated debate, as happened in couple of other language channels when they were forced to wind up the programme itself. Porkalam (Yudha Bhumi) and Jana Samksham in Kerala were two such examples – police have to go the extent of charging the group in the glare of cameras.

The third phase was a more focussed open enquiry in selected Lok Sabha constituencies with key candidates in the midst of a local community. In this **half** an hour live programme both locals and candidates were asked about performance of sitting candidate, validated with butting in of local public and followed by similar exposition with opposing candidate. Big Fight appeared without preconceived position. It did not try to drive people towards certain set positions. Rather it left the participants and viewers ponder about the issues in a open ended way. The anchors did not allow cockfight like situation for viewership that poll programmes on other channels went about.

Over a period of **30 days**, (March - April) with **two** daily interactive programmes, Big Fight had involved more than 200 political leaders in

*Contd. on next page*

any of the six part pre-poll survey based full page reports, *Mint* tried to influence voters. The emphasis was more on enlightening voters without indicating who is the likely winner or the seats that parties are likely to get. (*Mint* New Delhi – March 10, 11, 16,17, 2009).

**Saakshi Model**

As against the *Mint* model, *Saakshi* daily newspaper in Telugu reproduced prominently on its front page a pre-poll survey conducted by A C Neilson – ORG – Marg for NTV channel (March 2009). Only the number of seats that contending parties were projected to get in the Andhra Pradesh Assembly election was presented graphically. In the coverage of the pre-poll survey on the first day neither the NTV channel nor Sakshi had referred to any issues or factors that concerned voters – not even by way of explaining why or how a party was projected to get the seats, that it had forecast. Where as, on the other hand, Saakshi did not report at all another survey by the Week magazine (April 3) but Saakshi's opponent, Eenadu, published that survey prominently with a two column headline. This was because this survey predicted Congress party to get only 125 seats in the Assembly against claims of much higher number by its leaders and also the other survey of Neilson.

*Contd. from previous page*

actual discourse and some 10,000 people in all must have personally witnessed the live telecast debates and a few even intervened. Big Fight took the debate beyond TV viewers and gone beyond bites, beyond showcasing "same old" faces, and trivialization of poll campaign into a more serious and voter activating exercise.

This programme was unique in terms of its structure, scope, participation, substance and in terms of role of the two anchors. Some other news channels in Andhra Pradesh too took to Big Fight like programmes but not with similar fineness or success in so many respects.

*Mint* March 13, 2009

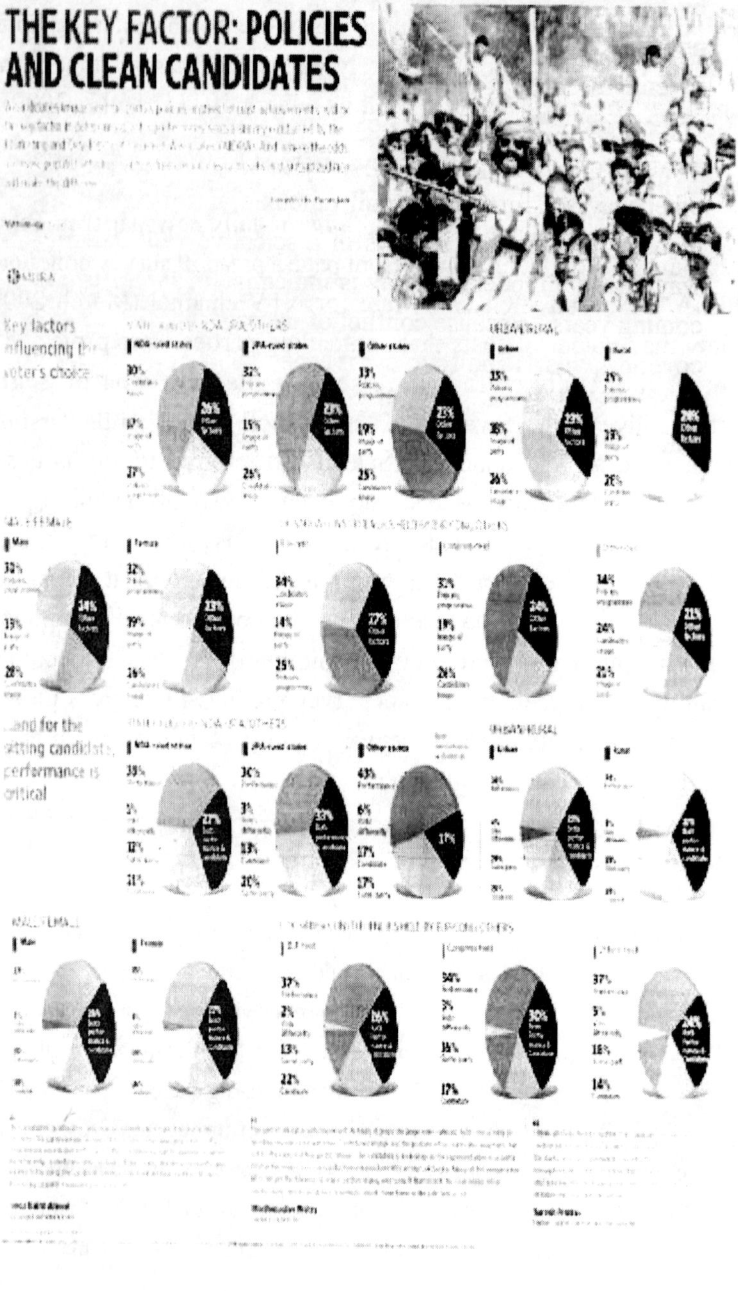

# THE KEY FACTOR: POLICIES AND CLEAN CANDIDATES

Key factors influencing the voter's choice

...and for the sitting candidate, performance is critical

The difference in the two models of covering pre-poll surveys by two different news media is in their intention. While *Saakshi* newspaper was trying to sway voters using a survey, Mint was trying to enlighten voters presenting survey findings more sensitively and objectively. Whether 2009 Lok Sabha poll marked the beginning of news media using poll surveys more sensitively and together with other ways of forecasting poll outcome and processes, instead of featuring and hyping surveys in a selective and blatantly partisan way. Saakshi model in a way is indicative of things to come in the coming years. Because conflict of interest aspect of news media in covering polls and poll surveys is becoming critical in poll campaigns.

**Political Parties**

2009 poll had seen political parties taking to poll surveys more seriously than the news media as in the earlier years. In that process, the thrust of surveys had shifted from projection of outcome to selection of party candidates.

It is good that political parties / leaders have recognised the significance of field surveys towards maximing opportunities in an electoral democracy. Instead of limiting to news media and party organization for inputs to poll campaign, they are now conducting their own poll surveys, instead of limiting to those of news media. 2009 Lok Sabha poll has amply proved this change. Most parties, national and regional, had gone for their own multiple surveys in 2008 – 2009. The 2009 Lok Sabha poll has in fact signalled proliferation of surveys of all kinds and in that process some leaders got into a syndrome of surveys at the cost of the grassroot level cadres and organisation. The sensitivity to strengths and limits of surveys and skill to discriminate and take a desegregated view is limited in political parties - may be to one or two persons even in the case of the two major national parties. The parties should now go about organising orientation programmes to functionaries the same way they do now for "spokespersons" and those incharge of "press relations". Some national political parties in 2009 Lok Sabha poll were inundated with survey reports as a part of bio-data of aspiring individual candidates adding to chaos in "candidate selection process". Criterion for selection tended more in some cases on the basis of such surveys rather than field record of aspirants.

The parties tend to engage their "own people" (no women psephologist so far has been popped up by parties or the media) for conducting poll surveys as if the pros and cons of going for an independent professional. There was no evidence that has made parties any wiser. The kind of critical appraisal that such internal surveys require is different. Also, certain myths like more the sample size more reliable a sample survey is more indicative and reliable. Political parties should avail surveys not just close at the heels of an election schedule but well before. Parties would be better of building their own data base on polls at headquarter such a way that it is easily retrievable, reprocessed and updated. Digital strategy with availability of digital maps and desegregated socio-economic profiles should bring new orientation of parties to surveys. Party leaders should know better how to respond or react to surveys covered in the public media both when the surveys are favouable and unfavourable.

**e-surveys by 2014**

The rethink about poll eve surveys evident in 2009 is bound to usher in a more inclusive era of public opinion surveys by 2014. Communication technologies are experiencing an exponential growth, similar to the broadcast media's growth in the last decade, which in turn will engender new opportunities to think beyond and change the very paradigm of poll surveys in news media.

By 2014 when the next Lok Sabha poll is expected in the normal course, we could expect considerable shifts in the poll campaign strategies. By then more poll surveys would be e-based and will be accompanied by a much higher level of web campaigning. But field survey will continue to be most relied source. Campaign momentum will flow from a collection of these online initiatives. Most newspapers and channels have already taken to e-surveys by way of SMS polls, on-line surveys and live phone-ins in one context or another. Even regional language newspapers and channels are also doing so, most of them on the front page or as part of news or discussion programs on TV. There is already an outbreak of popularity contests of all kind of topics, often to the extent of perpetuating relatively frivolous news. So far such initiatives have not become a serious information input as in the case of field surveys in media. This is mainly because of the limited representative character, relevance of the topics, anonymity of response, and the way such response is presented in the news media. However, the speed with which the number of cell phones are getting added across all sections of people, including rural sectors, will definitely elevate the importance of e-surveys in the coming years.

With broadband connectivity rapidly multiplying and penetrating more districts, the number of serious poll-eve e-surveys is bound to be far more in the next Lok Sabha election. Furthermore, the character of survey culture is bound to change once phone numbers reaches a billion mark; Cable TV connections and internet connectivity are estimated to go beyond 100 million by 2014. By then the number of PCs and television sets are also estimated to increase by 50 percent. That is by 2014 there will be more than 50 million PCs and 140 million television sets in the country. Population covered by these new media by then is likely to be two-thirds of urban and more than one-third of rural households. However, the distribution of this connectivity will not be representative of the large base of voters in the country and only about ten percent of Lok Sabha constituencies will provide a balanced voter base to undertake reliable e-surveys. By 2014 the country will have next generation communication networks with voice over internet protocol and by then the composition of the electorate too would see a "new generation" voters who could be more involved and active in responding to e-surveys. Many more parties/candidates will have internet based or digital strategies.

Although Mobile Association of India claimed 57 million users of internet, leading communication think tank, CMS, estimates that no more than 12 million could be voters for targeting during poll campaigns. Political websites by parties attracted different voter bases. According to Komoli Medu, Advani's site in 2009, for example, attracted more women and that of Rahul Gandhi's Website attracted more youth. But what is interesting to give an idea of emerging scene is that a relatively high percent of educated users claimed visiting Advani's website between March 1 to 30 April 2009 (Mint, May 16, 2009). By 2014, the political Parties will become even more web savvy with websites becoming campaign hubs, candidates becoming internet driven, and news media looking for more ways of availing digital media for expanded interactive coverage. Polling agencies too will gear up and be way ahead in understanding and monitoring these new tools focusing the technology for the betterment of country and electoral politics. There are however a plethora of issues that need to be surmounted before the above envisioned scenario is brought to fruition. The issues range from SMS polls to e-surveys.

**SMS Polls:** SMS polls and phone-ins have been part of discussions of channels and newspapers for some time now. The SMS polls by different media channels are mostly for "yes / no" type responses and the results are typically presented via graphs. Neither the ones on TV nor those on the front pages of newspapers, rarely indicate the methodology details including the number of total responses received and from where or who they were. Also, the telephone numbers for responding to the TV polls is never given in advance nor known uniformly to viewers/readers. There are instances where since the participants in the program were informed about such a poll in advance, the responses were "pre meditated", "organized", or even "prompted" by political parties/leaders or participants. Even otherwise, it is obvious that such SMS or phone-in polls do not represent the respective universe concerned with the subject or voters of a constituency. SMS polls in news media now are misleading more often because of complexity or irrelevance of the very questions and yes/no analysis. The questions posed through this medium are not completely amenable to yes-no type responses. News media have also adopted SMS and phone-in polls in a big way. Due to the interactiveness of SMS polls and competitiveness among news media, SMS polls have become regular feature of all media and of all type of programs. News channels use SMS polls not only in the context of elections and politics but also in many other contexts like business, sports and social issues –on a daily basis. With increase in the phone connectivity and their spread across segments of population and reduced tariff, SMS and phone-in polls are acquiring potential for e-polling among certain sections of voter base like CEO's or decision makers.

Realizing that SMS has become the new media for election canvass, the Election Commission has banned in 2009 use of SMS as part of election campaign 48 hours before polling. But participation in SMS polls of news media was not specifically banned. On the eve of Delhi State election in November 2008, SMS message was sent by Chief Minister of Uttar Pradesh and leaders of BSP to voters even after the campaign had come to a stop officially. In fact, even on the day of polling SMS messages were sent out, even (exit) poll findings were sent out in between polling phases as a part of swaying voters.

By making these e-surveys more representative, mass media can make them far more important as tools for deepening democratic culture in the country. (1) First, master list of telephone numbers including cell phones and e-mail addresses should be available; one could then select appropriate category of respondents. The phone number or e-mail of news media to respond by viewer should remain constant (instead of changing from time to time or poll to poll as now), (2) Channels should come to an understanding with phone companies for a reduced (nominal) tariff and in fact should soon have "toll-free" numbers. (at present they are looking at these polls as a revenue earning opportunities) (3) Importantly, viewers should have opportunity to know in advance what the broad subject is likely. SMS polls in daily newspapers imply 24 hour time to respond, live discussion based SMS polls on channels, however, require setting up of specially designed on-line response system.; (4) News media should indicate the total responses while presenting instead of giving only "Yes – No" percentages.

For a more reflective e-survey of voters, what is also required is desegregated directories and profile of users of phones, of all kind for broadband connections and TV households. The sooner these directories are available, faster e-surveys will become the norm. By 2014 we could expect altogether new research agencies taking to e-surveys which would be faster and less expensive. But to ensure representative character as to male-female, age groups and even socio-economic background, considerable preparatory work is needed and new research methodologies and tools need to be experimented from now onwards. Toll free easy numbers (paid centrally) if available for research agencies on dedicated basis would change the scope and significance of e-surveys assuming that no new law prohibiting random digit dialing of cell phones is drafted.. Research methodology of surveys will go through dramatic changes introducing new opportunities and challenges because of technology diffusion. Research agencies need to experiment with full scale e-surveys in some constituencies of Chennai, Mumbai, Bangalore and Kolkatta and Coimbatore.

The methodology of e-surveys and the way they are presented in news media deserve experimentation. In e-surveys it will not be possible to the kind of number of questions and the kind of probing that is possible in personal interviews. E-surveys have to be more focused and yet more sensitive in the enquiry. There is need to establish linkage between personal interview based surveys with the on-line ones. How reaching out to those who do not have access to news media and newer communication technologies will remain a challenge.

The 2009 Lok Sabha poll has signaled the transition of electoral politics with new generation voters coming to forefront in all political parties. The next election scheduled in 2014 should signal India moving towards tele-democracy. With e-survey becoming hallmark we need to gear up so that e-surveys could be reflective, representative, and inclusive. All this however should not mean dampening citizen activism or alienation of any section of people from grass root politics. This requires that voters' understanding about relevance of surveys in a democracy is positive. Their receptivity and skills to respond to such e-surveys need to be promoted. Only then the process of transition could be expedited and meaningfuls.

# 10

# The Way Forward

Scientifically conducted field surveys could be of immense help in many decision making situations and for strategizing future courses including electoral fortunes. At the same time, if surveys are not objectively conducted or/and presented transparently, they could be misleading and even counter productive. The surveys conducted in the context of elections to States assemblies and Lok Sabha require sensitivity about methodology particularly when the survey findings are used for psephological exercise. When surveys try to analyse complex processes as in the case of elections in the era of a coalition politics, should not be taken as an end in themselves. They can only be supplementary inputs. They cannot be viewed as definitive and conclusive mid way in an electoral process, particularly by news media and political parties.

Surveys obviously bring out what is popular but that need not always be what is right – even assuming methodologies used are unbiased and have used neutral measuring instruments. It is relevant to recall what UK's Labor Party leader Roy Hatterslay had said in 1996 about surveys - they are "a major disincentive to ideological politics as they make politicians believe that they can choose between principle and popularity". In fact, Professor Robert Worcestor of

UK's leading public opinion agency (Mori) went to the extent of observing that "when opinion surveys get into hands of politicians and spin doctors, as they tend to more often these days, they become a threat to democratic culture". This could be said even about news media, going by the ways they use poll surveys.

If poll surveys cannot motivate and activate civic sense and societal concerns, they have the potential to blunt "free and fair" conduct of elections and snub voter activism. When news media relies on surveys too much, it could dampen the very spirit of democracy. Having ventured into conducting poll eve surveys in India and their use by news media more than three decades ago, this author is concerned at the twists and turns these surveys have seen through also the way they were used by news media initially and have been handled by political parties now. Political parties/leaders have taken to surveys as a means and end and in the process to the point of their becoming counter productive to the very democratic culture.

One reason for such a situation is the lack of sensitivity about poll surveys - the methodology and limitations. Lack of transparency in the way surveys are conducted in fact magnifies the problem. There is no evidence of such an understanding or realization even among those who are the prime perpetrators of poll surveys – the news media. And yet there is no effort or concern on any ones part to take on the task. There cannot be any doubt that poll surveys do serve democratic processes and could make a difference. If poll surveys do not make any real difference when covered in the news media, why so many are anxious to sponsor, relie on and hype them in the news media.

There has to be a distinction between the scope of poll surveys conducted for the news media, from those conducted for political parties or for individual leaders or candidates. The methodology of such surveys cannot be the same when conducted to analyse poll factors or for projecting a poll outcome or for selecting new candidates or deciding about the sitting candidates or for evolving a campaign strategy.

News media are an essential part of the democratic processes and their role in ensuring "free and fair" polls is paramount. Poll coverage by the news media has become survey centric in the last decade. CMS Media Lab has brought out how discussions in media are structured and even tailored sometimes, particularly by channels based on surveys. And channels are relied far more and by many more voters and cadres. The Election Commission's curbs have come handy for a relook about the way polls are conducted and covered. A rethink in this regard is already evident in 2009. These initiatives need to be taken forward and proactively. Curbs on media use of poll surveys in 2009 have somewhat made news media realize the limitations of surveys. Innovatively taken up poll eve coverage could motivate voters, stimulate civic activism, engage citizens and enlighten party cadres. This is what some channels had experimented in 2009 or tried to. The limitations of rating centric approach of news media is a constraint, in that process, in their taking initiatives for a more inclusive, interactive and engaging approach to poll coverage.

Research agencies engaged in conducting poll surveys would be appreciated far more than at present if only they treat such poll eve opportunities beyond commercial concerns and on an ad-hoc basis. More over, it is in their own interest. The findings of surveys should enhance the very scope of democracy rather than constrain it. Research methodology requires constant update and modification with regards to design, sampling and even analysis as electoral scene is constantly changing. Research methodologies used by research agencies should get discussed periodically in open forums with participation of academic faculties and civil society.

While those research or psephology agencies engaged by political parties / candidates could engage whoever they want, those who conduct for news media should be identified and conflict of interest, if any, should be indicated. The responsibility for transparency should be of the news media itself. News media should realize that implications of poll surveys going wrong or being misused will effect credibility not only that particular media but eventually of the entire news media.

Psephology and surveys are not necessarily the same. A psephologist projects seats taking into account survey inputs along with other considerations. With too many journalists and even political activists getting into psephological exercises and being described as psephologists, the problem gets complicated. A journalist could function better as an investigative analyst and come up with more reliable figures than a psephologist. It is in the interest of news media to make this distinction and avail of the strengths of both. A journalist, a political activist and an analyst working together can make a better sense of surveys and enlighten citizens far more. This is what channels often try. Some correctives always help and are worth considering. The polls during 1998 – 2009 have lessons for every one – news media, research agencies, political parties and the Election Commission. All of them need to *think of correctives and alternatives*. To mention a few: News media should go beyond – in terms of their sources; personalities covered, concerns in the context of elections; self – discipline in the profession of journalism is far better. Such a discipline and transparency is needed even more in the very functioning of psephologists and research agencies and their methodologies. It is high time that there are guidelines (their own) both for news media in using poll surveys and for survey agencies in disclosing methodology. The Election Commission should be pro-active in the case of news media's role in the context of free and fair elections. In fact, it should have similar consultations with news media as it does with political parties.

This author was an advocate of restraint on publication of poll surveys but only in between polling phases. But after seeing how 2009 Lok Sabha election, spread over a month involving five phases, was covered by news media, he has to rethink about that position. The urgency is for transparency and sensitivity among the decision makers in the news media. Competition between news media is only one way of bringing innovations in the way a campaign is covered. As such, the onus should be on the news media to be aware of pros and cons of poll surveys and ensure transparency. Editors Guild,

News Broadcasters Association and such other professional bodies have to be deeply concerned because even isolated instances or error could erode credibility of the news media as a whole. The Election Commission should also bring into picture news media, same way as political parties are in the interest of free and fair elections.

Political parties or even corporates cannot be stopped from having embedded psephologist, or commissioning poll surveys, but they should restrain from passing on such surveys to news media as independent surveys or selectively. Political leaders should know limits of surveys and avoid in their own interest getting into a survey syndrome as they are now more and more. Political parties and leaders as well as news media would be better off in the long run of not getting into a trap of poll surveys. The power of such surveys is to the extent they are critically appraised first and viewed with long term perspective. Surveys are useful tool if used to serve the needs and ambitions of people more rather than the whims of the media or parties.

An alternative model for media covering polls should be sensitive to its implications for various sections of public. The coverage should not be pre-emptive of citizen participation and assertions should be explanatory, not conclusive. Important is to alert or warn about limitations. Participative, interactive, reflective and representative character of poll related programmes deserves to be enhanced as much as possible. Survey findings should not be hyped beyond a point in such a way that they are viewed as suggestive or recommendatory and even persuading. News media should seek out and involve public in drawing sense of poll surveys in a more democratic way of reporting.

For a country of India's size and regional complexities, one or two institutions devoted to election studies are not enough. Longitudinal studies can not be expected to be taken up by individualised outfits or one person polling agencies. Even market research agencies however big they may be, can be expected to fill the vacuum. Universities are the right place. The Election Commission perhaps should take initiative in this regard. We have many missing links in our understanding of voting bahaviour despite so many polls claiming big samples and as if sample survey approach is good enough. India needs truly independent and decentralised research endeavours in this regard. The CSDS model too has its potential.

2009 Poll was a turning point in many respects. It had signalled a transition of party politics in India to a newer phase with innovative young people of change coming to the forefront. Their positive outlook including towards interactive and digital media indicate shifts in the paradigm of electoral politics. 2014 Lok Sabha poll would see more of that. Poll surveys and psephological exercise can no longer be merely quantitative and news media can no longer be preemptive in the style of their coverage of polls. Websites, emails, text messages, digital campaigning and social networks will be far more serious source. But for them to be reflective, special efforts are required for citizen to become more sensitive, articulate and active in availing these sources and in *responding or giving cooperation to surveys*. Only then surveys become true instruments of participative democracy and for good governance. E-surveys are less expensive, more attentive and can be faster but not necessarily without flaws. They have the potential to increase reliability of surveys. Nevertheless efforts from now on have to be to generate representative samples.

# Index

**R**